S0-ASU-961

TRANSFORMING RURAL WATER GOVERNANCE

TRANSFORMING RURAL WATER GOVERNANCE

The Road from Resource Management
to Political Activism in Nicaragua

SARAH T. ROMANO

THE UNIVERSITY OF
ARIZONA PRESS

TUCSON

COLORADO COLLEGE LIBRARY
COLORADO SPRINGS, COLORADO

The University of Arizona Press
www.uapress.arizona.edu

© 2019 by The Arizona Board of Regents
All rights reserved. Published 2019

ISBN-13: 978-0-8165-3807-2 (cloth)

Cover design by Leigh McDonald
All photos are by the author except where noted.

Publication of this book is made possible in part by the University of Northern Colorado's Fund for Faculty Publication.

Library of Congress Cataloging-in-Publication Data are available at the Library of Congress.

Printed in the United States of America
♾ This paper meets the requirements of ANSI/NISO Z39.48–1992 (Permanence of Paper).

In the absence of an effective state, civil society groups have important roles in service delivery, while at the same time mobilizing society to demand better governance. This means, of course, that civil society organizations will sometimes face the need to transform themselves (e.g. from service delivery to advocacy), a task fully as difficult as transforming society.

—DEEPA NARAYAN, *BONDS AND BRIDGES: SOCIAL CAPITAL AND POVERTY*

[Nicaragua] has potable water committees, which are expressions of society, expressions of the community, which aren't part of the government, and which in an autonomous and self-sufficient manner promote and provide water and sanitation service, principally potable water, in their own community.

—CARMEN PONG, COSUDE, MANAGUA, NOVEMBER 19, 2009

We have to formalize ourselves.

—POTABLE WATER AND SANITATION COMMITTEE (CAPS) MEMBER, MANAGUA, NOVEMBER 9, 2009

Contents

Illustrations

Figures

Maps

Boxes

Tables

Preface

"You have to fall in love with the project." These were some of the first words Jessenia Rivera from the province of Nueva Segovia, Nicaragua, said to me after I sat down next to her. The November 2009 national-level meeting of the Potable Water and Sanitation Committees (CAPS) was beginning, and Jessenia and dozens of other water committee members from across regions were filtering into a large room with seating organized circularly. I had arrived to the capital, Managua, days earlier to start my dissertation field research. In that moment, the start of ten months of independent research was an exciting continuation of years of interest and exploration on the topics of water politics and collective action in Latin America. Jessenia's words conveyed her unflinching personal commitment to serving her community. Yet, they also seemed to lend insight into a larger story about water management and access in Nicaragua, the "second poorest" country in the Western Hemisphere, where roughly half the national population resides in rural areas, where state services are limited. Her words, as I would learn, spoke to the hard work and level of commitment necessary for contributing to community health and well-being through managing water resources. They also foreshadowed collectively held understandings of the volunteerism, and indeed "love," invested in community-based water management that months of in-depth field research would reveal.

Two years before starting my dissertation field research, I had participated in a meeting of the Coalition for the Right to Water (CODA) in the department of Jinotega in the northern highlands.[1] The meeting convened staff members of community development and environmental nongovernmental organizations (NGOs) who had been involved in a national anti–water privatization social movement that was coming to an end with the passage of a new water law declaring water a *bien público* (public good). Coalition members raised questions about the limited engagement of the Potable Water and Sanitation Committees (CAPS) in the primarily urban-based movement that had begun in 2000. Even though I had spent three months in the capital, Managua, during anti–water privatization organizing in the winter of 2004–5, I had not heard about CAPS. As small, community-based groups of residents, CAPS were tasked with managing water resources and infrastructure in the country's rural areas. As I would learn, CAPS numbered in the thousands.

Coalition for the Right to Water members, some of whom represented organizations already working with CAPS on issues pertaining to rural water access, had been strategizing about how to integrate water committees into national debates and discussions on fresh water. In the north, NGOs had also been playing a crucial role in promoting CAPS' legal recognition vis-à-vis the state. Despite decades of rural water management and service provision in Nicaragua, CAPS still lacked any legal status. Water committees were not passive actors in these processes of political activism. Rather, with the crucial support of allies, they were emerging in the public view as advocates for their organizations and communities.

"I never imagined that these four letters would be printed on fabric, much less on a hat, much less on a shirt," Jessenia expressed to me in June 2010, almost seven months after we first met. "Today we've come to light. As CAPS we're living. And living with strength, because I feel that as CAPS, we're really strong." Jessenia tied CAPS' increasing collective visibility to NGO and multilateral organizations allying with water committees at a national level: "Thank God and thank APN [Norwegian People's Aid], because APN gave us their hand. First we began with SIMAS [Latin American Information Service for Sustainable Agriculture] . . . and now APN is protecting us." Water committees' collaborative, multisectoral engagement in collective action across geographic and political scales reflected a transformation—namely, CAPS' transcendence of community-based *resource management* into the realm of *political activism*.

For the vast majority of individual water committee members, this would be a new role, distinct from the everyday labors of managing water systems and service. Resource management and service provision are inherently political: charging residents fees for service, determining rules for household water shut-offs and reconnections (including whether or not such rules will be enforced), and negotiating access to water sources with local property owners constitute just a few of the highly political endeavors CAPS undertake as part of their day-to-day work in their communities. Yet, this local work did not reflect political *activism*. Starting in the mid-2000s, CAPS' collective push for political and social *change*—activism's main thrust—would propel them onto a national political stage and into new roles as they demanded recognition.

Grassroots Water Crises in Global Context

A key point of departure of this book is an important empirical reality: many of the most acute water crises globally are "everyday" crises experienced in impoverished rural areas and urban slums across the Global South. While rarely headline making, these crises characterized by inequitable access to sufficient and clean water affect over one billion people globally. What is less known, though, is that *millions* of these same global citizens are at the forefront of responding to the challenges of climate change, deforestation, megahydraulic projects, and other threats to accessing water as a critical resource. Citizen-driven efforts to secure water raise important conceptual and practical questions for academics and policy makers. Although some have been grappled with, gaps remain in regard to our understanding of the diversity of community-based water management (CBWM) regimes globally, the role they play in managing resources essential to life and livelihoods, and how they relate to state policies and decision-making processes beyond the grassroots realm in which they are socially grounded.

One salient area of inquiry concerns the "below the radar" political and legal status of many CBWM regimes. Across Latin America and the Global South, formal decentralization initiatives or state policies have devolved decision-making authority for environmental management and forms of service provision, such as water and electricity, to local governments. These initiatives may *mask*—or worse, displace—preexisting, nonstate management and service provision arrangements. That is, although compensating for inadequate state reach or limited state capacity to manage or distribute resources, many community-based water management regimes typically lack formal state recognition for the work they perform. This omission matters, in part, because the work is most often legally assigned to a government actor on paper. What do state actors owe—in terms of financial resources, technical assistance, political inclusion, and more—to nonstate actors fulfilling *state* roles and responsibilities? A lack of recognition can preclude access to state support and resources. Lacking recognition and legal backing is also particularly significant when residents carry out this work in contexts of high levels of poverty and underdevelopment— and where residents increasingly experience the impacts of acute environmental degradation and climate change that undermine efforts to secure freshwater access in their communities.

In beginning this project, I wanted to understand how water committees had emerged, worked, and thrived across diverse political regimes in Nicaragua. What did it mean, in practice, that CAPS in Nicaragua did not have official state recognition? How had this influenced the evolution of their organizations and water management over time—including how water committees thought about their work and its significance? If state actors were not consistent or viable sources of support to rural communities, with whom were water committees working to secure rural water access? The mobilization of CAPS during and in the wake of anti–water privatization organizing made it clear that their work and its significance were not confined to their communities. The political activism of CAPS introduced the question of how community-based organizations, previously disconnected in geographic and political terms, were able to organize quickly into *transcommunity* networks as multiscalar bases for seeking political recognition and inclusion. Moreover, how would CAPS' consequential, albeit de facto, work as water managers and service providers come to bear on their engagements with state actors in their quest for legal recognition? Water committees' mobilization in the context of extreme partisan polarization and central government efforts to co-opt autonomous civil society organizations made these questions more puzzling. What kind of autonomous, broad-based collective action would be possible in the context of polarization and democratic erosion?

Transforming Rural Water Governance: The Road from Resource Management to Political Activism in Nicaragua tells the story of how CAPS have transcended their rural localities and responsibilities as resource managers and service providers to engage in fundamentally new forms of political activism and advocacy. In so doing, the book contributes to a growing line of inquiry around the role water users and managers play in democratic decision-making and policy processes that shape water use and access. Water committees' transformative process from engaging in local resource management to a broader sphere of collective work encompassing political activism has resulted in CAPS coming into public view as unique and indispensable agents in the water and environmental sectors.

Tracing this process of transformation, the book draws attention to how grassroots water management and service provision contribute to a basis for multiscalar concerns and activism. It also reveals how this grassroots work strengthens demands for legitimate inclusion in water governance processes "beyond" the local level. In particular, the book highlights the character of CAPS' collective action in the form of new transcommunity and multisectoral networks that have drawn upon old and produced new working relationships across diverse social and political actors in Nicaragua. This is a story that lies at the intersection of Latin American politics, social justice and mobilization, and environmental policy and change. It is my hope that the book does justice in explaining the efforts of rural social actors to achieve political recognition and legal standing, as well as informs regional understandings of citizen-driven, multisectoral efforts to confront "everyday" crises of water use, access, and distribution.

Acknowledgments

This book is the product of the profound influence and support of many people.

The mentorship of my advisor, Don Share, greatly influenced the path I took as an undergraduate at the University of Puget Sound. Don's political economy of Central and South America courses were eye opening and inspiring, and owing to Don's encouragement, I enrolled in the Center for Global Education's study abroad program in Guatemala, El Salvador, and Nicaragua my junior year. Thank you to Adrienne Burk, not only my godmother, but a mentor before, during, and after graduate school who has supported me with thoughtful and honest guidance at several critical junctures over the years and helped me to become a stronger writer and scholar.

During graduate school, I was fortunate to benefit from the dedicated and involved advising and mentoring of Kent Eaton, Jonathan Fox, Ronnie Lipschutz, Tom Perreault, and Margaret Keck, each of whom influenced the course of my work and provided valuable guidance that supported my success. I am especially grateful for the mentoring of Kent Eaton and Jonathan Fox during and after graduate school. I have been inspired by their scholarship and have benefited greatly from their guidance and support over the years.

I am also grateful for the generous financial support that was crucial to my ability to carry out international research provided by the Fulbright Institute for International Education, the UCSC Chicano/Latino Research Center, the UCSC Department of Politics, the UC Pacific Rim Research Program, and the University of Northern Colorado Summer Support Initiative.

In Nicaragua, countless individuals and organizations have supported and befriended me. A constant, deep source of support has come from the Miranda Rodríguez family in Batahola Norte, Managua. Thanks so much to Guillermo, Jeniffer, Daniela, René, Iris, Jaqueline, Alan, and your children for welcoming me into your home and for sharing meals, holidays, and much laughter over the years. A heartfelt thank you to Josefa Rodríguez Poveda, my friend as well as host mom. I am forever grateful that your family shared a life with me: Chavala, my Nicaraguan-American Shepard mix who has been my friend and partner in crime for the last fourteen years! Thank you as well to Kathy McBride, Mark Lester, Juan Carlos López, and all the staff at Center for Global Education in Managua who have supported, hosted, and fed me on numerous occasions since my first time in Nicaragua.

This project would in no way have been possible without the numerous Potable Water and Sanitation Committee members in Nicaragua who shared their work and stories with me, brought me into their communities and meeting spaces, and embraced me as both friend and researcher. Special thanks to Delia Aydeé Tamariz, Esperanza Soza, José Francisco Salgado, Misael Blanchard, Florentín López, Marbelly Tremenio, Jessenia Rivera, and Miguel Ángel Úbeda. I am deeply indebted to you all and continue to be amazed and inspired by your work.

My sincere gratitude to a number of organizations and individuals in Nicaragua whose direct support, time, and guidance made writing this book possible: Eduardo Zamora; Roberto Stuart; Rosibel Kreimann; Edgard Bermúdez; Raúl Díaz; Harmhel Dalla Torre and the staff at La Cuculmeca; Mirna Rojas and Francisco Altamirano and the staff at ADEMNORTE; Javier Mendoza, Benjamín Martínez, and the staff at ODESAR; Denis Meléndez and the staff at MNGR; Martín Cuadra; Lourdes García; Francisco Baltodano; Gilberto Arauz; Carlos Pacheco; Heddy Calderón; and Anielka Figueroa. I have learned so much from all of you.

I extend my deep gratitude to Andrea Solorzáno and Karen González, who spent many hours meticulously transcribing my interviews. I also owe a special thank you to Henry, Norman, Eleda, and Daniel for ensuring that I traveled around Managua with ease and in excellent company.

Many friends made up an important community of support for me during my field research. Thank you to the following people for sharing meals, living spaces, hiking excursions, dance outings, and good conversation: Christine Goffredo, Amanda Otero, Meg Gray, Victoria Kabak, Emma Yorra, Greta

Tom, Sara Riegler, Erick Moncada, Guillermo González Prado, Claudia Dieta, Yumi Rydlun, Héctor Iván González Brioso, and Amanda Eastwood. My time in Nicaragua was much richer because of you all. Special thanks to Thomas LaVanchy, who has been both a dear friend and collaborator with me in the field.

I am grateful to the University of Arizona Press, including Allyson Carter and Scott De Herrera, among many others, for working with me and supporting this project. Thanks to Sonya Manes for her meticulous copy editing of my manuscript. Thank you, as well, to several anonymous reviewers who helped me to sharpen and clarify this book and the story therein.

It is an understatement to say that I would not be who I am or where I am today—and would never have written this book—without my family, including my parents, Marti and Dennis, and my brother, Michael. I owe my sense of social justice to my parents, whose life work has reflected a commitment to improving people's lives and protecting the environment. Thank you to my father, Dennis, for his unwavering support and encouragement, especially during some challenging periods over the years; thanks, Dad, for reminding me that I *can* do much of what feels impossible in the moment. Thank you to my mother, Marti, who served as an indispensable editor of the entire book and with whom I share deep interests in environmental justice and social activism— interests and passions that, on my end, are a direct result of our conversations and joint learning over the years about water, climate change, and the role of people in pushing for change from below. Mom, you have taught me so much about activism and what it means to be an engaged local and global citizen. Thank you for being my model of what is possible in this life as not only a teacher and scholar but also an activist.

Lastly, I extremely grateful for my husband, Kevin Cody, without whom I wonder whether I would have made it through the final stages of completing this book. Thank you, Kevin, for your thoughtful feedback on my book chapters and for being my day-to-day source of love, support, and encouragement. I am so lucky to have you.

Abbreviations

ADEMNORTE	*Asociación para el Desarrollo de los Municipios del Norte* (Association for the Development of Northern Municipalities)
AMNLAE	*La Asociación de Mujeres, Luisa Amanda Espinoza* (Nicaraguan Women's Association "Luisa Amanda Espinoza")
AMPRONAC	*Asociación de Mujeres ante la Problemática Nacional* (Association of Women Confronting the National Problem)
ANA	*Autoridad Nacional de Agua* (National Water Authority)
APN	*Ayuda Popular Noruega* (Norwegian People's Aid)
ATC	*Asociación de Trabajadores del Campo* (Rural Workers' Association)
CAPS	*Comité/s de Agua Potable y Saneamiento* (Potable Water and Sanitation Committee/s)
CBWM	Community-based water management
CDS	*Comités de Defensa Sandinistas* (Sandinista Defense Committees)
CISAS	*Centro de Información y Servicios de Asesoría* (Center for Information and Consulting Services)
CODA	*Coalición por el Derecho al Agua* (Coalition for the Right to Water)

CONAPAS   *Consejo Nacional de Agua Potable y Saneamiento* (National Council of Potable Water and Sanitation)

COSUDE   *Agencia Suiza para el Desarrollo y la Cooperación* (Swiss Agency for Development and Cooperation)

CPC   *Consejo del Poder Ciudadano* (Citizen Power Council)

DAR   *Dirección de Acueductos Rurales* (Direction of Rural Aqueducts)

DNRM   Decentralized natural resource management

ENACAL   *Empresa Nicaragüense de Acueductos y Alcantarillados Sanitarios* (Nicaraguan Water and Sewerage Company)

EPA   *Ejército Popular de Alfabetización* (Popular Literacy Army)

FISE   *Fondo de Inversión Social de Emergencia* (Emergency Social Investment Fund)

FSLN   *Frente Sandinista de Liberación Nacional* (Sandinista National Liberation Front)

GPAE   *Grupo de Promoción de la Agricultura Ecológica* (Group Promoting Agroecology)

IADB   Inter-American Development Bank

IMF   International Monetary Fund

INAA   *Instituto Nicaragüense de Acueductos y Alcantarillados* (Nicaraguan Water and Sanitation Institute)

INETER   *Instituto de Estudios Territoriales* (Institute of Territorial Studies)

JS-19   *Juventud Sandinista* (Sandinista Youth)

MAGFOR   *Ministerio Agropecuario y Forestal* (Ministry of Farming, Livestock, and Forests)

MARENA   *Ministerio del Ambiente y los Recursos Naturales* (Ministry of the Environment and Natural Resources)

MAS   *Ministerio de Acción Social* (Ministry of Social Action)

MINAS   *Ministerio de Energía y Minas* (Ministry of Energy and Mines)

MINSA   *Ministerio del Salud* (Ministry of Health)

MNGR   *Mesa Nacional de Gestión de Riesgos* (National Risk Management Board)

NGO   Nongovernmental organization

ODESAR	*Organización para el Desarrollo Económico y Social para el Área Urbana y Rural* (Organization for Economic and Social Development in Urban and Rural Areas)
PAHO	Pan American Health Organization
PLANSAR	*Plan de Saneamiento Básico Rural* (National Basic Rural Sanitation Plan)
PLC	*Partido Liberal Constitucionalista* (Liberal Constitutionalist Party)
PRACS	*Programa Rural de Acción Comunitaria en Salud* (Rural Community Health Program)
RNDC	*Red Nacional en Defensa de los Consumidores* (National Consumers' Defense Organization)
RRAS-CA	*Red Regional de Agua y Saneamiento para Centroamérica* (Regional Water and Sanitation Network of Central America)
SERMUNIC	*Departamento Nacional de Servicios Municipales* (National Department of Municipal Services)
SIMAS	*Servicio de Información Mesoamericano sobre Agricultura Sostenible* (Latin American Information Service for Sustainable Agriculture)
SINAS	*Sistema Nacional de Información de Agua y Saneamiento Rural de Nicaragua* (National Information System of Rural Water and Sanitation)
SNV	Netherlands Development Organization
UNAG	*La Unión Nacional de Agricultores y Ganaderos* (National Union of Farmers and Ranchers)
UNICEF	United Nations International Emergency Children's Fund
UNO	*Unión de Oposición Nacional* (National Opposition Union)
UNOM	*Unidades Nacionales de Operación y Mantenimiento* (National Operation and Maintenance Units)
USAID	United States Agency for International Development
WHO	World Health Organization

TRANSFORMING RURAL WATER GOVERNANCE

Introduction

From Resource Management to Political Activism

Amid a national anti–water privatization social movement, organizations constituting the Coalition for the Right to Water (CODA) met in the Northern highlands city of Jinotega, Nicaragua, in early September 2007 to discuss strategies for influencing the implementation of a new national water law passed several months earlier. The CODA had formed in 2005, an offshoot of another coalition, the Alliance against Water Privatization. Since 2000, diverse environmental, human rights, labor, and consumer advocacy organizations had been organizing to influence the management trajectory of the country's freshwater resources.

Starting the same year, the Cochabamba, Bolivia, "Water Wars" loomed large globally and across Latin America, conjuring images of skyrocketing water costs in cities and privatization of community wells in rural and semirural sectors.[1] In 1999, a $21 million loan package from the Inter-American Development Bank in the wake of Hurricane Mitch had stipulated the commercialization of the water sector in Nicaragua. Perceiving commercialization as a step toward privatization of the state water company, ENACAL, civil society organizations mobilized. Numerous consumer defense, human rights, and community development organizations engaged in street protests and demonstrations in front of ENACAL's head office in the capital. When the government passed the National Water Law (Law 620) in 2007, legislation prompted by antiprivatization organizing, it set forth a comprehensive legal framework for management of the country's freshwater resources and put a de facto end to anti–water privatization organizing and protest.

The group of roughly ten representatives of domestic NGOs began the CODA meeting by reflecting upon the process of the National Water Law's development. Participants expressed reservations about aspects of the law, even though a series of government consultations with businesses and the NGO sector had allowed for civil society input on its development. According to one participant, an article of the law stating that water service would not be privatized had been formulated "almost in secret." Members of CODA, and other social movement participants, perceived this article as a way to leave the door open to different forms of water privatization. For example, what protections would there be against private ownership of water *resources*? Similarly, there was concern about the law's emphasis on private industrial production and agriculture, potentially undermining the law's proclamation of water as having a "public character" and being a *patrimonio nacional* (national heritage). Even though Law 620 listed prioritization of water for human consumption over all other water uses, how would this translate into much needed attention to pervasive issues of water quality and access at a national scale?

Urban NGOs had taken center stage during anti–water privatization organizing in the early to mid-2000s, demonstrating in front of ENACAL and in other sites in the capital, Managua, and meeting to strategize contributions to the development of the new national water law. The CODA meeting in Jinotega in 2007 reflected this, as did the coalition itself, which was constituted by various NGOs with offices across capital cities within Nicaragua's departments. Yet, a new, little-known actor was about to emerge on the national political scene: the Potable Water and Sanitation Committees (CAPS), who were individually constituted by small groups of residents within rural areas and who had, since the mid-1970s in Nicaragua, taken leadership on the construction, maintenance, and administration of their communities' small-scale water systems such as wells and gravity-fed systems.

Like their global counterparts, CAPS function as part of common property regimes, or social and "institutional arrangements for the cooperative (shared, joint, collective) use, management, and sometimes ownership of natural resources" (McKean 1996, 1). Within Nicaragua, CAPS form around the construction of local water systems intended to serve a delineated community of users, or residents living within "small" communities of five hundred or fewer residents. Working with NGO staff, community members approve a

FIGURE 1 Anti–water privatization protesters in front of the state water company, ENACAL, in December 2004.

set of bylaws to guide local water management and service provision. In practice, CAPS constitute the community leadership as groups of roughly five to ten residents elected in community assemblies who then follow through with implementing local rules. These rules include provisions for elected leadership turnover on the water committee; financial management of community funds; local environmental stewardship; and participation of system beneficiaries in water management responsibilities, which include system maintenance and payment for water service.

The mission of CAPS to provide universal access to clean water within their communities is not easy to fulfill. Legally, state agencies, including the Ministry of Environment and Natural Resources (MARENA) and the Ministry of Health (MINSA), are responsible for ensuring the potability of drinking water. In practice, however, water testing is unevenly performed, and provisions such as chlorine tablets for water tanks are unevenly distributed across communities and regions. Moreover, although some rural water systems have basic technical components to support cleaner water—for instance, filtration using sand, dirt, and rocks built into gravity-fed systems in the highlands—many CAPS and rural residents are unaware of the actual potability of their "potable" water systems. While access to water via CAPS-managed wells and in-home or public water taps constitute an improved water source for residents, factors such as upstream/downstream water users and uses, environmental change, and population growth challenge the ability of CAPS to ensure comprehensive and consistent access to clean water. Strikingly, extreme drought and increasing climatic variability in Nicaragua (particularly for communities along the *corridor seco* [dry corridor] in the Central American region) are producing circumstances in which, at times, systems lack water flows entirely.

Despite the difficult circumstances they face, CAPS, as part of a rural water management model, have persisted since they first emerged in the 1970s—and their numbers have grown. By the 2000s, CAPS managed over five thousand water systems in Nicaragua, uniting upward of thirty to forty thousand rural residents in the day-to-day work of securing access to water for domestic use. Although functioning largely in isolation from one another as service providers, CAPS constitute a large-scale resource management scheme for over an estimated one million rural residents—a sizable portion of the country's small population of six million residents, almost half of whom lived in rural areas when the government last documented rural water projects (see table 1). Yet strikingly, as research for this book revealed, many urban-based actors, including government officials, had no idea that CAPS even existed.

This social and political "invisibility" in spite of CAPS' large-scale presence in rural areas helps to explain what might otherwise seem a surprising set of facts: CAPS were not centrally engaged in "public" debates on water privatization nor the process of consultation and design of the National Water Law (Law 620), despite their integral role in freshwater management. More startlingly, when the law passed in May 2007, rural water committees were completely absent from the law's content. It wasn't until August 2007 that CAPS briefly appeared in the law's regulations—a mention that amounted to a narrow recognition for the purpose of establishing the state's regulatory authority over water committees without conferring legal status to CAPS as organizations.

Why had CAPS lacked a visible presence or audible voice leading up to Law 620's passing—a heightened moment of national-level debate and dialogue on the future of freshwater resources in Nicaragua? What could be done to change this status quo of procedural exclusion and to engage rural residents in national level debates and dialogue on an issue to which their work was

TABLE 1   Rural Water Projects and Beneficiaries by Region

Region[a]	Water Projects	Houses in Region	Beneficiary Houses in Region	Population in Region	Population Served in Region
I	1,344	123,158	30,343	658,827	169,780
II	1,218	89,187	31,769	553,772	193,390
III	80	12,990	11,002	84,140	69,003
IV[b]	334	44,702	25,173	262,855	155,680
V	704	37,269	14,035	228,630	95,325
VI	1,175	92,580	40,972	597,848	269,415
VII	58	NA[c]	NA	28,676	12,064
VIII	42	NA	NA	23,841	14,796
IX	63	NA	NA	38,988	16,784
Total	5,018	399,886	153,294	2,477,577	996,237

Source: These figures come from data collected in the Sistema Nacional de Información de Agua y Saneamiento Rural de Nicaragua (National Information System of Rural Water and Sanitation [SINAS]), a database created by the Nicaraguan government and international donors in the mid-1990s to document project implementation. These data reflect documented water systems and estimated population served through part of 2004 only.
[a] Each region corresponds to the following departments (see also map 1): (1) Estelí, Madriz, Nueva Segovia; (2) León, Chinandega; (3) Managua; (4) Carazo, Granada, Masaya, Rivas; (5) Boaco, Chontales; (6) Jinotega, Matagalpa; (7) Región Autónoma del Atlántico Norte (RAAN); (8) Región Autónoma del Atlántico Sur (RAAS); (9) Río San Juan (RSJ).
[b] Figures include twenty water projects in the RSJ and 163 in the RAAS.
[c] Data not available.

essential? It was with these kinds of questions that CODA members grappled in Jinotega as they met in the wake of Law 620's passing.

Not mentioned in the CODA meeting, however, was a transformative process underway as of 2005 in Jinotega's neighboring department of Matagalpa. Located to the south of Jinotega, Matagalpa is similarly nestled in the central northern highlands, where the region's agricultural sector, including large-scale coffee production, provides a livelihood for many rural residents. Owing to a crucial convening role being played by rural development organizations, most actively the Organization for Economic and Social Development in Urban and Rural Areas (ODESAR), the department was becoming the site of a new social innovation in the rural water sector: the formation of multi-CAPS networks serving to bridge individual water committees across localities and regions for the first time.

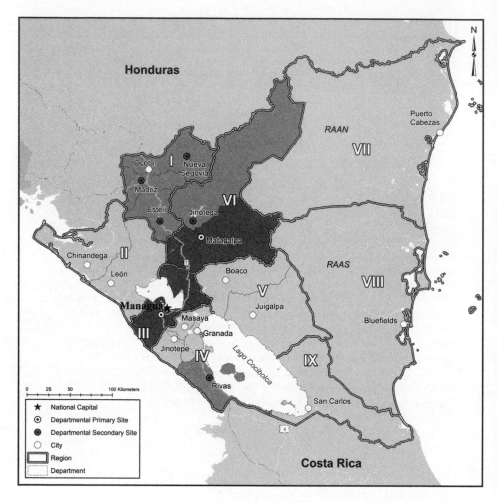

MAP 1 Regions in Nicaragua and departmental field research sites (map by Madeline Kelley).

Bridging not only individual CAPS members but also NGO and multilateral agency staff, "CAPS networks" at the municipal level in Matagalpa reflected new *transcommunity* as well as *multisectoral* instances of collective action with explicitly political aims. These primarily NGO-led bridging processes would draw strength from the bonds CAPS members shared as water managers and service providers at the grass roots across Nicaragua. Once united in network spaces, CAPS succeeded in cultivating a new collective identity and developing shared goals that would bear on unfolding public policy processes. By 2010, a

FIGURE 2 Residents collecting water at a CAPS-managed community water tap in Tejerina, Matagalpa, in 2010.

National CAPS Network in addition to dozens of municipal and departmental networks—including eight municipal networks and a departmental network in Matagalpa—would form across the country, engaging over a thousand water committee members.

Using new networks as a platform, CAPS pursued a paradoxical objective: to demand state recognition and support as well as to protect and promote the autonomy of their rural organizations and water systems. It does seem contradictory for nonstate water users and managers to seek to engage the state as a source of resources, protection, and recognition while at the same time wanting to preserve their uniquely independent and nonstate character. However, this engagement approach reflects a practical, as well as rational, response by societal actors.[2]

In a national context of fierce party loyalties and political polarization, pursuit of this objective created tensions during CAPS' mobilizing processes. However, partisan politics and the co-optive tendencies of the state toward civil society organizations would not inhibit an important achievement. In 2010, the efforts of water committees and their domestic and international allies culminated in the passing of the Special Law of Potable Water and Sanitation Committees (Law 722). The CAPS Law afforded water committees a pathway to official legal status as community-based organizations in addition to a formal political recognition of their work as water managers and service providers within the broader framework of freshwater management in Nicaragua. By the time President Daniel Ortega of the Sandinista National Liberation Front (FSLN) signed Law 722 in May 2010, the character and scope of many water committees' work had been effectively transformed. No longer engaged "solely" in resource management and service provision at the grass roots, CAPS had become effective political activists.

How did rural water committees become politically activated in Nicaragua? What factors explain CAPS' successful transcommunity mobilization to achieve a national collective presence and, ultimately, legal recognition from the state? This book traces the process of how water committees in Nicaragua transcended their rural localities and roles as water managers and service providers to engage in fundamentally new forms of political activism and advocacy vis-à-vis the state.

My central claim is that three interconnected factors proved crucial to explaining CAPS' process of political activation, mobilization, and ultimate achievement of legal recognition. These include CAPS' (1) de facto empowerment as community-based water managers and service providers and their legitimate authority in the water sector as a result, (2) their alliances with domestic and international organizations, and (3) their discourses that describe and outwardly project a locally grounded understanding of water governance.

While the book sheds light on water committees' empowerment, alliances, and discourses as each having independent explanatory power, these factors are best understood as interconnected dynamics and processes that contributed to CAPS' successful mobilization and advocacy. In one sense, these processes build upon each other sequentially. For example, CAPS' empowerment and legitimate authority as resource managers and service providers at the grass roots was a necessary precondition for their effective alliances with NGOs and multilateral agencies. That is, water committees' empowerment to manage water and distribute resources, and the legitimacy derived from this work, "scaled up" with them into network spaces convened and funded by NGO and multilateral staff. The experiences of CAPS and their legitimate authority in the water sector supported how ally-coordinated network spaces became productive sites of engagement where rural water committees cultivated a shared sense of goals and developed collective action platforms. Similarly, allies' convening and facilitation of network spaces and their dissemination of "products," such as published versions of CAPS' pronouncements on government policy, enabled the shaping and honing of water committees' collective discourses of water governance. As a result of ally-supported projection of CAPS' voices into the public sphere, these collective discourses functioned as a mechanism for CAPS to promote their experiences and understanding of rural water governance vis-à-vis state actors.

Water committees' empowerment, alliances, and discourses also have important iterative dimensions. For example, the bridging processes allies set in motion via CAPS networks at the municipal, departmental, and national levels served to generate bonds among previously disconnected water committees. In turn, these bonds translated into new working relationships across CAPS at the grass roots evident in new forms of collaboration such as intercommunity *intercambios* (exchanges) to learn about each other's water management and provision—activities that can be understood as further empowering water committees as resource managers and service providers. The legitimacy derived from CAPS' work at the grass roots has also been enhanced through their discourses of water governance, which have heightened awareness and understanding of the significance of their experiences as water managers and service providers among public officials in Nicaragua. The projection of CAPS' voices, and the ally-facilitated opportunity to talk directly to water committees, gave public officials and elected leaders at the national level a basis for knowing and understanding who CAPS are and what they do in rural areas. This new knowledge and awareness influenced public officials' perceptions of CAPS as having legitimate authority in the water sector and as meriting formal recognition.

Seeking Solutions from the Grass Roots: Rural Water Governance in Latin America

With 31 percent of the world's "permanently usable water" and significant portions of some countries' residents living in rural areas (Robson and Lichtenstein 2013, 6–7), Latin America is an important region for examining the persistent and perennial issues of insufficient and inequitable access to clean water for drinking and domestic use. Notably, even countries within the region that have abundant freshwater resources, such as Nicaragua, struggle to secure water access. It is striking that over a third of the population in Latin America does not have access to potable drinking water and that considerable access gaps exist between urban and rural areas within the region. There is an urban-rural gap in tap water coverage in countries with sizable rural populations (20–50 percent)—for example, Bolivia, El Salvador, Guatemala, Haiti, Peru—as well as in those, for example, Venezuela, with relatively small rural populations (12 percent).[3] In Nicaragua, where roughly 40 percent of residents live in rural areas, an estimated 33 percent of rural residents have access to tap water compared to 95 percent of urban residents—a 62 percent gap (World Health Organization and United Nations Children's Fund 2017).

The challenge of securing access to water and sanitation, and of rectifying inequities within and across regions globally, remains stark in the wake of major global initiatives to address these issues. These include the United Nations' International Drinking Water Supply and Sanitation Decade in the 1980s and the subsequent Millennium Development Goals (MDGs). The UN MDGs touted success in halving the number of people globally without access to piped water when the initiative officially ended in 2015. While this book focuses primarily on *water* management and provision, access to water and sanitation are fundamentally intertwined (see, e.g., Pacheco-Vega 2015b). Sanitation facilities such as sinks and flush toilets are dependent on water resources to exist and function. Moreover, sanitation-related practices—for example, waste disposal—must be managed in relation to water sources to avoid contamination of drinking water sources. The critical interconnection of water and sanitation is reflected in how government, NGO, and community-based initiatives rarely emphasize one without the other.

The problem of *securing* rural water provision owes to complex and overlapping geographic, financial, and political issues. In spatial terms, the geographic dispersion of rural communities make infeasible, in financial and infrastructural terms, connecting large populations of residents on a single water supply system. Small-scale water systems, including wells and small gravity-fed systems, while more appropriate to a rural community scale, are logistically challenging and still require significant financial and technical inputs—both immediate and long term—for system maintenance. Moreover, governments tend to lack the political will to supply water to rural populations. This failure relates to the political and social marginalization of rural constituencies, who are relatively more impoverished and receive less schooling than their urban counterparts (López and Váldez 2000). Thus, even though globally many residents in rural areas have come to expect national states to ensure drinking water access (see, e.g., Robinson 1998; World Bank 1993), this is not the dominant arrangement.

It could be argued that there is little "payoff" for governments to invest limited public funds in a sector of the population deemed less important in political terms. And, while the private sector is undoubtedly interested in the water *resources* of rural areas globally (see, e.g., Gerlak and Wilder 2012; Pacheco-Vega 2015a), an effective private sector role in securing large-scale and equitable water access in rural areas is unlikely. In short, rural water delivery systems are just not profitable where economies of scale are difficult to achieve and where residents have little to pay for their water service.

Who or what, then, confronts the "everyday" challenge of rural water provision? In Nicaragua, similar to other rural areas in Latin America and other Global South regions, residents tend to be at the forefront of addressing issues of water access, quality, and distribution. In the absence of water distribution infrastructure, residents may access directly from freshwater sources such as springs, rivers, and lakes; in so doing, they confront issues related to water quality and access in terms of time and energy spent collecting water—a task falling mostly to women and children. Yet across Latin America, roughly eighty thousand community-based groups such as CAPS in Nicaragua enable water access through small-scale infrastructure to an estimated forty to seventy million rural and semirural residents (Dupuits and Bernal 2015) (see map 2). Within Central America, CAPS are part of a regional phenomenon of community-based water management and provision; an estimated twenty-four thousand water committees operate across the region, enabling "improved" water access to roughly 25 percent of the region's rural inhabitants (FANCA 2006).

Integrated to varying degrees into state legal frameworks, these groups—simultaneously constituting waters users, managers, and service providers—often operate without a legal status. Indeed, systems of customary rights, wherein residents depend upon local *usos y costumbres* (uses and customs), are still prevalent in rural areas for resource and environmental management globally (Fuys and Dohrn 2010; Perreault 2008). The de facto existence of resident-driven water provision confirms the importance of a non-state-centric view of water governance (Pahl-Wostl 2009). Certainly, "irrespective of whether policymakers like them or not, and regardless of whether states recognize them or not, analysis requires acknowledging that systems and sources of norms and laws need not be formalized or institutionalized by the state to matter" (Roth, Boelens, and Zwarteveen 2015, 465).

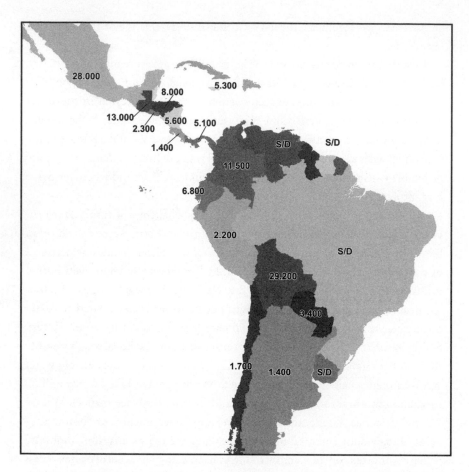

MAP 2 Community-based water systems in Latin America and the Caribbean (map by Madeline Kelley). Data obtained from CLOCSAS (Confederación Latinoamericano de Organizaciones Comunitarias de Servicios de Agua y Saneamiento), "Antecedentes, evolución y potencialidades," June 2017, p. 16. "S/D" means no data available; decimal points represent commas (e.g., 28.000 = 28,000).

This book reinforces this conclusion: resident-driven water management and service provision in rural areas prior to the passing of the Special CAPS Law in Nicaragua reveal decades of highly consequential work and outcomes for lives and livelihoods. Water committees' work would have remained materially and socially consequential even in the absence of a formal state policy recognizing CAPS. While outside the scope of this book to examine in depth, the CAPS Law's recognition of water committees in Nicaragua raises the question of what *kinds* of state policies in the region affect water users' associations and *how* (see chapter 5).

Despite the significant contributions of water users' associations globally to resolving the problem of rural water access, scholars and policy makers should be wary of seeing a nonstate, community-based "solution" as either equitable or fully sustainable as a model of rural water management and provision. For instance, the local social contexts that embed community-based resource management may be characterized by gendered, socioeconomic, and ethnicity-based inequities that have led scholars not to romanticize community-based resource management, nor to presume homogeneity along these dimensions in examining "communities" (Boelens 2009; see also Meinzen-Dick and Zwarteveen 1998). Internally, communities can reflect similar inequities and forms of exclusion that are visible in broader societal terms. Moreover, related both to equity and sustainability, provision of water and sanitation is inherently expensive for rural communities, sometimes prohibitively so. This restriction explains why the construction and maintenance of infrastructure such as piped water systems, latrines, and toilets are rarely endeavors financed or undertaken solely by rural residents themselves. While many governments exhibit a kind of "benign neglect" of rural areas in terms of critical service provision, the work of NGOs and multilateral agencies (e.g., the United Nations Children's Fund [UNICEF]) since the 1970s has entailed a drawing in of the state into collaborative work to provide water and sanitation services to rural populations. Community-based water management "is now being taken up by a number of countries as *the* approach for providing rural services" (Schouten and Moriarty 2003, 5). It is important to note that in the case of rural drinking water, this trend reflecting state engagement in the sector does not reflect the drawing *back in* of the state after retrenchment in the context of global neoliberalism; rather, state actors were rarely engaged in rural water provision to begin with. Instead, increasing international attention to and energy behind expanding rural water access has prompted a greater state role as governments facilitate this primarily international investment in the sector.[4]

The "model" of community-based water management has inherent weaknesses. For example, rural residents responsible for the ongoing administration and maintenance of water systems are usually unevenly trained and equipped across regions and communities. This discrepancy owes to the diversity of state and nonstate actors involved in the sector and their different approaches to projects, and it has an impact on how well rural residents can ensure long-term system functioning as well as things such as the quality or, more specifically, the potability, of the water flowing through their potable water systems. Moreover, working in an unofficial capacity in relation to state policy intersects in largely negative ways with increasingly acute ecological and environmental issues. Long-standing threats such as large-scale deforestation and megahydraulic projects and "new" ones such as climate change and water privatization have produced conflicts and affected resource management imperatives in Latin America (Hoogesteger and Verzijl 2015; Kuzdas et al. 2015; LaVanchy, Romano, and Taylor 2017; Perreault 2006). Without a doubt, a rapidly changing ecological context has and will continue to put compounding pressures on residents as resource managers and service providers. Rural residents are on the front lines of environmental change, including climate change; yet, they contribute little to the problem of accelerating climate change and, in contrast to state actors, do not possess the means to curb the fundamentally *global* trend of a warming planet.[5]

This landscape of environmental change impinges upon the work of water users' associations such as CAPS in Nicaragua in terms of water quantity and quality. Indeed, one Nicaraguan newspaper's reporting of some CAPS being "out of work" owing to drought reflects the kind of existential threat climate change poses to water committees as social organizations (Pérez 2010). Not surprisingly, climate change and environmental stewardship constitute important threads motivating CAPS' political activism and influencing how they talk about their work as resource managers and service providers.

Many of the challenges CAPS confront are not new. Why did CAPS become politically activated in Nicaragua in the early to mid-2000s? What explains *how* they successfully engaged in transcommunity and multisectoral mobilization to achieve a national collective presence and, ultimately, legal recognition from the state? Three factors—empowerment, alliances, and discourse—explain CAPS' transcendence of localities and engagement in new forms of political activism. Understanding these factors, including how they dynamically interrelate, requires engaging with and building upon an interdisciplinary scholarship.

Contributions of the Book

Through bringing into focus understudied dimensions and processes pertaining to contemporary rural water management and provision, this book contributes to the literatures on common property regimes, social capital, and decentralization.

Common Property Regimes in Multiscalar Perspective

This book reveals the importance of a more nuanced understanding of the role that community-based groups such as CAPS in Nicaragua play in their communities—and in their countries. Providing substantial empirical evidence refuting Garrett Hardin's supposedly unavoidable "Tragedy of the Commons" (1968), common property regime scholars have contributed to our understanding of how resource users' associations collectively manage shared resources: pastures, forests, fisheries, and the like. These scholars have pointed to a number of elements associated with successful commons management: small group size, locally devised systems of rules, clearly delineated resource boundaries, and effective local monitoring arrangements that external government authorities do not undermine (Becker and Ostrom 1995; Feeny et al. 1990; Gibson, Williams, and Ostrom 2005; Ostrom 1990, 2002). As small groups of residents, CAPS function much like common property regimes in their management of water.

One understudied dimension of common property management this book brings into focus is how resource managers often have a simultaneous role as providers of critical and public services. Indeed, CAPS are not only resource managers but also water and sanitation *service* providers. Part of the significance of this dual role is that as common property organizations, CAPS fulfill a role legally assigned to the state. Water provision is also a role associated with the state in the popular imaginary. This association has implications for understanding the legitimacy and authority ascribed to common property organizations providing water service and hence constitutes an important dimension of common property management. Because "they exercise public authority" (Lund 2006a, 673), nonstate organizations such as CAPS in Nicaragua benefit from "the legitimacy that follows from control of public decisions and service delivery" (Ribot 2011, 8). Christian Lund characterizes organizations that "take on the mantle of public administrative authority [including] legitimated administrative operations" (2006a, 678) as "twilight institutions." Although nongovernmental, CAPS and other twilight institutions demonstrate the "state qualities of governance" (2006b, 685) via their public functions.

Through introducing the concept of "organic empowerment," this book explicitly seeks to acknowledge the ways in which common property organizations cultivate legitimacy and authority through their de facto empowerment to manage resources. An organic empowerment contrasts with a formally state-conferred authority and set of responsibilities via decentralization (see below). Beyond an initial moment of empowerment resulting from the construction of a potable water system, the day-to-day labors of water management reveal an *evolving* empowerment at the grass roots that strengthens as well as generates new capacities to sustain local water access. These dynamics engender a sense of ownership and autonomy in local water management and infuse water committees with legitimacy vis-à-vis system beneficiaries; these dynamics can become self-reinforcing as water provision is sustained over time.

This book does not endeavor to reproduce detailed descriptions of community-based arrangements for managing water as they exist in Nicaragua and elsewhere in the Global South; many other scholars and practitioners have produced these kinds of accounts.[6] Rather, this book focuses on the dimensions of local commons management that surfaced as important for understanding CAPS' multiscalar, politicized forms of collective action. Explaining these collective, both multiscalar and multisectoral, organizational processes constitutes the central explanatory task of the book.

Notably, emphasis on factors such as ownership, autonomy, authority, and legitimacy at the grass roots are distinct from the traditional common property scholarship's emphasis on institutional factors, for example, group size and monitoring arrangements. Attention to these social and relational dimensions of common property management reveal *understudied* dimensions of common property management. These dimensions are important; for example, the perception of resource management organizations as legitimate authorities is a precondition for successful resource management. For instance, collecting water users' fees and engaging residents in sustaining local water management regimes—through activities such as reforesting around water sources—depend upon water system beneficiaries' perception of CAPS as legitimate authorities in their communities. In the Nicaraguan case, examining CAPS' organic empowerment as water managers and services providers also reveals how rural residents' capacities in the sector oftentimes exceed those of urban-based state actors. Of importance, this bottom-up form of empowerment has come to bear on top-down efforts to restructure the water sector: CAPS have leveraged their de facto water management roles and responsibilities to contest their political exclusion and promote the passage of a new law "decentralizing" responsibilities to their rural organizations.

Highlighting rural residents' dual role as common property managers and public service providers helps to understand a second analytical contribution of this book: an expanded frame of analysis accounting for when and how community-based resource managers "scale up" (Fox 1996) politically. Arguably, conventional common property regime theory's emphasis on microlevel institutional characteristics proves insufficient for understanding increasingly complex landscapes of environmental governance. For example, multiscalar dynamics impinging upon local resource management regimes—global neoliberalism, the related policy trend of privatization, and socioecological trends such as accelerating climate change—compel scholars to expand frameworks for understanding community-based resource and environmental management. How and under what circumstances do local resource users and managers act collectively *across* and *beyond* their communities? Indeed, in focusing largely on these microlevel regimes in isolation from one another, common property theory leaves the political mobilization and organizing of common property organizations, such as CAPS in Nicaragua, outside the frame of analysis.

Organic empowerment serves as a conceptual bridge between common property regime and decentralization frameworks because it draws attention to the empowerment of grassroots, including "unofficial," actors in resource governance and facilitates examination of how locally grounded capacities and the legitimacy they generate may influence state policies. In examining these processes, this book contributes to a growing body of scholarship revealing how community responses to state water policies and extralocal politics prompt multiscalar responses. A multiscalar approach to grassroots water management builds upon scholarship that has sought to capture the cross-scalar mobilization and collective action of water users and managers in response to local injustices or external threats (Boelens 2008; Hoogesteger 2012, 2013; Hoogesteger and Verzijl 2015; Llano-Arias 2015; Perreault 2003, 2006, 2008; Romano 2012; Shiva 2002; see also Fox 1996). As scholars have revealed, "local" resource and environmental management regimes often clash with policies and decision making at higher political scales. For example, opposition to state policies that alter water ownership or management arrangements may be particularly vibrant and assertive among communities intimately involved in water extraction, use, and conservation at the grass roots. This opposition owes to the necessity of water for life and livelihoods and the intimate connection between water and processes of identity formation, as well as the de facto control of water resources on the part of communities and user groups who contest losing certain prerogatives (Boelens 2008; Boelens, Getches, and Guevara-Gil 2010; Perreault 2006, 2008; Romano 2012). In Latin America, the multiscalar political mobilization of water users' associations has been characterized by demands and debate related to issues of water quality and access and to the financing, repair, and legality of water systems, in addition to legal recognition of grassroots water management organizations.

This book contributes an analytical emphasis on how locally grounded experiences in day-to-day resource management affect interactions and relationships beyond the local. In particular, the book argues that experiences and sentiments, including a sense of ownership and autonomy cultivated at the grass roots, "scale up" with water committees as they act collectively beyond their communities. Once speaking with a collective voice and having a platform to engage with public officials, the social and relational dimensions of grassroots resource management and service provision serve to strengthen CAPS' political position vis-à-vis state actors. In other words, CAPS' sense of, and claims to, ownership, autonomy, and authority over rural water systems have affected how state actors perceive and treat CAPS as legitimate authorities and experts in the water and sanitation sector.

In revealing how the empowerment of rural water users and managers has the potential to come to bear on interactions and negotiations with state officials, this book highlights the continued need to study grassroots resource management and service provision within a larger social, political, and ecological context. This entails embracing an analytical frame of analysis both attentive to and transcending of common property scholars' focus on primarily microlevel dynamics of commons management.

Reconceptualizing Decentralized Natural Resources Management

This book's findings support a reconceptualization of decentralized natural resource management (DNRM). Specifically, I seek to integrate a focus within the scholarship on societal actors participating in water governance and service provision who operate "below the radar" of state policies and legal frameworks. One shortcoming of the conventional decentralization scholarship is its overlooking of local, or subnational, resource management falling outside the realm of official state policy. This owes to scholars' primary focus on examining policies that shift government decision-making, including management and regulation authorities and responsibilities, to lower levels of government (Agarwal and Gupta 2005; Bergh 2004; Crook and Manor 1998; Larson 2004; Larson and

Ribot 2004; Ribot 1999, 2007, 2011; Ribot and Larson 2005). This granting of power to state actors at the subnational level typically entails displacing primary state authority at the national or federal level.

In contrast, this book sheds light on nonstate actors who constitute a de facto (and large-scale) decentralized resource management and service provision scheme. Specifically, CAPS' empowerment to manage resources—what I call an "organic empowerment"—emerged in the *absence* of official state devolution of decision-making authority. Given the emphasis of conventional decentralization theory, it is significant, first, to recognize that the government is not always performing a function or service prior to subnational actors taking it on. Second, it matters that subnational actors with primary decision-making authority and responsibility are not always governmental actors. Notably, scholars have focused on the *participation* of civil society actors in governmental decision-making at subnational levels. Empowering residents or nonstate organizations to participate in resource and environmental management in theory improves management effectiveness; local actors contribute better information to projects and spending decisions and are likely to be more invested in outcomes than nonlocal politicians and public officials (Agarwal and Ribot 1999; Narayan 1994; Ribot and Larson 2005). Nevertheless, highlighting the political and legal contours of local resource management and service provision matters for distinguishing, first, if this work has a primarily state or nonstate character, and second, if this work has been formally recognized in law or remains in a legal gray area.

In regard to legality, the decentralized natural resource management scholarship does not fully account for what, in empirical terms, constitute ex-post facto devolutions of state authority. That is, the existence and operation of unofficial resource management and service provision regimes *prior to* their formal recognition in law raise questions regarding the nature and meaning of administrative decentralization. In the Nicaraguan case, community-based water management had been an empirical reality for decades when the CAPS Law recognizing rural water committees was passed by the National Assembly in 2010. As the book reveals, decades of unofficial water management at the grass roots influenced the interest in, and perceived imperative to, pass the CAPS Law. In empirical terms, the law also reflected a kind of "decentralization from below" (Larson 2004) given water committees' direct and energetic role in helping to shape the law's contents and promote its passage.

In Nicaragua and regionally in Latin America, political recognition and formal legal standing of water users' associations cannot be viewed as panaceas to the problems and challenges of community-based resource management and service provision. This reality is evident in the scholarship on users' associations managing irrigation water in the Andean region (see, e.g., Boelens 2009; Roth, Boelens, and Zwarteveen 2015; Seemann 2016). Nevertheless, this book takes as an important point of departure the quest for recognition on the part of drinking water users' associations to achieve greater political voice and inclusion in decision making—part of which manifested in demands for formal legal recognition from the state.

Drawing together the scholarships on common property management and decentralization is one of the principal theoretical contributions of this book. Through granting greater attention to state policies in the first and the role of unofficial actors in natural resource governance in the second, this book contributes a more comprehensive accounting of not only grassroots resource management but also the multiscalar collective action of locally grounded, nonstate water users and managers such as CAPS in Nicaragua.

Social Capital: From Bridges to Bonds

In addition to bringing into focus consequential, yet politically unrecognized, actors in resource governance, the book seeks to explain the *transformation* of CAPS from resource managers and service providers to political activists. How do CAPS and other grassroots social actors scale up their collective action in ways that contribute to collective political efficacy? Engaging with and building upon theories of social capital, the book confirms and advances a specific relationship between two forms of social capital: bonding and bridging. Bridging social capital, or those connections, networks, and relationships across difference—be it socioeconomic, sectoral, or class-based (Anderson 2010a; Granovetter 1983; Narayan 1999; Woolcock and Narayan 2000)—contrasts with "bonding" social capital, or "relations among family members, close friends and neighbors" (Woolcock 2001, 13; see also Adler and Kwon 2002). While bonding social capital has been criticized for promoting narrow and exclusive interests, bridging social capital has been found to facilitate entry into new political and economic arenas because of the "cross-cutting ties" (Narayan 1999) it entails.[7]

This book's main contribution to theories of social capital includes documenting the conditions under which bonding social capital, and the positive synergies among the people who share it, *transcend* the geographic, social, and political boundaries of these "tight-knit" groups. In so doing, this book provides evidence that, first, bonding social capital does not impede action and solidarity across different actors (in terms of, e.g., geographic location or social class), and, second, bridging social capital facilitates the spread of bonding social capital. Indeed, rather than impede integration into broader wholes, high levels of bonding social capital, or social solidarity (Woolcock and Narayan 2001) among water committees at the grass roots, intersects with bridging social capital to realize the full potential of the former. In other words, locally grounded, and oftentimes materially resource-poor, actors often must *bridge* with differently endowed actors to gain mobility (Granovetter 1983), support "social action that is politically and economically efficacious" (Evans 1996, 1124), and/or gain access to certain resources such as "talent or expertise" from "outside the community" (Hyman 2002, 200–201).

In sum, opportunities for people in bonded social groups to connect to socially different actors, and thus gain access to greater or different resources, can serve as an antidote to insularity and disconnection from broader wholes. This corroborates other scholars' findings that social capital solely at the microlevel may be insufficient for accessing the resources necessary for economic advancement or political gains (Bebbington et al. 1993; Fox 1996; Krishna 2004; Woolcock and Narayan 2000). Indeed, this study's empirical findings reveal that bonding social capital can be highly beneficial toward achieving collective goals—including those promoting inclusivity across diverse societal actors—when it has not produced hostility toward or encouraged exclusion of other groups (see also Collins, Neal, and Neal 2014; Hyman 2002; Larsen et al. 2004; Narayan 1999; Ohmer 2010). The book builds upon this finding by demonstrating how bonding social capital not only serves as an important precondition for collection action and civic engagement at other scales but also can grow and *spread* when bridging social capital facilitates the coming together of previously disconnected social actors who share similar experiences at the grass roots.

Researching Water Governance across Scales

I conducted research for this book across twelve years, from 2004 to 2016, with most research conducted from 2009 to 2010. Starting in 2004, this study entailed eighteen months of fieldwork in Nicaragua, with ten consecutive months spent in the country from October 2009 to May 2010. The following sections outline my analytical approach, case selection rationale, and data collection methods.

Analytical Approach

As an endeavor to document and understand new forms of organizing and collaboration, this research reflects a multiscalar process tracing approach. As a within-case analytical approach, process tracing uses "careful description" to document empirical patterns or relationships toward developing causal explanations (Beach 2017; Collier 2011). Process tracing is an apt methodological approach for capturing "novel political and social phenomena" and starting to make sense of these through "gaining insight into causal mechanisms" (Collier 2011, 824). As a new phenomenon, water committees' political mobilization to form advocacy networks in Nicaragua required not only documentation of these processes but also a systematic assessment of how different components of this mobilization worked together dynamically to effect the outcomes of new advocacy networks, including official state recognition. In methodological terms, the three factors discussed in the book (i.e., the independent variables discussed in chapters 2–4) were inductively derived as factors explaining the outcome of collective action across scales and ultimate achievement of formal integration into state legal frameworks (i.e., the dependent variables).

This book reflects an emphasis on detailed descriptions and the importance of sequencing (Collier 2011). Descriptions of processes such as CAPS' cultivation of water management capacities over time at the grass roots and their development of political and legal knowledge in network spaces allow for insight into what Collier refers to as "recurring empirical regularities" (2011, 824). In turn, patterns observed across interactions as well as those understood from interviews and historical documents support this book's formulation of causal inferences—that is, how parts of a process connect and influence one another. For instance, this book's documented pattern across rural communities of CAPS' initial empowerment to manage resources at the time of water system construction constitutes what Collier calls a "snapshot in time." In dynamic perspective, this empowerment has influenced a trajectory of capacity building and water committees' cultivation of legitimate authority as resource managers and service providers at the grass roots.

This book's analytical emphasis on sequencing includes attention to how the three interrelated factors of empowerment, alliances, and discourse build upon each other in ways that ultimately supported CAPS' legal recognition. This entailed attention to how dynamics at one scale connect to those at another. For instance, water committees' organic empowerment at the grass roots served as an important *precondition* for allies' ability to elevate CAPS within a national level political scene. Grassroots processes and outcomes thus consequentially inform those at broader and higher scales of collective action.

Case Selection

This book reflects a single-country case study of water committee mobilization. Because the research objective was to understand a national-scale phenomenon within Nicaragua, the book does not integrate a negative case of nonmobilization. From an empirical perspective, it would be possible to examine systematically why some water committees did *not* participate directly in this mobilization (either at the national or subnational levels); however, this line of inquiry falls outside of the scope of what this book is attempting to achieve in terms of explaining the mobilization that did occur at a national scale. Aligning with this objective, within-case analysis focused on several geographic sites and respective actors as a way of providing detailed descriptions of CAPS, their allies, and these multisectoral organizing processes toward developing an understanding of how mobilization occurred and with what outcomes (see map 1, above).

The "within-case cases" of CAPS networks and respective participants reflect the inherently multiscalar and multisectoral character of water committees' organizing processes and outcomes. Because municipal, departmental, and national CAPS networks constituted interconnected sites of new collaboration between and among CAPS, NGOs, and multilateral agencies, examining each of these sites was fundamental to understanding water committees' transcendence of the "local" and seeking of political recognition.

As reflected across the chapters, the main protagonists in this story include individual water committee members and their allies and NGO and multilateral agency staff, at multiple scales of water governance. At the subnational level, I selected the department of Matagalpa to study processes of CAPS' empowerment at the grass roots and *subnational* (i.e., municipal and departmental) CAPS network formation and operation. This region is home to the first CAPS networks in the country. In addition to having the oldest networks, Matagalpa was described by key informants during early research in 2006 and 2007 as having the most vibrant, established, and well-organized networks nationally. These characteristics made the department an apt site to examine not only the origins of CAPS' mobilization and political alliance building but also to gain insight into how new networks were functioning in the mid- to late 2000s. Within Matagalpa, several networks were examined: the Matagalpa

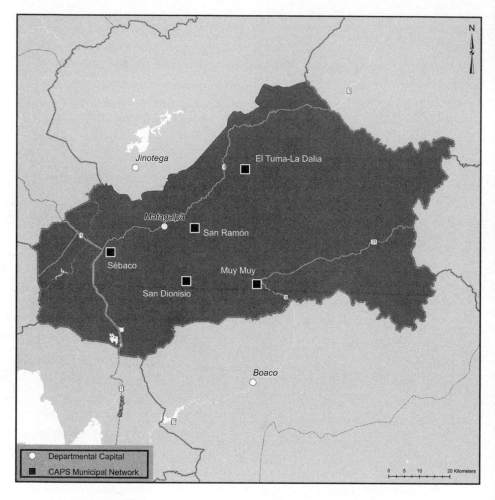

MAP 3 Municipal networks of Potable Water and Sanitation Committees under study in Matagalpa (map by Madeline Kelley).

departmental CAPS network linking CAPS from across municipalities and five municipal-level networks—El Tuma–La Dalia, Muy Muy, San Dionisio, San Ramón, and Sébaco. These networks were selected because they allowed for examining a range of experiences owing to date of formation, with San Dionisio being one of the first municipal CAPS networks, forming in 2005, and Sébaco one of the most recent, forming in late 2009. These cases provided the opportunity to look for variance as well as similarities regarding how CAPS allied with NGOs and multilateral agencies to pursue collective objectives via new networks. For comparative purposes and to expand my data set, I conducted secondary research on municipal-level networks in the municipalities of Estelí, La Trinidad, Pueblo Nuevo, Jinotega, and Palacagüina, which are also located in the central-northern highlands of Nicaragua in the departments of Estelí, Jinotega, and Madriz (see map 1).

As the sole collective body at the *national* level, the National CAPS Network was a necessary body to examine toward understanding CAPS' transcommunity, multiscalar, and multisectoral mobilization processes.

Data collection methods

The primary methods adopted for this study included semistructured interviews, participant observation, and analysis of primary and secondary documents. Over 190 semistructured interviews were conducted with key informants from 2004 to 2016. The interviewees selected for this project reflect the central protagonists of this story: CAPS, and their allies, in addition to key governmental actors.

Semistructured interviews with CAPS members were conducted as both individual and group interviews across different geographic and political scales. Owing to the multiscalar processes under study, interviews entailed talking to water committee members from across geographic regions. Semistructured interviews were conducted, first, with *individual* water committee members. Some of these interviews were scheduled in accordance with community-based events and assemblies, municipal- and national-level network meetings, and other local and regional events.

Second, I conducted *group* interviews with the elected leadership bodies of individual CAPS and municipal CAPS networks across several municipalities in Estelí, Jinotega, Madriz, and Matagalpa (see above). Municipal-level group interviews were conducted with CAPS networks' *juntas directivas* (boards of directors) in four Matagalpa municipalities: El Tuma–La Dalia, San Ramón, San Dionisio, and Sébaco.[8] Group interviews with CAPS' elected leadership bodies of twenty-two different communities were also conducted across the course of research from 2007 to 2016 and have informed this book's characterization of CAPS as common property organizations. These CAPS represented communities primarily in the departments of Matagalpa and Jinotega. Interviews with CAPS leaders (or members) emphasized water committees' roles and responsibilities at the grass roots, working relationships with urban-based

NGOs and multilateral agencies and their staff, and relationships with and perceptions of state actors in the water and sanitation sectors as these pertained to rural water management and CAPS new networks.

Interviews with staff at domestic NGOs and multilateral organizations similarly reflected the multiscalar and multisectoral nature of this research. I conducted semistructured interviews with rural and community development organization staff in their offices in Matagalpa, Jinotega, and Estelí, as well as with national-level NGO and multilateral agency staff in organizational offices in the capital, Managua. The latter included, among others, staff at UNICEF, CARE International, Swiss Aid, Norwegian People's Aid (APN), and the World Bank Water and Sanitation Program. As I had with individual water committee members, I took advantage of CAPS network meetings and local and regional events as sites to conduct both semistructured and informal interviews with these water committee "allies" who were in attendance.

Last, interviews with state actors were consequential for learning about public officials' awareness and knowledge of rural water management and their experiences, when applicable, of working with rural water committees. Interviewees included staff at state agencies and ministries, including the Nicaraguan Water and Sanitation Institute (INAA), the Nicaraguan Water and Sewerage Company (ENACAL), the Ministry of the Environment and Natural Resources (MARENA), the Ministry of Health (MINSA), the National Council of Potable Water and Sanitation (CONAPAS), the Institute of Territorial Studies (INETER), and the Emergency Social Investment Fund (FISE). I also interviewed local and national elected officials, in addition to municipal government staff in the areas of water and sanitation and citizen participation.

I conducted extensive observation to deepen my understanding of CAPS' work within rural communities in addition to the formation, operation, and growth of CAPS networks. At the local level, this observation took place during site visits to observe CAPS members and residents (or system beneficiaries) interacting in community meetings, performing water system construction and maintenance, and engaging in community events (celebratory inaugurations of new sanitation infrastructure or intercommunity exchanges, etc.). During site visits in Matagalpa, Jinotega, Estelí, and Madriz, I also received tours of communities and their respective water systems.

At the municipal level, I attended and observed fifteen CAPS network leadership meetings and municipal-level assemblies hosted by network boards of directors. I also attended four departmental CAPS network meetings in Matagalpa. At

FIGURE 3 The author and CAPS members of the community of El Bosque (Muy Muy, Matagalpa) visiting the water system storage tank in July 2016. Photo by G. Thomas LaVanchy.

the national level, I attended four, two-day National CAPS Network meetings—sixty-four hours total of meeting time. These all-day meetings (three in Managua and one in Matagalpa) provided the opportunity not only to observe CAPS' and their allies' work, interactions, and conversations in network spaces but also to conduct semistructured and informal interviews with organizational staff and CAPS members representing different regions over shared breaks and meals. I was also able to observe various forums and events including the National Land Fair (hosted in Matagalpa in 2010) and multi-CAPS trainings and workshops hosted by NGOs (various municipalities). Participant observation was also conducted at the Central American Community Water Management Fair in Costa Rica (March 19–22, 2010) to gain comparative insight into the CAPS and their Central American counterparts as community-based water managers.

Review and analysis of primary and secondary data sources significantly informed the contextualization of interview and observation data gathered for this book. These sources included official sets of notes from CAPS' meetings at the national and subnational level provided by NGO staff, NGO and multilateral organizations' websites and published hard-copy materials, newspaper articles, national legislation, historical as well as recent government reports and documents, and the academic theses and other published scholarship of Nicaraguan researchers.

Outline of the Book

Chapter 1 of this book situates CAPS within Nicaragua's historical and contemporary landscape of dictatorship, revolution, popular participation, and public goods provision. A central goal of the chapter is to give the reader an understanding of why and how the model of community-based rural water management emerged in Nicaragua, paying particular attention to state-society relations and the interaction of domestic and international factors across time. An additional goal is to provide insight into *why* CAPS began to mobilize politically in the mid-2000s. Notably, while conventional wisdom would cast water committees as a legacy of the Sandinista Revolution (given their reflection of the kind of "self-help" and citizen-driven organizations promoted in the 1980s), this chapter reveals a more complex history of rural CBWM regimes that is not attributable to the policy agenda of any one political regime. The chapter provides evidence for a generalized pattern in spite of major regime changes across time: while the state has tended to support international, donation-based investments in the sector, assistance to rural communities by outside actors in the wake of system construction has been extremely limited as well as geographically uneven.

Chapters 2 through 4 constitute the primary analytical chapters of the book addressing the main research question. They reflect an examination of three interrelated and mutually dependent factors explaining CAPS' mobilization processes and ultimate achievement of legal recognition, outlined in the next three subsections.

"Organic" Empowerment and Cultivation of Legitimate Authority

Chapter 2 examines how CAPS' empowerment as water managers over time has infused them with legitimacy and authority vis-à-vis water system beneficiaries. As later chapters reveal, this organic empowerment supports water committees' recognition as consequential actors and legitimate authorities in the water and sanitation sector once they scale up politically. The chapter demonstrates how CAPS' organic empowerment emerges out of the day-to-day labors of water management and environmental stewardship at the grass roots, reflecting how, in practice, empowerment may be *either* a formally conferred *or* de facto access to and control over local resources entailing significant decision making, capacity building, and leadership. Organic empowerment serves as a conceptual bridge between decentralization and common property frameworks because it, first, draws attention to the empowerment of grass roots, including unofficial, actors in resource governance, and second, facilitates examination of how locally generated capacities and legitimacy "scale up" to influence grassroots actors' engagement in public policy processes. With relevance for CAPS' engagements with state actors, the chapter sheds lights on how rural residents' "everyday" work at the grass roots has generated organizational and technical capacities that tend to *exceed* those of urban-based actors in the water and sanitation sector.

Alliances

Drawing on theories of social capital, chapter 3 details how allies have been of crucial importance to water committees' ability to mobilize across communities. CAPS' main allies include domestic NGOs and multilateral organizations. Bridging social capital reflected in CAPS-ally collaborations have created opportunities for water committees to connect across regions and pursue a collective political agenda. It is important to note that the collaborative opportunities facilitated by allies via the CAPS networks have served, in practice, as an antidote to the potential isolation resource managers and service providers experience when working in dispersed rural communities. Once CAPS and allies are "bridged" in new transcommunity network spaces, bonding social capital is generated via water committees' sharing of similar experiences at the grass roots and via development of shared goals and objectives as CAPS. In this way, bonding social capital ultimately comes to support CAPS' political activism. The chapter documents three main contributions allies have made toward supporting CAPS' multiscalar collective action and pursuit of legal recognition. These include facilitating water committees' (1) physical mobility and political visibility, (2) political and legal capacity building, and (3) access to state channels of representation.

Discourses of Water Governance

Chapter 4 examines the discursive dimensions of CAPS' political activation and emergence as a collective actor in water governance. I examine three interconnected discourses, akin to collective action "frames" as examined in the vast social movements literature. These include discourses of autonomy, ownership, and state roles and responsibilities in the water sector, which reflect how CAPS members achieved a way of understanding and describing their work that arose from their on-the-ground experiences in water management. These discourses also shed light on CAPS' organic empowerment as resource managers and service providers, including their day-to-day, historical and contemporary, experiences in their de facto roles at the grass roots. Discourses circulated within and emerged from CAPS networks in a way that has fostered collaboration across urban-rural, sectoral, and partisan divides and promoted CAPS' recognition as a distinct actor in water governance vis-à-vis state actors. Notably, the Nicaraguan state's failure to discursively delineate CAPS within national legal frameworks for water governance gave water committees leverage to shape public perceptions of their organizations and work as they advocated for formal recognition. In other words, CAPS' invisibility in policy frameworks and debates meant they benefited from a relatively "blank" discursive terrain as they mobilized. Perhaps most surprising about CAPS' discourses in light of existing theories of collective framing is how effective they were in garnering an apparent consensus among CAPS participating in networks. Media outlets and state actors followed suit, with the buy-in of the latter being all the more counterintuitive as they were the principal target of CAPS' policy interventions. The chapter contends that "representation by omission" may support grassroots groups who have high empirical credibility through limiting conflict and contention in framing processes.

Chapter 5 moves beyond the initial years of the CAPS networks to examine the implications of legal recognition for rural water committees—what has become, in regional terms in Latin America, a sought-after strategy for improving rural water sectors on the part of diverse state and nonstate actors. The chapter draws initial conclusions about how the CAPS Law (Law 722) has affected water committees in financial, organizational, and political terms. As much of the scholarship on recognition or formalization policies in Latin America remains critical of attempts to "legalize" community-based water management regimes, this chapter draws attention to the differences characterizing drinking and irrigation water management in the region and the potential implications of these for assessing policies. The chapter argues that early on in its implementation, the CAPS Law has functioned as a double-edged, and in some ways, blunt, sword, in terms of effects on water committees and their work. The chapter contends that recognition and legalization policies are not panaceas and that understanding the on-the-ground contours of water governance requires looking "beyond the law." In empirical terms, this means transcending a narrow focus on state legal frameworks and their documented impacts as a metric for assessing the everyday issues grassroots water managers and service providers confront.

The final chapter summarizes the main argument, findings, and theoretical contributions of the book. Additionally, I use the concluding chapter to discuss some of the main practical and policy implications of CAPS' story of mobilization. This includes drawing attention to the particular challenges of rural water management and service provision in the Global South, the increasingly critical intersection between water and climate change, and important role of activism for promoting more equitable and sustainable water governance.

The Unlikely Backdrop of Partisan Polarization and a Co-optive State

This book goes to press as Nicaragua finds itself mired in political protests and violence: over three hundred people have been killed, mostly young men and boys, and thousands wounded, in antigovernment protests since the first largely publicized protest on April 18, 2018. The violence has been devastating; it has also been perpetrated and supported by the government of President Daniel Ortega of the Sandinista National Liberation Front (FSLN), despite its denial of this claim. The immediate impetus for the protests was the government's announced reform to a social security policy that would increase employees' contributions while decreasing the amount distributed to pension holders (Semple 2018).[9] The state-sponsored violence that has met the protests presents a starkly contrasting reality to the Ortega administration's public presentation of its government as promoting "peace, justice, and development."[10] Recently, state repression has taken the sinister turn of attempting to silence dissent through increased raids on opposition media outlets and human rights organizations as well as the detention of journalists (Robles 2018).

This moment of crisis of resistance, violence, and repression has much significance in relation to this book. In part, this is because, as Father Román of Masaya posits, it may be "impossible for things to go back to the way things were before" in Nicaragua, in political terms (Phillips 2018, n.p.). It is also because the factors contributing to the crisis have been "in the making for more than a decade and reveal a deepening crisis of legitimacy for the Ortega administration" (Morris 2018a, 2018b, n.p.). In fact, the current political situation in Nicaragua represents the pinnacle of antidemocratic tendencies that constituted the backdrop to the organizing processes of water committees and their allies described in this book. As CAPS moved from local collective action for managing resources to network formation for political and legal recognition, they did so in a context of extreme partisan polarization and co-optive state tendencies vis-à-vis civil society organizations.

Deep partisan commitments and related polarization along party lines have deep historical roots in Nicaragua, tracing back to struggles between liberals and conservatives in the nineteenth century and adopting its more contemporary face in relation to the 1979 Sandinista Revolution (Tijerino 2008). During the Revolution, which ruptured the more than forty-year Somoza dynasty (1936–79), civil society developed in close relationship to the state and party. Indeed, clear state-party-society divides did not exist. When Nicaraguans elected the FSLN's Daniel Ortega in 2006, it was a reelection: Ortega had held the presidency during the Sandinista Revolution from 1985 until 1990, the year in which the Revolution ended abruptly with national elections. In 2007, Ortega decreed the creation of municipal- and community-level Citizen Power Councils (CPCs). Promoted and mandated by FSLN authorities as the exclusive vehicles of citizen participation at the subnational level, the CPCs presented challenges to CAPS' own embracing of political pluralism and striving for the organizational autonomy of their organizations and networks. Harsh criticism of the CPCs as a party tool and exclusive partisan space accompanied a broader narrowing of space for autonomous civil society, including the repression of dissent, resulting from Ortega's election (Anderson and Dodd 2009; Chamorro, Jarquín, and Bendaña 2009; Prado 2010; Stuart 2009).

Nevertheless, in the mid-2000s, CAPS under study for this book were able to mobilize across partisan divides and with relative autonomy from state actors without being subsumed within or displaced by the Citizen Power model. Although water committees worked across partisan divisions, reflecting the character and ethic of their community-based work, CAPS often discussed the significance of political polarization for their work. As Jessenia shared with her water committee *compañer@s* during the November 2009 National CAPS Network meeting in Managua, "I hope we don't allow our municipalities to continue becoming politicized, because water doesn't have a political color, or religion, or belief system." As an independent professional consultant working with the National CAPS Network, Eduardo, explained in a June 2010 interview, "The community wisdom has been not to have a partisan political color, and this richness from the grass roots has been conserved at different levels" of CAPS' organizing.

At the time of research, the threat of party/state co-optation of CAPS networks was evident in several forms. For example, the Ortega government worked to displace the Municipal Development Councils with the Citizen Power Councils as partisan bodies geared toward implementing the FSLN/Ortega agenda at the subnational level. Some CAPS spoke of experiences with local government seeking to engage with new networks; however, this engagement—particularly among water committees whose members were not aligned politically with the FSLN—was met with skepticism. The Sébaco municipal CAPS network secretary Delia once related how a local government official offered to disseminate CAPS municipal network assembly invitations across communities; however, the FSLN government official invited Citizen Power representatives, as opposed to CAPS representatives, to the meeting. (Not surprisingly, Citizen Power reps were largely at a loss of how to engage in technical discussions about water management.) This demonstrates that CAPS networks risked being undermined by party-aligned CPCs and were subject to the pressures under which local elected officials operated given the top-down mandates of the Ortega administration. Notably, in some predominately FSLN municipalities, water committees welcomed government involvement. Some CAPS networks, like those in El Tuma–La Dalia and San Ramón, were spatially integrated into local government spaces (i.e., these served as CAPS' meeting sites) and saw regular and welcomed participation of local government staff alongside NGO staff.

At the national level, the political proclivities of Ortega's FSLN provided a favorable context for CAPS' activism, the pursuit of legal recognition in particular. Because of national FSLN leaders' rhetorical commitments to "popular power" and democratic participation, it is not surprising that Sandinista lawmakers were eager to pass the CAPS Law. It is important to recognize that the interests of the Ortega administration and Sandinista lawmakers to "hang their flag" on a new law contributed to the political will and desire to pass the CAPS Law (Law 722). However, it would be wrong to see the law as primarily the product of a top-down, state- or party-led, process to recognize CAPS as water managers and service providers. In practice, the outcome of the CAPS Law must be attributed to how water committees, in bottom-up fashion, took advantage of a political opening in national-level politics to push their grass-roots agenda as they become politically activated and increasingly visible in the water sector in the late 2000s. Moreover, CAPS' and their allies' concerns with maintaining water committees' autonomy and mitigating potentially divisive politics within new network spaces suggest a fear of partisan co-optation.

As were the late 1970s and the early 1990s, the eve and end of a revolutionary era, respectively, the current political moment constitutes a critical juncture for organized popular sectors and social movements in Nicaragua. The violence and repression in Nicaragua have coincided with calls for Ortega's resignation as president, along with that of his vice president and wife, Rosario Murillo. The international community is paying attention: human rights organizations such as Amnesty International, and foreign governments, including through the regional Organization of American States, are condemning the violence. The Interdisciplinary Group of Independent Experts of the Inter-American Commission on Human Rights labeled the violence crimes against human-ity under international human rights law.[11] In July 2018, the U.S. government imposed sanctions on three Nicaraguan officials deemed complicit in human rights violations. Some Nicaraguans are even calling for international interven-tion to remove Ortega—a controversial plea given the United States' history of unsavory intervention in the country.

It remains to be seen how the current crisis, including heightened polar-ization and state repression, will affect Nicaragua's vibrant popular sector in the intermediate and long term. Regarding CAPS' transcommunity networks: during field research in 2016, it became clear that the National CAPS Network (in contrast to dynamics observed in 2009 and 2010) was struggling to gain the ear of national officials as they endeavored to carry out a national-scale survey of water committees. A lawyer who had worked with the National CAPS Net-work on Law 722 posited that the government was refusing to work with CAPS' national leadership because the president of the network and NGO consultant were not politically aligned with the FSLN. Arguably, in the wake of the passing of the CAPS Law in 2010, the national movement of water committees lowered in political importance for the party and national government officials. State-society relations are fluid and dynamic, and, needless to say, social change can backslide. However, at the end of 2018, CAPS networks at both the national and subnational levels continue to function. For the hundreds of water committee members who have engaged directly in CAPS networks, and the thousands whose local organizations are being integrated into formal legal frameworks through following the new law's formal registration process, it seems almost "impossible for things to go back to the way things were before." It is hoped that this story of CAPS' mobilization—including their cultivation and assertion of a collective, autonomous political voice—offers insights into the potential for activism and social change even in unlikely and evolving contexts.

ONE

Rural Water Service from Dictatorship to Democracy

Why and how did a large-scale model of rural community-based water management (CBWM) emerge in Nicaragua? What explains the political activation of community-based water managers to form new transcommunity networks in the 2000s? Understanding the rupture in Potable Water and Sanitation Committees' (CAPS) roles as resource managers and services providers requires situating CAPS within Nicaragua's historical and contemporary landscape of dictatorship, revolution, and neoliberal democracy. This chapter pays particular attention to state-society relations and the interaction of domestic and international factors across time that have supported and at times challenged nonstate participation in water management and service provision.

The emergence of CAPS presents a historical puzzle, since conventional wisdom would encourage drawing a direct relationship between the invigorating organizational effects of the Sandinista Revolution and CAPS as a "self-help," popular sector organizational form. Yet, CAPS' emergence and proliferation reflects a more complex history—one not entirely attributable to the policy agenda of a single political regime. For example, the number of rural water systems increased greatly *subsequent* to the electoral defeat of the Sandinistas in 1990 (see table 2 for estimated rural water projects through 2004). Moreover, CAPS' origins must be examined in a way that transcends a narrow focus on domestic policies and political institutions. This is because there has been a significant *international* influence on the evolution of community-based water

TABLE 2 Rural Water Projects by Regime (1960–2004)

Departments (and Region*)	1960–79	1980–89	1990–2004	Total Water Projects
Estelí, Madriz, Nueva Segovia (I)	0	209	1,135	1,344
León, Chinandega (II)	0	58	1,160	1,218
Managua (III)	0	15	62	80[a]
Carazo, Granada, Masaya, Rivas (IV)	54[b]	70	121	334
Boaco, Chontales (V)	0	7	697	704[c]
Jinotega, Matagalpa (VI)	NA[d]	101	1,068	1,175[a]
Región Autónoma del Atlántico Norte (VII)	NA[d]	NA	11	58
Región Autónoma del Atlántico Sur (VIII)	0	0	42	42
Río San Juan (IX)	0	19	42	63[a]
Total	54	479	4,338	5,018

Source: These figures come from data collected in the National Information System of Rural Water and Sanitation (SINAS), a database created by the Nicaraguan government and international donors in the mid-1990s to document project implementation. These data reflect water systems constructed through part of 2004 only.

*See map 1 in the introduction for a map of regions.

[a] These numbers are greater than the sum of projects noted across regimes because dates were not available for some projects, and hence were omitted for this table.

[b] Eighty-nine of a total of 143 water systems constructed by 1980 in Region IV were documented as "urban" water systems and were thus omitted for the purposes for this table. It is likely that many of the fifty-four remaining systems serve urban, or at least periurban, neighborhoods as well. With the exception of three projects, this region's projects from 1960 to 1979 have been attributed to the state water company, ENACAL, an institution not created until 1998. It is much more likely that these projects were supported financially by the World Health Organization (WHO) through coordination with the Ministry of Health (MINSA), as there is evidence of collaboration between these two entities toward a "Water Service Plan" starting in 1972 (RRAS-CA 1998, 10).

[c] This number reflects 163 water projects constructed in the RAAS and twenty in the Río San Juan.

[d] Dates were not available within SINAS for most RAAN projects.

management regimes in Nicaragua, regionally in Latin America, and globally across developing country contexts. Indeed, the regional phenomenon of CBWM suggests CAPS are more than mere reflections of changes wrought by a domestic revolution.

This chapter argues, first, that political regimes across time in Nicaragua have presented both opportunities and constraints to effective resident-led rural water management and provision. That is, despite major regime changes and respective ruptures in state-society relations across time, NGOs and multilateral agencies—in many cases coordinating with state actors—have supported the construction of rural water and sanitation projects. Moreover, support to rural residents in the wake of water system construction has been extremely limited in financial, technical, and organizational terms. At times, no support has been available to residents left to care for water systems. While this pattern of state-society synergy and postsystem construction neglect repeats across regimes in Nicaragua, the chapter does draw attention to how each regime has presented unique opportunities as well as constraints for CAPS' emergence and effective functioning over time.

A second argument of the chapter is that NGOs and multilateral agencies leveraged a political opportunity in the early 2000s to activate and engage CAPS around the issue of water privatization and within public policy processes. Specifically, domestic and international organizations prompted water committees to mobilize in relation to the threat of water privatization in the early 2000s and, later, to the government's passing of the National Water Law (Law 620) in 2007. In the eyes of CAPS and their allies, Law 620 maintained a problematic status quo of leaving water committees "below the radar" of formal state policy in Nicaragua. This was especially the case in relation to this new law establishing a framework for comprehensive management of the country's freshwater resources. Seeking water committees' formal legal recognition became a central goal motivating the formation of CAPS networks at the municipal, departmental, and national levels.

Understanding CAPS' collective mobilization and its significance for the water sector and state-society relations requires understanding this activity within a unique historical context. The years leading up to the overthrow of Somoza in 1979 and the decades since reveal dramatic transformations in political practices and institutions in Nicaragua. These changes include the expansion of "everyday" Nicaraguans' role in public governance, including resource management and the provision of goods and services, over time.

The Somoza Dynasty (1936–1979)

Counterintuitively, community-based arrangements for rural water management and service provision began to emerge in Nicaragua during a period of politically repressive dynastic rule. Constituting an authoritarian political regime, the Somoza family ruled the country from 1936 to 1979, precluding political pluralism and residents' access to formal institutional channels.[1] Anastasio Somoza García took national power in 1936 with the support of the U.S. government, inheriting control over a military-security force, the National Guard, which the U.S. Marines both created and trained starting in 1927. In 1957, Somoza García was succeeded by his son, Luis Somoza Debayle, followed by his other son, Anastasio Somoza Debayle, in 1967.

The regime's repressive apparatus depended upon political patronage, military might, and concentration of national wealth and resources. As the country's military, the National Guard functioned as a mechanism to control the urban and rural populace and came to be known as the Somozas' "private army." The Somozas' concentration of political and military power was accompanied by their massive concentration of wealth: the family had substantial economic investments in banking, finance, cotton, tobacco, and sugar; Anastasio Somoza García, the patriarch, had wealth amounting to between $10 and $60 million by 1945 (Booth 1985, 68). This wealth reflected the country's broad patterns of economic inequity that ensured most Nicaraguans would live in conditions of extreme poverty. For example, the poorest half of rural Nicaraguans in 1972 had an average income of $35 per capita monthly (Kaimowitz and Thome 1982, 225). Cast in slightly different terms, the poorest 50 percent of income-earning Nicaraguans in the late 1970s earned 15 percent of the national income, while the richest 5 percent earned 30 percent (Booth 1982, 85).[2]

Historical documents reveal that the Somozas invested little in public services, including water, until growing international attention to water and sanitation in the 1970s interrupted the regime's tendency to leave public services underdeveloped, particularly rural services and infrastructure.[3] During this era, the Nicaraguan "government spent less of its budget on health and education than any other nation in the region," including Costa Rica, El Salvador, Guatemala, Honduras, and Mexico (Booth 1982, 85). Most of the regime's investments in water and sanitation were limited to urban areas, and formal responsibility fell to local governments for their development. These responsibilities were not necessarily fulfilled. A 2004 report by the Nicaraguan government and the Pan American Health Organization cites that the National Department of Municipal Services (SERMUNIC) was decreed in 1955 to ensure "planning, designing, and constructing potable water projects in the urban sector and administering those municipal aqueducts that because of administrative, technical, and financial issues were not cared for by the appropriate municipal government" (Government of Nicaragua and PAHO 2004, 27).

Notably, then, shifting international political economies of development help to explain the burgeoning attention to *rural* water and sanitation in Nicaragua in the 1970s. For example, the United States Agency for International Development (USAID) issued the Rural Community Health Services Grant to Nicaragua in 1973, which in 1975 created the Rural Health Action Community Program (PRACS) (Donahue 1983, 267–68). A "complementary" program, the National Basic Rural Sanitation Plan (PLANSAR), was created in 1977 under the domain of Nicaragua's Ministry of Health (MINSA). The National Basic Rural Sanitation Plan also depended upon the financial support of USAID, and a year later, support from the World Bank, and would grant attention to rural sanitation in part through the construction of potable water systems in rural areas (Donahue 1983; Government of Nicaragua and PAHO 2004). Like other sectors during the Somoza era, the health sector, subsuming water and sanitation, was based upon a "vertical power structure of control and patronage" (Donahue 1983, 266). Similar to the community- and neighborhood-based strategies that would follow in the Sandinista era, however, rural health programs sought to utilize volunteer "rural health collaborators" at the community level who would conduct educational work locally and work as an intermediary between residents and health clinics and programs. During the Chinandega Seminar of 1976, the U.S. and Nicaraguan governments articulated a "concept of community organization," the overarching purpose of which was to encourage greater state attention to the rural health sector (Donahue 1986, 16–17).

Conventional wisdom has it that the Somoza era emphasized a lack of investment in the general population. However, attention to rural health, including provision of water and sanitation, did begin in Nicaragua before the Sandinista Revolution. Several caveats apply. First, not surprisingly, the impetus for this attention was *external* to the Nicaraguan state and the Somozas. That is, Nicaragua's bilateral relationship with USAID and relationship with multilateral agencies such as the World Bank during this period explain "domestic" efforts to stimulate community-level organization and involvement in public services, including health. Second, potential advances in rural water and sanitation infrastructure via international donations were stunted by the Somozas' tendency to divert foreign funds (Donahue 1986). Third, donations for water systems had an urban bias. The National Information System of Rural Water and Sanitation (SINAS), for example, shows that an estimated 143 water projects had been constructed by the end of the 1970s. All of these were in the department of Managua and 89 (62 percent) of these were listed, counterintuitively, as *urban* aqueducts.[4] The best indicator of the construction of rural water systems under Somoza is the estimate that improved water access had reached 7 percent of the rural population by the end of the decade (RRAS-CA 1998) (see figure 4).

The Somozas' repressive modes of governance negatively affected new community health programs. The government carried out "violent repression of any political dissent in the very areas in which the PRACS [Rural Health Action Community Program] and PLANSAR [National Basic Rural Sanitation Plan] programs were operating" (Donahue 1983, 268). The regime also selectively

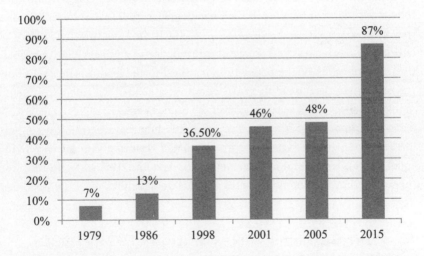

FIGURE 4 Improved water access in rural areas, 1979–2015. Data in this chapter referring to "improved" water access include water accessed via the following technologies: piped water into individual households (via gravity-fed or electrically pumped systems), public taps serving multiple households (via gravity-fed or electrically pumped systems), public wells (hand dug and drilled), and household wells (hand dug and drilled) (RRAS-CA 1998, 35). The estimated rural population in Nicaragua for each of these years is as follows: (1) 1979, 50 percent; (2) 1986, 40 percent; (3) 1998, 45 percent; (4) 2005, 44 percent; (5) 2015, 42 percent (World Bank 2018). Sources: INAA 1989; Medrano et al. 2007; FANCA 2006; Government of Nicaragua and PAHO 2004; RRAS-CA 1998; PAHO 2017.

implemented programs to monitor dissent. For instance, a 1976 USAID report suggests that Somoza encouraged implementation of these programs in two northern regions with high levels of rebel activity, Estelí and Matagalpa, because this would help to monitor antigovernment organizing (Donahue 1983). Community-based health programs thus became "a mode of community organization which enhanced control and fragmentation" (Donahue 1986, 11) and aligned with the regime's strategy of controlling the populace and quelling dissent.

Notably, this era would see the emergence of sectoral patterns that would prove perennial in Nicaragua. A 2007 report reflecting the collaboration of the Nicaraguan government and multilateral agencies including the World Bank Water and Sanitation Program and UNICEF expressed a sobering take on the relationship between rural residents and extralocal project supporters (including multilateral agencies such as the report's authors) in the decade leading up to Somoza's overthrow: "Upon finishing the projects, its implementers would leave the site without training the population in management of the systems, whether they were imported hand pumps or small gravity-fed systems. In the case of latrines, in many cases these were not utilized, due to an inadequate participation and education of the population in regard to the health benefits accompanying appropriate use of these" (Medrano et al. 2007, 75). In short, although uniquely subject to active repression in the Somoza era, CBWM arrangements depending upon rural residents received little financial or technical support in the wake of water system construction, and residents were often left ill-equipped to manage and care for new water systems. This pattern of limited support to rural communities would persist across regimes.

The Sandinista Revolution (1979–1990)

The 1980s were of crucial importance to the construction of space for collaborative organizing efforts between state and society, paving the way for the proliferation of grassroots water committees in rural areas.[5] When the 1979 Sandinista Revolution broke the bonds of over forty years of dictatorship in Nicaragua, it embarked the country on a course of dramatic political, social, and economic change. Once in power, the Sandinista National Liberation Front (FSLN) sought redistribution of the country's material wealth and political power in part through cultivating mass participation in public life. The promotion of popular engagement and empowerment not only had ideological underpinnings consistent with the Sandinistas' conception of democracy but also served as part of the new regime's governing strategy regarding provision of basic goods and services.

When the new government took power in 1979, Nicaragua was in physical as well as financial ruins. The effects of the revolutionary war only compounded the effects wrought by over forty years of corrupt rule by the Somoza family on the country's current and future ability to invest in public services. As Laura Enríquez (1985) and others have noted, Nicaragua's dependent capitalist development under Somoza produced great inequality of wealth domestically and negatively affected the ability of the Nicaraguan state to accumulate income to provide public goods and services.

In addition to inheriting a severely drained public resource base, the Sandinista regime faced intense political and military aggression during the Contra War (1981–88). The new government was forced to direct much of the available public funds toward defense spending for political survival. As noted by Smith, "by 1985, defense spending had grown to more than 50 percent of the [national] budget, leaving much less money for more productive uses" (1996, 48).[6] The war thus significantly undermined the financial capacities of the Nicaraguan government to implement its social agenda to enhance and expand public welfare. In this context of resource shortages and war, the new regime depended upon its broad base of societal support to achieve its political objectives and to meet the basic survival needs of the populace.[7]

Prompted by the ideological proclivities and practical needs of the regime, civil society began to flourish in Nicaragua. Crucial to an evolving popular sector were the Sandinista "mass organizations" and their role in political representation and societal mobilization.[8] The mass organizations had a dual imperative: "to defend and deepen the process of revolutionary transformation and to channel [societal] demands to the government" (Serra 1982, 95). Thus, in contrast to the popular movements and activism of prerevolutionary Nicaragua, the mass organizations explicitly worked *with* those in power, versus pushing against them. Nicaraguans not only took up arms as part of popular militias for the defense of the regime against internal and external threats; they also coordinated with the state and party, the FSLN, to carry out tasks fundamental to economic productivity and daily social and political life. Much writing during the revolutionary era viewed the 1980s as serving to establish "the groundwork necessary for the construction of an effective civil society—that is, a society in which the majority is able to exercise decisive influence over the state through its own autonomous social and political organizations" (Coraggio and Irvin 1985, 29).

The close relationship of the mass organizations with state and party limited the extent to which popular mobilization during this period may be viewed as an effective *counterweight* to the state or political parties (Gilbert 1988; Luciak 1995, 2001). Where autonomy was approached, it was relative. As Jonathan Fox notes, "Whether the Sandinistas represented the mass organizations or vice versa is a matter of debate, hinging on the empirical question of the varying degrees of internal democracy and autonomy of the mass organizations" (personal communication, October 29, 2012).

Albeit with limited autonomy from state and party, the mass organizations fulfilled important governance functions in the context of the new regime. Several of the most prominent mass organizations included the Sandinista Defense Committees (CDS, previously the CDCs), who most directly "filled the vacuum left by the disintegration of the Somocista state and economy" (Ruchwarger 1987, 91). The defense committees distributed food and medicine, rebuilt houses and roads, carried out vaccinations against infectious disease, and treated the ill or those wounded from counterrevolutionary, or Contra, violence. The CDSs were also charged most literally with defending the Revolution, participating in civil defense as neighborhood watch groups in urban areas. Also contributing to the day-to-day production of public goods and services were members of Nicaraguan Women's Association "Luisa Amanda Espinoza" (AMNLAE; previously AMPRONAC), whose members worked as educators in the national Literacy Crusade, contributed to the development and implementation of childcare facilities, and engaged extensively in policy formation and advocacy. Additionally, the Sandinista Youth (JS-19) participated actively in the Popular Literacy Army (EPA), who comprised more than seventy thousand youth and other mass organization participants (Serra 1982, 108) and who succeeded in reducing national illiteracy from 50 percent to 13 percent (Ruchwarger 1987, 111).[9] By the end of the 1980s, an estimated half million Nicaraguans had participated in Sandinista initiatives via the mass organizations (Serra 1991).

Greater numbers of urban-based residents were directly incorporated into the Revolution's political and socioeconomic projects during the 1980s; this owes primarily to residents' participation on a block-by-block basis in the urban-based defense committees. Yet, rural residents also engaged in new government projects and initiatives. The dramatic restructuring of land ownership and the implementation of the national literacy campaign are two excellent examples of how national Sandinista initiatives affected daily life within rural areas: roughly 43 percent of rural families received land as part of the agrarian reform (Baumeister 1995, 247), and in the central northern highlands, including the departments of Matagalpa and Jinotega, illiteracy was reduced from 66.7 percent to 20.2 percent (Hanemann 2005).

Rural Nicaraguans benefited from health and literacy campaigns and also participated in these; rural residents also engaged in new farmer cooperatives and workers' unions, which served as platforms for representation and demand making. Two mass organizations, in particular, were directly concerned with incorporating rural-based sectors. The Rural Workers' Association (ATC) and National Union of Farmers and Ranchers (UNAG) each incorporated different segments of rural workers. The ATC represented year-round agricultural laborers and small-scale *campesinos* (peasants), while the UNAG formed to defend the interests of medium- and large-sized farmers in addition to small farmers within the primarily state-run cooperatives. The UNAG has been regarded as the most politically autonomous of the mass organizations during the 1980s because of its members' assertion of interests vis-à-vis the state and the FSLN. Yet, even as "the most autonomous and assertive" mass organization, the UNAG had "to tailor its work to the demands of the State" (Quandt 1995, 268). By 1989, the ATC and the UNAG had an estimated 50,000 and 125,000 members, respectively (Serra 1991).

Beyond helping to constitute a governing strategy for the Sandinistas' socioeconomic and political agenda, the mass organizations were part and parcel of the party's vision for democratic development. The FSLN, as the "vanguard" party, saw itself as responsible for the political enlightenment and empowerment of the masses (Gilbert 1988). As "schools of democracy" (Serra 1982, 96), the mass organizations not only facilitated broad, cross-class mobilization at the grass roots but they also served as channels through which everyday Nicaraguans' interests and demands reached those in government and the FSLN. A provisional national legislative body, the national Council of State, represented twenty-nine organizations, including five mass organizations (the CDS, ATC, AMNLAE, JS-19, and the Sandinista Workers' Central), in addition to political parties and private sector organizations. Although the FSLN remained committed to direct forms of participation in the provision of public goods and services, such as security and health care, international as well as domestic pressure engendered political compromise that produced a hybrid system of government. Representative democratic features came to be institutionalized in the "Western-style constitution" passed in 1987 (Gilbert 1988; see also Reding 1991). The new Constitution created four branches of government (executive, legislative, judicial, and a Supreme Electoral Council), hence replacing the provisional legislature and Council of State. The significant overlapping membership between the FSLN and the mass organizations made it typical that leaders within the mass organizations would be appointed to posts within the party; in this sense the means of representation changed, but not necessarily those individuals doing the representing.[10]

Assessing the mass organizations leads to some notable urban-rural distinctions that reveal relatively less engagement of rural sectors in the social and political work of the Revolution. Significantly, data specifying demographics along rural-urban lines in the mass organizations are lacking. These data are most difficult to estimate or draw conclusions about for those organizations not obviously bound in sociogeographic terms, like the Nicaraguan Women's Association. However, available data suggest that revolutionary projects saw a relatively greater incorporation of urban sectors compared to rural. An estimated 115,000 Nicaraguans participated in mass organizations with rural bases, including the Rural Workers' Association and the National Union of Farmers and Ranchers. In contrast, those with urban constituencies—including the Sandinista Workers' Central, Sandinista Defense Committees, the Nicaraguan Women's Association, and Sandinista Youth—had an estimated participation of 721,500 to 801,500, nearly seven times the number of participants in mass organizations with rural bases (Gilbert 1988; Ruchwarger 1987). In the health sector after 1979, "rural areas were still weakly organized" relative to urban areas, and health programs emphasized care in urban areas over rural (Bossert 1982).

In addition to being relatively less mobilized than their urban counterparts by the Revolution's projects and initiatives, rural populations failed to achieve the same extent of political *representation* vis-à-vis the state during this decade. For example, the Council of State, the national representative body of the era, reflected an urban bias: fourteen of the mass organization seats represented urban constituencies versus four for rural (Booth 1985, 193). Rural Nicaraguans were "still not organized into a mass political movement" as were urban FSLN constituencies before the 1979 *triunfo* (triumph) of the Revolution, nor did they achieve the same levels of coordination and communication with the state and party during this era (Ortega 1990). This translated into a relative disorganization of the rural populace likely reflecting, as well, the legacies of repressive and manipulative political tactics wielded by the Somozas across the preceding four decades of rule.

There is a caveat when assessing urban versus rural social and political engagement during the Revolution. Rural and urban participation becomes more equalized in terms of numbers *if* one takes into account the rural residents who participated in the Sandinista-driven agricultural cooperatives. Citing a 1989 National Union of Farmers and Ranchers self-diagnostic, Luis Serra notes that 3,363 cooperatives had formed by the end of the 1980s, with an estimated 474,572 individual participants (1991, 51). Moreover, the mobilization of peasants to oppose the Sandinistas as part of the U.S.-funded Contra War also constitutes a significant form of rural mobilization wrought by the politics of the decade. Thomas W. Walker (1991) cites that there were over 15,000 Contra combatants mobilized by the mid-1980s, a number that by the end of the 1980s had reached 50,000, of which an estimated 40,000 were Nicaraguan peasants (Langlois 1996).

Historical accounts of the mass organizations mobilizing explicitly for *water* provision are scarce. Moreover, the available evidence shows little explicit or direct connection between state/party agendas and the popular sector's role in rural water and sanitation projects. Some have pointed to the role of the Sandinista Defense Committees and "voluntary labor" more broadly in the construction of water projects and latrines (see, e.g., Bossert 1982; Gilbert 1988; Serra 1982, 1991). Yet, there is little to no documentation of these arrangements or forms of participation in rural areas, and hence limited popular or scholarly historical understanding of residents' roles in the development of the water and sanitation sector. The role of Nicaraguan civil society in the management and provision of water has not been systematically delineated.[11]

Did the revolutionary government's ideologically driven initiatives matter for explaining the emergence of CAPS? Sadrach Zeledón Rocha, mayor of the city of Matagalpa in the mid-2000s and former FSLN deputy in the National Assembly, cited the Revolution, including the "popular initiative" and "volunteer work" it fomented, as a key factor in the construction of new rural water systems during the 1980s. Zeledón, who had previously served as the city's mayor during the 1980s, described the volunteerism of this era as the "organizational seed" for the formation of CAPS in regard to water and other groups charged with day-to-day tasks in the areas of health and education (interview, March 25, 2010), a clear reference to the Sandinista Defense Committees and other mass organization efforts to implement vaccination and literacy campaigns. The director of the Nicaraguan Water and Sanitation Institute, Gilberto Arauz, who also worked with the Office of Rural Aqueducts (DAR) in the 1980s, corroborated this direct connection between the invigorating organizational effects of the Revolution and CAPS as an organizational form: "As we were in the revolutionary era, there was a committee for everything . . . a countless number of committees. So the potable water committees formed too, that's how it happened" (interview, August 19, 2008).

Undoubtedly, the Sandinista Revolution constituted a dramatic rupture in political, social, economic, and cultural terms in Nicaragua that supported the emergence of CBWM regimes. However, the Sandinista era shares with the Somoza era overlapping tendencies characterizing the evolution of the water and sanitation sector. First, as in the Somoza era, state actors in the 1980s facilitated foreign contributions to the sector; indeed, the decade saw a marked increase in the number of international agencies supporting rural water and sanitation, owing in part to a growing international interest in the sector on the part of Global North governments and NGOs. Across the decade, the government facilitated sectoral coordination with a number of NGOs and multilateral agencies, including CARE International, the Swiss Agency for Development and Cooperation (COSUDE), the United Nations Children's Fund (UNICEF), the Netherlands Development Organization (SNV), Norwegian People's Aid (APN), Swiss Aid, KfW, and Agua para la Vida. Domestic proclivities matter for understanding how this international interest in water and sanitation came to bear in Nicaragua: the Sandinistas' broad socioeconomic agenda prioritizing access to health and basic services dovetailed with international donor agendas around increasing access to water and sanitation and agencies' model of involving residents, explicitly, in this endeavor.

As a result, the number of water systems proliferated during the revolutionary decade. By the end of the 1980s, over 480 rural water systems had been constructed in Nicaragua. The period from 1980 to 1986 saw water and sanitation coverage of the rural population double, from 6 percent to 13 percent. In urban areas, coverage rose from 67 percent to 77 percent (INAA 1989) (see figures 5 and 6; note monetary value reflects local and U.S. currency, respectively). While in absolute terms foreign donations to the sector were greater during the 1980–86 period, the data show investments of the Nicaraguan government steadily increasing while those of foreign agencies sharply decrease—particularly in 1984 and again in 1986. It is not clear what explains the dramatic increase and decrease in spending on rural water and sanitation projects on the part of the

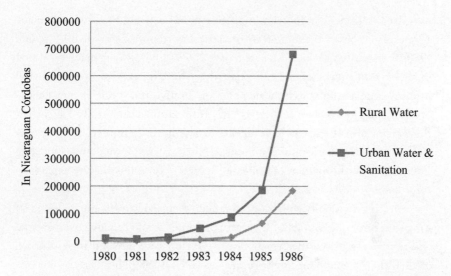

FIGURE 5 Domestic investments in urban water and sanitation and rural water projects, 1980–86. Source: INAA 1989.

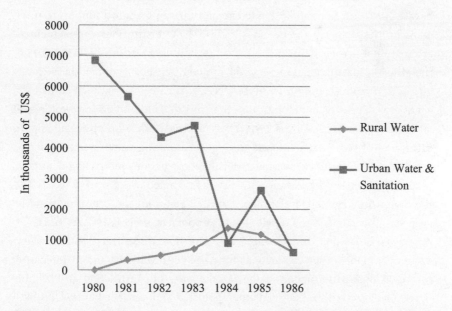

FIGURE 6 Foreign investments in urban water and sanitation and rural water projects, 1980–86. Source: INAA 1989.

national government and foreign cooperation, respectively. However, one plausible explanation for the drop in external support to projects in the mid- to late 1980s is suggested by John M. Donahue's (1989) finding that much spending in the area of preventative health halted as the Contra War destroyed vital infrastructure and increased the demand for curative and specialty care. Development and aid agencies such as CARE International and UNICEF shifted their financial and material investments to aiding those injured in the war as well as to meeting basic nutrition needs of Nicaraguans in war zones (Donahue 1989, 261–64). This pattern of decreased spending on infrastructure extends to rural water projects as well.

Reflecting continuity with the Somoza era, financial investments reflected an urban bias: from 1980 to 1986, 81 percent of domestic and foreign governmental and nongovernmental investments in the sector were directed toward urban areas, with 19 percent directed to rural areas (INAA 1989). Similarly, as increasing numbers of rural residents became beneficiaries of new water systems, rural communities continued to receive limited outside involvement in rural water management and service provision after system construction.

Despite these patterns, it is noteworthy that the Sandinista state developed new sector institutions and extended greater human technical support to rural communities than did the previous regime. New institutions complemented international involvement in the sector, providing a national counterpart to the growing international presence in the country. For example, the Nicaraguan Water and Sanitation Institute (INAA) became the national regulatory agency for the sector, both urban and rural, in 1980. Despite having weak regulatory capacities in rural areas, INAA was charged with supporting the implementation of rural water projects through elaborating water system designs, providing some technical assistance during construction, and paying a portion (~20–30 percent) of the administrative costs associated with the work of CARE, the Swiss Agency for Development and Cooperation, and other multilateral agencies. This entailed the development of booklets, such as INAA's *Guide for the Organization and Administration of Rural Aqueducts*, which outline water system components and instructions for basic organizational and maintenance functions required to support systems in the wake of construction. In 1985, the government created the National Operation and Maintenance Units (UNOM) as a form of rural technical support (Baltodano and Olmedo 2008). From 1987 to 2007, there were regional delegations of INAA's Office of Rural Aqueducts in the departments of Matagalpa, Estelí, León and Chontales, among others, each intended to provide technical support to multiple municipalities through operation and maintenance staff.

Historical documents reflect the domestic-international synergy that supported the proliferation of rural water systems. A 1981 report authored by INAA, the Nicaraguan Ministry of Health, and the International Bank for Reconstruction and Development (part of the World Bank) documented water project expenditures as reflecting the following sources: 18.3 percent from external sources (i.e., international), 9.4 percent from government sources, and 72.3 percent from community sources, with community expenditures including labor and local materials (Martínez and González 1981, 17). In supporting roughly 70 percent of the costs, international agencies would provide construction materials such as pipes, transport heavy materials, and conduct trainings for community members. The Nicaraguan government would fund public employees' salaries and provide stipends for food and travel associated with water projects (interview, Francisco Baltodano, February 3, 2010).[12]

In contrast to the Somoza era, the revolutionary era's fomenting of greater associational space for organizing supported its objective of imbuing rural residents with responsibility for the management of new water systems. Notably, some engagement in water projects aligned with mass organization objectives. For instance, a 1981 Ministry of Health (MINSA) report stated that "rural communities will have a great participation [in water projects] through the mass organizations, in this case the C.D.S. [Sandinista Defense Committees]; this participation will be made effective through community contributions like money, labor, and the attainment of local materials" (Martínez and González 1981, 8). Facilitating a pattern of benign neglect of rural water systems and users in the wake of system construction was state actors' *intention* to leave systems in local hands. A 1989 INAA report asserts that water system beneficiaries "should accept and comply with the responsibility of operating, maintaining and administering water projects, having INAA with functions of help and consulting only" (INAA 1989, n.p.).

Neoliberal Democracy (1990–2006)

The Sandinista Revolution ended with elections in 1990 that set the country on course of neoliberal economic and political reform. The Nicaraguan population at large had suffered great loss and emotional wounds during the Contra War (which coincided with the social and organizational shifts described above): over thirty thousand Nicaraguans—roughly half combatants and half civilians—lost their lives during the war, and twenty thousand sustained wounds, many of them severe (Smith 1996). When conservative president Violeta Chamorro, of the National Opposition Union (UNO), was elected, she reactivated the government's relationship with financial institutions, including the International Monetary Fund (IMF), as well as with development agencies that had been hostile to the FLSN, for example, USAID, to facilitate economic structural adjustment (Prevost 1999). This shift included the renewed promotion of export-oriented agricultural production and a reduced role of the state in the provision of public goods and services (Anderson and Dodd 2005; Baumeister 1995; Rocha 2007). In social terms, Chamorro's economic policies worked to undermine improvements in the standard of living for impoverished Nicaraguans that the Sandinistas had prioritized, albeit in the financially limiting context of the Contra War. Coverage of health care and other social programs was reduced, and poverty and unemployment increased (Anderson and Dodd 2005; O'Kane 1995).

The subsequent conservative presidencies of Arnoldo Alemán (1997–2000) and Enrique Bolaños (2001–6), in addition to continuing the economic neoliberalization begun under Chamorro, saw "erratic support for democratic institutions, corruption, and scandal" (Anderson and Dodd 2005, 241). The now-infamous pact constructed in 1998 between Alemán and Daniel Ortega—at the time a Sandinista member of the National Assembly—has been criticized as contributing to the demobilization of the grassroots civil society cultivated during the 1980s (Grigsby 2005). The pact served to further the power of the FSLN and Liberal Constitutionalist Party (PLC) through a series of reforms, including political gerrymandering and new requirements to securing party representation as a way to restrict competition from third parties. In sum, the pact undermined both the legitimacy and integrity of Nicaragua's fledgling representative democracy (see, e.g., Anderson and Dodd 2009; Brown and Cloke 2005).

In a context of ideological rupture and democratic weakening at the national level, the booming number of rural water systems post-1990 demonstrates the sustained and increasing relevance of international activity in the sector. Notably, a concerted strategy emerged on the part of the government and collaborating multilateral agencies to build and integrate more attention to capacity building into the process of implementing rural water and sanitation projects. By 1996, there were twenty-three regional National Operation and Maintenance Unit promoters across the departments of Boaco, Chontales, Chinandega, Estelí, Jinotega, León, Managua, Madriz, and Matagalpa in order to extend capacity building and technical support to rural communities.[13] Some sectoral assessments indicate that rural residents perceived limited support from staff of both the decentralized (i.e., municipal) and regional support models, with 65.2 percent and 77.7 percent, respectively, reporting "little help" or "no help" from government Operation and Maintenance Unit staff (Baltodano and Olmedo 2008). These data are not surprising given that some municipalities did not even have a staff person devoted to rural water and sanitation projects. Significantly, Nicaragua's Municipalities Law (Law 40) "does not obligate local governments to manage water and sanitation systems" (Medrano et al. 2007, 167). Thus, although "attempts to persuade mayors of the importance of [Operation and Maintenance] units within a decentralization framework were made" (52), the political will of a given mayor tended to determine whether operation and maintenance staff were hired. Given this local discretion, international involvement helps to explain an otherwise paradoxical increase in access to water and sanitation in rural and urban areas in the context of privatization and a "shrinking state" in the 1990s.

Beyond financial and technical support for rural water projects, domestic NGOs and multilateral organizations became increasingly consequential to the sector's evolution in the 1990s in the sense that they engaged rural communities in a host of social and economic issues, much as the state and FSLN did in the 1980s.[14] For instance, many NGOs developed trainings for new water committees on topics such as gender, community organization, system maintenance, and water quality. The sector regulatory agency INAA integrated these trainings into the accepted and government-promoted "project cycle" in the 1990s (Medrano et al. 2007). Although NGO, multilateral agencies, and state actors intended training and technical support for initial project stages only—that is, through system construction—they were an improvement from earlier project cycles that did not offer capacity-building elements.[15]

Related to the broader trends wrought by neoliberalism, this period saw contradictory tendencies regarding how the state approached developing public and private capacities in water and sanitation. In important ways, a tension existed between, on the one hand, an evolving, synergistic relationship among NGOs, multilateral agencies, and state agencies and, on the other, the policy trend of the sector's privatization. Of particular relevance to the water and sanitation sector, the Inter-American Development Bank (IADB) approved a loan in 1999 of US$13.9 million to Nicaragua for the "modernization" of water and sanitation services in the wake of the highly destructive Hurricane Mitch.[16] The loan called for establishing public-private partnerships to manage the water and sewage systems in four municipalities (Chinandega, Jinotega, León, Matagalpa) in addition to earmarking funds for a private management contract for the state water company, the Nicaraguan Water and Sewerage Enterprise (ENACAL). The loan-stipulated restructuring of ENACAL would "prioritize activities for the improvement of operational efficiency through a business strengthening program" (IADB 1999).

A trend toward increasing private sector involvement in the sector was also evident in President Bolaños's (2001–6) executive decree number 109 in 2004. This decree assigned formal responsibility for the rural water sector to the Emergency Social Investment Fund (FISE), an entity functioning with a high dependence on loans and private contracting to carry out much of its "social" investing (Government of Nicaragua and PAHO 2004). Even prior to the decree, transfer of resources from the central government to the regional- and municipal-level Direction of Rural Aqueducts (DAR) offices had begun to diminish (interview, Jorge Rojas, March 12, 2010). Because Decree 109 shifted responsibilities from the state water company, ENACAL, to FISE, it prompted the closing of all the regional and decentralized DAR offices at a national scale, thus diminishing the human capital previously cultivated within the rural water and sanitation sector.

Despite the loss of state capacity in the sector during this period, the number of water projects reflects the continued high level of external donations: by the mid-2000s, over five thousand rural water projects had been constructed in Nicaragua, entailing an estimated thirty thousand to forty thousand rural residents engaged in the day-to-day work of securing access to water for domestic use. Financial investments continued to reflect an urban bias—even as almost half of the country's population continued to be classified as rural into the early 2000s. From 1998 to 2003, US$25.3 million of the state water company's investments in water and sanitation were invested in rural areas versus US$120.5 million for urban areas (Government of Nicaragua and PAHO 2004, 135). In other words, the state directed roughly 83 percent of ENACAL's investments toward benefiting 56 percent of the population. In absolute terms, "improved," or piped, water access had reached an estimated 36.52 percent of the rural population by 1998 (Medrano et al. 2007).

What explains the political activation of community-based water managers, who had come to be known as the Potable Water and Sanitation Committees (CAPS), in the mid-2000s? Part of the answer can be found in the active response of popular sectors within Nicaragua to the trend of privatization. This national-level response began fomenting in the wake of the Inter-American Development Bank loan's package in 1999 and grew in response to the government's bid solicitation process in 2001 for the privatization of the country's largest hydroelectric generator, HIDROGESA, located on Lake Apanás in the department of Jinotega. Residents on and near the lake demanded inclusion in decision-making processes affecting the power generator. Some residents expressed concern that concession of the plant signified an eventual privatization of the lake. The government's consultation-based contract with a Chilean company in 2005 for the "modernization" of the state water company, ENACAL, provoked further suspicion of a government orientation toward privatization (Romano 2012).

Much of the initial impetus for CAPS' network formation emerged from their exclusion from primarily urban-based anti–water privatization organizing of the early to mid-2000s. Notably, staff at domestic NGOs making up the Coalition for the Right to Water (CODA) saw a timely opportunity amid anti-privatization organizing to interrupt this political exclusion and draw CAPS into public debates concerning water governance. Mobilizing water committees would not only enhance participating NGOs' and other social movement actors' strategy to propel the passing and influence the implementation of Law 620; it would also serve to shed light on CAPS as materially consequential organizations in water governance.

One CODA member, the Organization for Economic and Social Development in Urban and Rural Areas (ODESAR), engaged CAPS to form the first municipal network in Matagalpa in 2005. The organization had formed in 1990 with roughly twenty Sandinista-affiliated ex-mayors from the departments of Matagalpa and Jinotega with a mission of "awakening the individual and collective consciousness of women and men who find themselves disadvantaged and in conditions of poverty" (ODESAR 2017) in order to support social change and the cultivation of citizenship. Working in the area of water system construction in addition to social and economic development more broadly, ODESAR had previous connections to water committees across communities in Matagalpa. As explained by staff member and eventual facilitator of

Matagalpa's departmental network Javier Mendoza: "We talked about organizing the committees . . . We started there, calling them and presenting the idea: did they want to be organized in that way? Because we also realized that the committees didn't even know each other from one community to the next. Even though they were there in their communities, no one knew what a water committee was. . . . And from here, within ODESAR, came the idea of how to unite them in a municipal movement" (interview, June 21, 2010).

Water committees working with ODESAR in various areas of rural development responded favorably and enthusiastically to the prospect of expanding their organizational presence and goals. The Potable Water and Sanitation Committees also expressed interest in confronting a potential policy shift toward privatization, which they perceived as a threat to communities' de facto control, and sense of ownership over, community-based water systems. That is, although urban water systems were targeted for increased commercialization, Article 4 of the proposed National Water Law stated that "potable water service will not be the object of any privatization, direct or indirect." This language impressed upon civil society actors, including CAPS, that the door would remain open to privatization of water *resources*, even if formalized service arrangements would remain public.

Within Matagalpa, a second NGO was also integral to the formation of municipal-level CAPS networks: the Association for the Development of Northern Municipalities (ADEMNORTE). While the organization has since dissolved due to insufficient funding, ADEMNORTE worked for over ten years in support of rural water and sanitation projects. While similar in vision and mission to ODESAR, ADEMNORTE formed in 2002 with four staff members who had previously worked in the government's DAR office in Matagalpa (the last office of which closed in 2007). The NGO thus formed with the participation of individuals who had experienced and witnessed the limited organizational, technical, and financial support to communities. The association sought to provide more holistic support to communities before, during, and in the wake of new water and sanitation projects through employing a multidisciplinary work team of engineers, hydrologists, and administrators to support project planning, design, implementation, and sustainability. When ADEMNORTE supported the creation of the municipal CAPS network in Sébaco, Matagalpa, several CAPS members within the municipality were already actively engaged in the new National CAPS Network that had formed in 2005. One result of this political engagement at a national level was the phenomenon of water committees who had worked with ADEMNORTE on water projects approaching the NGO for support in political mobilization at the *municipal* level.

Return of the FSLN (2007-present)

The 2006 election of President Daniel Ortega entailed the return of the Sandinista National Liberation Front, or the FSLN, to power at the national level.[17] Ortega's presidency was quickly mired in political controversy. This controversy owed, in part, to his decreeing of a new model of direct democracy that stood in conflict with existing channels of citizen participation as outlined in Nicaragua's Municipality Law (Law 40) and the Law of Citizen Participation (Law 475). For example, the Citizen Power Councils (CPCs) undermined the functioning of existing Municipal Development Councils (CDMs) through supplanting them with new partisan-aligned bodies. Like the preexisting model, the Citizen Power Councils were established "to have Nicaraguans organize and participate in the country's development in an active and direct way" (Stuart 2009, 5). In the view of many critics, however, the CPCs were narrowly focused on the partisan agenda of the FSLN.[18] Overall, the model received harsh criticism as an alleged party tool of the FSLN to co-opt and control rural and urban civil society toward implementing the government's social programs and building political allegiance through clientelism (Chamorro, Jarquín, and Bendaña 2009; Prado 2010; Ruiz 2009).

Despite the criticisms, years after Ortega's election reflect an increased prioritization of water as a social investment. One important institutional shift in the water and sanitation sector was the government's adoption of a demand-based approach to water projects within the Emergency Social Investment Fund (FISE). This approach focused on upon rural populations' asserted needs, in contrast to the previous model, which awarded project funds based upon which municipality could offer the highest *contrapartida* (contribution) to projects. Water became the "automatic priority" at the subnational level, according to a FISE staff member in Estelí, elevating rural water projects above investment areas such as schools and infrastructure such as roads. The numbers support this assertion: in 2008 and 2009, the FISE in Nicaragua spent 35 percent and 30 percent of its budget, respectively, on water and sanitation projects, constituting the most significant expenditure at the subnational level and contrasting with much lower spending in this area in throughout the 1990s (Government of Nicaragua and PAHO 2004).[19]

Increased government attention to the rural water and sanitation sector under Ortega must be understood as both a result of popular mobilization and a factor contributing to it. First, Ortega's election coincided with civil society activism opposing water privatization; indeed, Ortega inherited the opportunity to sign the National Water Law (Law 620) into law in 2007—an act which brought anti–water privatization organizing in Nicaragua to a close. Law 620 sought to introduce a framework for the "sustainable" and "equitable" administration, conservation, development, and use of the country's water resources, as well as the "simultaneous protection of other natural resources, ecosystems and the environment." The law also established new nonstate decision-making roles, citing that "four representatives from users' organizations" will participate in a National Council of Water Resources (CNRH), charged with fulfilling a coordination and planning role for the sector.

Importantly, CAPS felt largely excluded from the popular sector consultations on the draft National Water Law as it evolved in the early 2000s—and, more important, had not had a role in elaborating the law's substance. In outlining new water sector decision-making roles for civil society organizations, Law 620 could have delineated specific roles for CAPS as rural water managers and service providers.[20] Moreover, the law made no mention of CAPS except in the Regulations, published in November 2007, which asserted: "In communities where the service provider [ENACAL] does not have coverage, systems will be administered by the community, specifically the Potable Water Committees, who will guarantee service to the community, all below the supervision and control of ENACAL." In the eyes of water committees and their domestic and international allies, asserting CAPS to be "below the control and supervision" of the state water company did not reflect a viable sector strategy. Moreover, the law did not accurately reflect the reality of the scope and scale of CAPS' work nationally in Nicaragua.

In 2008, CAPS member Esperanza of Muy Muy, Matagalpa, summarized the role of new networks in relation to concerns about legal changes to the sector: "Now at a national level there is a movement to form a national water network in order to develop a new special potable water committee law. Because we don't appear in any of the organizations that the national water law [Law 620] aims to form. The law doesn't recognize us. It's for this reason that we're working to formulate a potable water committee law so that, first of all, we have legal recognition as a source of support . . . if we have legal recognition, our projects can't be privatized" (interview, September 2, 2008). This testimony reveals that concerns about water privatization lingered among CAPS even after the passage of Law 620. Some individuals in the nongovernmental sector playing a role in the CAPS network formation shared this concern. Eduardo, one of the National CAPS Network facilitators affiliated with the Latin American Information Service for Sustainable Agriculture (SIMAS), shared his assessment that Law 620 did not close the door to the threat of privatization, as the law emphasized private-sector concessions and outsourcing. According to Eduardo, as well as other NGO staff working with CAPS networks, the shifting legal framework for the water sector created an important political opportunity for organized CAPS to influence its trajectory (interview, June 28, 2010).

The political mobilization of CAPS across territorial and political scales starting in 2005, preceding the passing of Law 620, reflected a quest for recognition and defense of past, present, and future water management and provision work. Notably, CAPS networks build upon historic, multisectoral synergies in the rural water and sanitation sector. Yet, CAPS' networks represented a new kind of relationship between these community-based actors and the organizations and individuals that support them. That is, the historical relationship between CAPS, NGOs, and multilateral agencies primarily served to support rural water provision; moreover, a key feature of rural water management has been the withdrawal of outside actors from rural communities after water systems are constructed. In contrast, CAPS mobilizing processes and networks constitute an inherently *multiscalar* as well as *multisectoral* collective action. Potable Water and Sanitation Committee networks have also become a strategic means to advance explicitly *political* and *policy* goals, including CAPS' recognition as rural, community-based resource managers and service providers.

Rural Water Provision at the State-Society Interface

Across diverse political regimes, NGOs, multilateral organizations, and the Nicaraguan government helped to facilitate the emergence of community-based water management regimes. Surprisingly, the government's promotion of rural residents taking on the management and administration of new rural water projects has been remarkably consistent in spite of major regime and ideological change across time. A significant shortcoming of the general pattern of state-society synergy in the sector concerns the limited technical, financial, and organizational support to rural communities in the wake of system construction. Moreover, underlying these patterns observed over time are the ways that each regime presented unique opportunities for as well as constraints to CAPS' emergence and effective functioning. For example, the turn to neoliberalism in the 1990s saw a shrinking of the public sector and an accompanying reduction in state capacity in the rural water sector. However, accompanying this shift was an increase in the number of domestic NGOs working in rural water and sanitation—helping to fill a "gap" in state support and resources. These NGOs would later be instrumental in promoting the transcommunity mobilization of water committees as they sought legal recognition.

A key centerpiece of the NGO-led strategy to mobilize rural water committees was the formation of a National CAPS Network and dozens of CAPS networks at the municipal level starting in 2005. As the first instances of CAPS' transcommunity collective action, these networks served to project rural water committees onto the national political stage, where they would become effective policy advocates. Yet, CAPS' omission from state policy frameworks and their political exclusion from the processes of designing these prior to the Special CAPS Law raise questions: How *did* water committees become empowered to manage water resources at the grassroots in Nicaragua? What experiences and knowledge did CAPS bring *into* network spaces—and with what impacts on these as platforms for political activism? The next chapter turns to these kinds of questions through an examination of CAPS' empowerment as water managers and service providers.

TWO

"Organic Empowerment" as a Grassroots Source of Legitimacy and Authority

"One of our achievements was buying 15 manzanas [37 acres] of virgin forest—the forest that's protecting our source and that of other water systems. We bought them using the tariffs from our users." CAPS secretary José Francisco, "Chepito" as his water committee colleagues and friends call him, stood at the front of a large hall next to flip chart paper resting on a stand. A slight man with a considerable presence, he stood before several dozen CAPS members hailing from various communities in Sébaco, Matagalpa, who convened in December 2009 to form a new municipal CAPS network. As the elected coordinator of the municipal CAPS network in San Dionisio, José Francisco, a local leader, had authority and knowledge from his organizational experiences to share with other water committee members toward supporting their local work.

The meeting was an opportunity for José Francisco to present how his community of El Zapote, San Dionisio, located along the corredor seco *(dry corridor) in Nicaragua's central highlands, had been innovative in organizational terms, effectively maintaining and expanding water service over time to include 165 families (up from 95 families in 1986 when the system was constructed): "In 1996 we started to have problems, so we reorganized so we could better undertake system maintenance and operation." Gesturing to the flipchart paper with twelve numbered quadrants, he explained: "Now we have twelve teams of people working on maintenance and operation of the water system. Each works on maintenance for one month with ten to twelve* compañeros. *Before the committee made repairs. Now the whole community does it." The CAPS had "problems," too, according to José Francisco: "Today the system's vida útil [useful life] has expired"*[1]*—how long would the community be able to keep the water system functioning? Local population growth and coffee plantations around the water source were also growing pressures on and threats to water quantity and quality. Some users were late in paying users' fees. And residents, or system beneficiaries, didn't always come to meetings.*

The experiences of the El Zapote CAPS would be echoed by CAPS from across regions as they shared stories in new network meetings and with me during visits to their communities. Sustaining water systems and service was hard work, challenged by perennial organizational, financial, and technological issues; it was also increasingly affected by ecological change, which has the potential to punctuate rural water management with crises such as the sudden destruction of water systems in storm-induced flooding. In my research, I had chosen to document "successful" cases of resident-led water management—that is, where water service was active. The "forest through the trees" that emerged was a landscape of significant achievements, including environmental stewardship and system repairs. The landscape, at the same time, reflected water committees' muddling through problems as they worked with commitment and out of necessity to ensure that water continued to flow to residents.

Since the 1970s in Nicaragua, community-based water management (CBWM) regimes have sustained small-scale water systems and rural water service. While these regimes are not always successful, many residents reflect having developed capacities enabling water service provision, such as the organizational skills and environmental services cultivated and practiced, respectively, in José Francisco's community of El Zapote, San Dionisio. However, the 2010 passage of the Special CAPS Law (Law 722) presented a puzzle regarding water committees' achievement of formal legal recognition for this work. In formally assigning roles and responsibilities to CAPS in the rural water sector, Law 722 mirrored other decentralization initiatives in terms of a devolution of authority and decision-making. Yet, CAPS' recognition via Law 722 reflected more than merely the government's embrace of the global trend of decentralization: community-based management of rural water systems was an empirical reality in Nicaragua at the time of the law's passing. To CAPS and the organizations working with them, the law significantly, yet simply, served to *codify* rural residents' long-standing contributions to water

FIGURE 7 José Francisco presents his water committee's organizational structure for system maintenance as part of a CAPS assembly to form a new municipal CAPS network in Sébaco, Matagalpa.

management at a national scale. Law 722 thus constituted an ex post facto decentralization as well a "decentralization from below" (Larson 2004) given water committees' direct and energetic role in helping to design the law and promote its passage.

The quick mobilization of CAPS in 2005 to form new networks and successfully pursue recognition raises the following questions: How had CAPS become "unofficial" water managers in rural areas, and what explained how this work had been sustained over time? How did water committees' process of empowerment at the grass roots influence the state's recognition of CAPS as water managers and service providers, and hence as legitimate authorities in the water sector?

This chapter argues that CAPS' experiences in Nicaragua reflect an "organic empowerment" of rural residents as resource managers and service providers at the grass roots. What I name an *organic* empowerment references a bottom-up process that evolves over time in the wake of a de facto conferring of roles and responsibilities to grassroots actors. That is, in the absence of formal state decentralization, rural residents *have* become empowered, albeit unofficially, to manage resources in their communities. In spite of—and, in ways, owing to—how outside support to rural communities has been limited temporally to an early phase of system construction, rural residents' work over time reflects an evolving empowerment as they cultivate skills and the knowledge necessary to maintain and administer water systems. Not only has this organic empowerment affected CAPS' legitimacy vis-à-vis residents for whom water access is facilitated; it has also has served to promote water committees' legitimacy beyond the communities in which they work, including in the eyes of public officials as CAPS have scaled up politically.

Organic Empowerment and Decentralization "from Below"

Conceptually and theoretically, the notion of an organic empowerment supports articulating the intersection of common property regime and decentralization frameworks. Independently, each of these scholarships has made outstanding contributions toward understanding the conditions under which state and non-state actors manage resources viably over time. However, neither fully accounts for forms of empowerment generated largely from below, which may, under certain circumstances, come to bear on top-down, state-led efforts to manage resources or design and implement water policy. For example, in examining the microlevel dynamics of resource management, common property scholars have paid relatively less attention to state policies and institutions and the myriad ways these matter for grassroots resource management. Yet, moments of state-led political and legal change—for example, formal decentralization or new legal frameworks such as those reflected in Nicaragua's 2007 National Water Law (Law 620)—create opportunities for grassroots actors to attempt to intervene in public debates and policy development. These opportunities may be seized upon when social actors feel threatened by such changes.

In contrast to common property regime frameworks, the scholarship on decentralized natural resources management emphasizes "higher" political and broader geographic scales through shedding light on state devolutions of decision-making authority to lower administrative levels. Scholars of decentralization have highlighted both subnational governmental and nonstate actors; however, this scholarship's emphasis on state policy has often left unofficial grassroots actors involved in resource governance outside the frame of analysis. For instance, a "properly empowered" resource management regime has been characterized as one that "operates with the freedom of any public, non-state organization with a *legal persona*" (Murphree 2009, 2559; emphasis added). Another take on empowerment asserts that for "legitimate community institutions" to be "enfranchised," decision-making "power comes through *empowerment*, which occurs when the decentralization of resource management gives not just responsibilities, but also rights, to local communities" (Kull, citing Ribot [1999] 2002, 58; emphasis in original). This emphasis on resource management actors formalized through state law reflects the significance of a legal status for obtaining political rights and protected roles in resource governance. Yet, at the same time, this emphasis results in a missed opportunity to examine alternative and nonstate sources of empowerment and legitimacy in natural resource management.

Drawing together the common property regime and decentralization frames of analysis sheds light on how—even in the absence of an official state policy conferring legal rights and prerogatives—resource users and managers can become "organically" empowered to manage water resources in their communities. As the director of rural water projects for the Nicaragua Integrated Watershed Project in the Department of Estelí, Francisco, asserted in 2010: "The CAPS are the cornerstones of the [rural] water systems. Government institutions don't help them, but in one way or another they are maintaining their systems" (interview, February 2, 2010). A notable pattern observed in the emergence of CBWM is that an *initial* moment of empowerment often results from outside financial, technical, and organizational investment in water infrastructure. In the Nicaraguan case, water committees' path to empowerment in terms of gaining access to and control over drinking water supplies has depended upon the resources devoted to water system construction on the part of NGOs, multilateral organizations, and state actors. This historical pattern reflects an initial moment of de facto, though not de jure, empowerment of CAPS as water managers and service providers.

Not dependent upon a legal state devolution of decision-making authority or control over resources, an organic empowerment is one that evolves at the grass roots, emerging out of the day-to-day labors and relationships associated with managing resources.[2] While outside financial, technical, and organizational support typically helps confer initial empowerment, organic empowerment draws attention to how empowerment can be *either* a formally conferred *or* de facto access to, and control over, local resources entailing significant capacity building, decision making, and leadership (see also Narayan 1994). Organic empowerment's emphasis on *nonstate* sources of power, authority, and legitimacy encourages expanding our understanding of empowerment within the decentralization literature: empowerment and the legitimate authority it may engender need not be derived from the state. This process of empowerment also presents an opportunity to examine how legitimate authority cultivated at the grass roots may scale up with community-based resource managers to influence interactions with state officials. This includes, in the Nicaraguan case, grassroots actors' efforts to influence a new state "decentralization" policy granting them, ex post facto, formal authority as community-based organizations.

How is legitimacy, and legitimate authority, cultivated at the grass roots? In contrast to common property regime scholars' emphasis on local institutional design (see box 1), an organic empowerment sheds light on how communities of users develop capacities over time in a way that engenders legitimacy vis-à-vis residents as water system beneficiaries. An organic empowerment entails ongoing and evolving processes of learning, capacity building, and exercising leadership through the work of managing resources. While CAPS interviewed and observed during the course of research do not reflect a representative sample,[3] empirical illustrations drawn from these cases generate insight into diverse dimensions of resource management that here serve as inductively derived indicators of CAPS' empowerment as water managers and service providers (see box 2).

Box 1 Common Property Regime Design Principles

1. Clearly defined boundaries for resource and its users (i.e., households and/or individuals)
2. Congruence between appropriation (i.e., resource extraction) and provision rules and local conditions
3. Collective choice arrangements by which "most individuals affected by the operational rules can participate in modifying" them
4. Monitoring arrangement by or accountable to the appropriators
5. Graduated sanctions for those violating regime rules
6. Conflict-resolution mechanisms
7. Minimal government recognition of appropriators' rights to organize
8. Nesting of the local regime within a larger system of institutions

Source: Ostrom 1990

Box 2 Dimensions of Water Management Demonstrating Empowerment

Technical
- Constructing water systems
- Repairing and replacing broken tubes
- Installing, maintaining, and reading water meters
- Cleaning water storage tanks and aqueducts
- Chlorinating water
- Shutting off / reconnecting household water supply

Financial
- Collecting users' tariffs
- Financial record keeping
- Making bank deposits
- Fundraising
- Appealing to NGOs, international agencies, and local governments for financial support of water projects

Organizational
- Maintaining water users' registry
- Convening and facilitating users' assemblies
- Organizing users for participation in water management activities
- Enacting formal rule changes
- Training incoming leaders
- Implementing relevant educational activities
- Coordinating with other community groups and state agencies
- *Design Principles 1–6*

Environmental
- Purchasing of land around water sources for conservation and protective purposes
- Reforesting around water storage tanks and recharge zones
- Day-to-day educational work and periodic campaigns to prevent and regulate deforestation, water contamination, and inappropriate or excessive water use

(continued)

Box 2 (*continued*)

Political/Legal

- Negotiating intracommunity access to water sources and land for water distribution systems
- Pressuring state agencies and public officials to enforce environmental regulations
- Advocating for legal recognition of local organizations and ownership over water sources/systems*
- *Design Principles 7–8*

Each of these areas of water management are meant to be illustrative, rather than comprehensive. Furthermore, they are not meant to imply that each CAPS interviewed and observed during research carry out all of these functions, despite having activity in each category.
*This reflects a new area of water committees' collective action once scaled up politically in new CAPS networks.

The technical, financial, organizational, environmental, and political/legal realms of CAPS' "everyday" labor at the grass roots encompass, but also transcend, the narrow institutional design principles. The concept of an organic empowerment thus seeks to expand common property frameworks, first, through highlighting a broader array of resource management roles and responsibilities and, second, through shedding light on the social dimensions of community-based resource management. Particular attention is paid to legitimacy as a relational dimension of common property management that infuses and may result from this work across all of the foregoing dimensions. Indeed, although it has been overlooked in the scholarship relative to an emphasis on institutional design, legitimacy as local buy-in and acceptance of authorities, rules, and norms (Kull 2002) constitutes part of the social engine propelling and sustaining the collective endeavor of resource management and service provision at the grass roots.

Cultivating Legitimacy and Authority through Practice

How have CAPS' empowerment and water management capacities evolved organically, outside of state legal frameworks, at the grass roots over time? The following sections examine how water committees' everyday practices have fostered and deepened their capacities in the technical, financial, organizational, environmental, and political/legal realms of common property management. These community organizations have faced circumstances that pose extreme threats to their sustainability, let alone effective functioning. Yet despite challenges, water committees have demonstrated the ability to navigate difficult circumstances to ensure water system functioning and "survive" as social organizations. This involves work that is self-initiated, self-directed, and proactive toward achieving the water management goal of universal water access. Moreover, water committees' complex and, in ways, sophisticated work engenders legitimacy vis-à-vis the residents for whom they facilitate water access, evident in system beneficiaries' payments of water tariffs, attendance at CAPS-convened community assemblies, and participation in water system maintenance.

In relation to other kinds of resource users' associations, such as forest councils or irrigators' associations, CAPS have derived additional legitimacy from serving as not just resource managers but also *service providers*. In other words, in providing drinking water, rural water committees fulfill a critical function associated with the state. Notably, CAPS' work cannot easily be taken over by state actors, who often lack the necessary capacities and local legitimacy water committees have engendered over time. Previous research in Nicaragua found that the more rural and geographically isolated CAPS tend to be those with *greater* capacities (compared to periurban, or semirural, communities) (Kreimann 2009). Rosibel Kreimann explained differential capacities by arguing that isolated communities have come *not* to depend on the support of state actors, while those closer to urban centers expect the state to invest resources toward supporting water access. Indeed, the laissez-faire approach of outside actors postsystem construction in Nicaragua has meant that contributions to rural water management and provision *capacities* have been extremely limited.

Related to the state's limited involvement in rural water management, CAPS' intracommunity capacities oftentimes exceed those of government officials legally assigned to work with rural communities in support of water management and service provision. Possessing greater knowledge and capacities than state actors in the sector, as well as locally cultivated legitimacy, has unwittingly supported rural residents' development of competencies. Once water committees scaled up to form new networks at the municipal, departmental, and national levels, their organic empowerment came to bear at other scales and in relation to state actors. In particular, capacities and legitimacy engendered at the grass roots bolstered arguments for the state's formal conference of legal recognition upon CAPS as legitimate authorities in the water sector.

Technical Capacities

Water committees in Nicaragua typically receive some minimal technical training from donor organizations and, in some cases, government staff, at the time of water system construction. Yet, because they are unable to depend on continued assistance, CAPS seek ways to sustain water provision as problems arise. Similar to water users' associations regionally in Latin America, CAPS' empowerment to access and control water can emerge out of users' "taking part in the organization, design and construction of the irrigation system"; moreover, users "consolidate and re-create their rights by maintaining and rehabilitating the system" (Boelens 2002, 145). One particular, increasingly prevalent, issue CAPS confront pertaining to maintenance and rehabilitation is that of water systems ceasing to function or verging on obsolescence, as most small-scale water systems are intended to last for fifteen to twenty years. According to a report issued by the Pan American Health Organization and the Nicaraguan government, an estimated 18 percent of the 4,886 documented water systems in the country were "out of use" as of 2002 (Government of Nicaragua and PAHO 2004). Some systems become defunct from old age, yet others break, and may fail to be fixed, because residents lack the technical skills or resources to maintain them.

Although NGO and multilateral agency staff include water committee trainings as part of their project cycle, the government has had very limited involvement in developing residents' capacities.[4] Even without training for certain tasks, however, CAPS may demonstrate having developed certain capacities, including the ability to innovate, in order to problem-solve. The engineer Rafael Díaz, who began work in rural water and sanitation in Nicaragua as part of UNICEF in 1988, expressed surprise that many CAPS function as well as they do without much initial or sustained outside support. He reported on the technical ingenuity he observed in one community in the municipality of San Isidrio: residents were utilizing old hand pumps imported from India that UNICEF had installed twenty to twenty-five years previously—and that in his opinion, should have ceased to function. Members of CAPS began to build their own spare parts for the system as repair needs arose. These technical innovations ensured that CAPS could function as resource managers and maintain water service to residents. As Narayan argued in regard to rural water supply projects in global perspective: "Once . . . [beneficiaries of water projects] are empowered, they are more likely to be proactive, to take initiative, and to display confidence for undertaking other actions to solve problems beyond those defined by the project" (1994, 8). Rafael recognized that some technical undertakings require external support, hence why some communities he worked with on system construction would reach out to him and UNICEF staff for help with tasks such as changing water pumps (interview, January 27, 2010).

While the capacities of individual CAPS vary, many pride themselves on having the faculties necessary to manage water systems technically and financially. An estimated 70 percent of communities have a resident sufficiently qualified to do basic plumbing work on systems (Government of Nicaragua and PAHO 2004, 100). The community of Compasagüe 1 in Muy Muy built the first rural aqueduct in the entire municipality in 1995 with support from a program of the Ministry of Social Action (MAS, created by the central government in 1993) that provided a small amount of funds for food while the community constructed the water system. The community collected donations internally from residents until there was enough money to buy needed materials. With contributions of residents in the form of *mano de obra* (labor), the community could avoid the costs of contracting with and paying noncommunity members to work: "We didn't bring in people from outside, and that was one of the advantages of the project. . . . We did everything, and because of that it cost us very little" (interview, August 22, 2009). The CAPS coordinator, Marlene, expressed another "advantage" her committee had going forward: "We have people who know how to plumb, who know how to build, and who know other skills we can use. Among ourselves we don't earn much. We don't charge much [from water users], but something, and we do the work." Another CAPS coordinator, Jessenia of Nueva Segovia, related a similar story: "I'm a plumber. . . . I used to say, what's the point of being the [CAPS] coordinator if I don't know how to work with PVC piping? How does it make sense to be a coordinator if I can't say to the plumber 'this is good, this is bad' because I don't know where the hell something goes? We have plumbers, technical experts, everything. The donor organization prepared us." When communities have to develop and hone capacities internal to the community, CAPS demonstrate the ability to be largely self-sufficient in regard to water management and provision.

Nevertheless, a lack of access to capable state actors in the sector means that communities often have no choice but to problem-solve independently—a

FIGURE 8 Residents of the community of El Naranjo, Sébaco, assemble and lay piping for their new gravity-fed water system in April 2010.

behavior that may also be reinforced through interactions with local governments. For instance, a government water *técnico* (expert; literally "technician"), in Pueblo Nuevo, Estelí, recounted his response to a resident's request to have him dismantle the community's well pump. He responded: "I told her that I had never dismantled that. It would be irresponsible of me to take it apart. I told her that people in the community were trained to do that. When they built the system, that well, they left one person [trained] who could put together and take apart that pump. 'You all, take it apart, see what's wrong with it, and the day that you do that if you want let's go together, to look at what's wrong, and we'll see how the mayor can resolve [the problem]'" (interview, February 4, 2010). For reasons unbeknownst to the técnico, the community was attempting to involve the local government in an operation for which they, supposedly, had the capacity.[5] Although the técnico believed the CAPS "should" have the capacity to dismantle the pump on their own, this seeking of support does not necessarily mean the capacity was absent, but rather that rural residents held certain expectations of local government officials.

An equally significant observation, however, is that government water and sanitation "experts" may have inadequate working knowledge of the infrastructure used by residents in their municipality. In Pueblo Nuevo, the public official could not perform a task necessary to the functioning of the characteristic water systems within the municipality. This shows that CAPS and communities often have no choice but to problem-solve independently. The knowledge and experience CAPS accumulate over time in their day-to-day work contribute to the ways in which they amass greater technical capacity in water system operation and administration than many public officials—who even as water and sanitation technicians may have little to no experience in the sector.

Financial Capacities

Technical issues related to maintenance intertwine with the financial dimensions of community-based water management. There is no comprehensive "study that reflects with specificity what happens in regard to the CAPS' finances at a national scale" (Government of Nicaragua and PAHO 2004); however, individual water committees reflect having developed financial skills as part of their water management and service provision. The capacities of CAPS to modify and implement local financial rules not only strengthens their ability to maintain and sustain water management but also generates legitimacy from the perspective of system beneficiaries.

Government decision-making with a history of spending limited public resources on urban, as opposed to rural, water systems and populations means CAPS have incentives to become as self-sufficient as possible in economic terms. Esperanza, the CAPS El Chompipe coordinator in the municipality of Muy Muy, expressed her committee's achievement of a degree of financial independence since forming in 2001: "The truth is that to this day we've survived without support from the municipality and without the support of the national government. The central government—none of the governments that have existed—have helped us economically in any way" (interview, August 21, 2008). Although the construction of water systems is rarely possible without significant external investment, rural residents' financial contributions to local water management and access start immediately upon receipt of a project; funds are not simply "gifted" to residents. In fact, water committees may resist the notion of receiving charity. Esperanza emphasized a desire for support to CAPS, but not for a mere "gift": "We don't want [the government and NGOs] just to give us things. Because never, of all of us CAPS who are organized, do we want them to give away things to us. We want them to help us" (interview, August 21, 2008).

In practical terms, CBWM models require significant contributions, both physical and financial, from residents. In the case of the community of Compasagüe 2, USAID supported the project with financing, the domestic Organization for Economic and Social Development in Urban and Rural Areas (ODESAR) assisted with system construction, and community members gave a financial support of 460 córdobas (US$22) per household. This financial contribution is something that people took "from their *gallinitas* [savings]," as a CAPS member expressed. Additionally, Compasagüe 2 system beneficiaries each invested fifty hours of physical labor into the project.

Arguably, the capacity to collect user fees (between $0.23 and $2.85 a month per household for water service) reflects the legitimacy of CAPS as local authorities. The capacity to collect user fees does not necessarily translate into the community having sufficient funds to ensure system sustainability under all circumstances, however. In La Reina, San Ramón, the water system is living in "a year of grace," according to CAPS vice-coordinator Miguel Ángel. Miguel Ángel reported that his CAPS has a savings of 42,000 córdobas (US$2,000) accumulated from the 10 córdobas (US$0.50) tariff each household pays per month, which Miguel Ángel emphasizes as largely symbolic: "I don't consider it a payment. It's an economic contribution for the project, because to have water twenty-four hours a day is really quite impossible for other communities. And we actually have this ability. It's 10 córdobas, which is nothing, it's symbolic" (interview, March 2, 2010). Even "symbolic" user fees, though, can give water committees the ability to purchase inexpensive system components needed for fixing and replacing broken or leaking tubes and other basic repairs.

Small user fees do not necessarily allow a community to accumulate sufficient funds to make significant system repairs, however. The La Reina CAPS, for example, had pipes in need of replacement that would cost an estimated 100,000 córdobas (US$4,761). Needed repairs stood beyond the community's financial means. Fortunately, after requesting assistance from CARE International in 2010, the community received approval for a renovation of the water system in 2011. While the La Reina CAPS confronted a system overhaul that required depending upon outside actors, the income generated from user fees has proven adequate for the CAPS' day-to-day maintenance costs.

Some communities depend on water meters as a mechanism to ensure that payments correspond to household water usage. Mirna, staff member with the Association for the Development of Northern Municipalities (ADEM-NORTE), explained that her organization promotes meters when supporting new water projects. The philosophy of ADEMNORTE reflects that of many rural development organizations: that meters allow individual household payments to be differentiated by the actual amount of water consumed and also help to conserve water, as people tend to reduce their household water usage when paying according to a meter reading (interview, April 10, 2010). Typically, community institutions such as churches, schools, and *casas comunales* (community houses) are excluded from water metering and payments.

Household meter installation is often met with resistance. Members of CAPS working with ADEMNORTE in the communities of Molino Sur and La Labranza, Sébaco, embraced the challenge of convincing residents of the benefits of meters, going "door to door" to "sensitize" residents to the idea. Marbelly, the secretary of La Labranza's CAPS, praised the consciousness-raising effect that meter installation has had in her community as users learn to waste less water. Delia, CAPS treasurer of Molino Sur, a community downstream from La Labranza, asserted during an intercommunity exchange with CAPS members from Las Sabanas, Madriz: "You should always fight for meters in your community to moderate" water usage; otherwise, there may "not be enough" for everyone (April 29, 2010). The experience of receiving water meters has enhanced both the capacities and confidence of Marbelly and Delia as resource managers. System beneficiaries' ultimate buy-in to meters is indicative of their trust and support for CAPS as community-based water managers and service providers.

Beyond sound financial practices—safe storage of community funds and the like—and the capacity to collect users' fees, tailored and flexible bylaws and norms support effective common property management (McKean 1996; Ostrom 1990). While not emphasized in the common property scholarship, the ways in which community rules and norms reflect the local contexts and lived realities of residents can have a significant legitimacy-enhancing effect on common property organizations. Notably, CAPS' rules "on paper" do not always work in favor of expanding or ensuring water access. A staff member of a Matagalpa-based NGO, PRODESSA, shared a community's experience wherein CAPS' bylaws stipulated a one-time payment of two hundred dollars—roughly equivalent to the minimum monthly salary in Nicaragua—to gain access to the community's water source, a provision he claimed limited access to this necessary resource (interview, August 22, 2008).

The CAPS participating in this study, however, told a different story of community norms grounded in the day-to-day socioeconomic realities of residents. In short, norms reflected water committees' valuing of universal and consistent access over rigid payment structures.[6] The CAPS Compasagüe 2 coordinator Marlene emphasized how poverty affects people's ability to pay—and hence committees' willingness to implement the bylaws: "We don't implement [our rules] because we have few resources. Most of us women leave to harvest coffee each year. When we get back, most of us pay 120 córdobas for water service for the year all at once. . . . Not applying the regulations is a challenge to our [water] project, but it's not because we don't want to, but rather because we have few resources, because we understand each other" (interview, August 21, 2009). Reflecting common property design principle 3, CAPS make accommodations for residents engaged in seasonal labor who do not have a constant flow of monetary resources during the year. In La Labranza, where residents' financial circumstances and abilities to pay fluctuate throughout the year, the CAPS remains "flexible" according to Marbelly, "because we're the same family" (interview, December 11, 2009). Receiving late payments has not been deemed a problem: "Even though we're flexible, we don't have problems."

The tendency not to cut off residents' water supply negates many CAPS' bylaws that stipulate cutting water for nonpayment of user fees or lateness. Bylaws such as this may reflect the influence of NGOs and state actors at the time of system construction and CAPS formation. Financial decisions to disregard the rules often reflect appropriate accommodations given local circumstances. They also may constitute sound economic decisions—since with strict adherence to the formal rules CAPS might not collect *any* payment from certain households. Molino Sur's CAPS' treasurer, Delia, proclaimed proudly that the only cases of water shutoffs in her community have been by request only; for example, a household may request a shutoff when leaving the community for short-term or seasonal work. Beyond fluctuations in income throughout the year, conditions of poverty affect CAPS' implementation of financial rules. As Carlos of Compasagüe 2 emphasized: "We have understood the necessities of the people, their difficulties. . . . If someone is poor, he can't pay the tariff" (interview, August 21, 2008). An important and perennial issue CAPS confront also comes into view when considering their financial management strategies: rural water systems are inherently expensive, and sustaining them proves challenging in local contexts with high levels of poverty. "Breaking" the rules, some of which have been "imported" in terms of being developed in initial project phases with outside actors, reflects a local embeddedness generating a social legitimacy vis-à-vis residents.

While the amount of money collected for water service varies across communities, CAPS demonstrated the exercise of local discretion in the use of their funds, sometimes choosing to support activities or endeavors understood as socially or economically beneficial to the community or individual residents. The La Labranza and Molino Sur CAPS felt financially secure enough to innovate in the use of the CAPS' funds to advance their communities' sanitation goals: both CAPS made small loans available to families so their households could pay a portion of the costs associated with the installation of bathrooms and new plumbing that a Spanish NGO, CIC-Bata, supported. Each household had paid back their individual loan by the end of the year. Marbelly, who had been an elected member of the La Labranza CAPS for ten years, showed off her new bathroom with pride: she did most of the installations herself, including the water piping.

FIGURE 9 Delia, CAPS treasurer, in her home office in the community of Molino Sur (Sébaco, Matagalpa), where residents drop by to pay their water bill (July 2016).

Another local arrangement CAPS have deemed to support their water management and service provision is that of providing a stipend to CAPS members whose tasks depend upon certain technical expertise or whose work is particularly time consuming relative to other elected committee positions.[7] The San Lorenzo, Boaco, CAPS pays the person in charge of operation and maintenance 700 córdobas a month (less than other communities reported), in addition to gifting him 700 córdobas at Christmas and "pardoning" him from paying his water service for the year. According to CAPS coordinator Luis Adolfo, "we have wanted to rotate the position, but the community says no" (interview, February 18, 2010). Luis Adolfo calls this "a small help" to a community member who is "poor." Delia's Molino Sur CAPS, which collects over four thousand córdobas (US$190) a month from users' fees, spends 2,500 córdobas (US$119) a month as stipend payments to certain committee members, including those in the areas of finance, operation and maintenance, and health. Delia receives a stipend of US$47 a month working as the Molino Sur CAPS treasurer; this stipend does not, to use her example, provide enough money for her to buy any needed medicines. However, she explains, it would be hard to relinquish her position—which she says is "full time"—because no one else in the community has "agreed to be elected" to do this work. Delia described working seven days a week in the CAPS' office, a small room with hard-packed dirt floors at the front of her house, where she attends to community members who arrive sporadically to pay their bill or perhaps request that their water be shut off during a period of leave. She expressed wanting to resign from the CAPS to rest and to find work that would provide a "livable" income. Yet, for the foreseeable future, she described her work on the CAPS as "permanent."[8]

Organizational Capacities

The organizational dimensions of CBWM are difficult to disentangle from the financial and technical situations and problems CAPS encounter. Fundamentally, however, these aspects concern water committees' ability to implement their bylaws, including the engagement of water users, or system beneficiaries, in water management. Although CAPS' rules may vary by community and region, these typically include provisions for elected leadership turnover, participation of system beneficiaries in water system maintenance, household payment for water service, local environmental stewardship, and financial management. The ability of CAPS to implement, enforce, and, when necessary, modify rules must be seen as evidence of their organizational capacities as water managers and their role as leaders. Residents' compliance with these rules—whether via explicit coercion or not—speaks to CAPS' legitimacy as local authorities.

Because of their experiences working with and receiving training from domestic and international organizations (for example, ODESAR and CARE International, respectively), many CAPS implement similar financial and organizational procedures. Delia refers to the Nicaraguan Water and Sanitation Institute's (INAA) Guide for the Organization and Administration of Rural Aqueducts as her *machetito* (little machete), indicative of how she has been able to harness the government guide as a valuable tool in her work as treasurer. From outlining a recommended process of forming a CAPS to detailed discussion of how to organize effectively for local water provision and management, the INAA guide has enabled those who use it to overcome some of the problems plaguing the community in the past—such as theft of CAPS', and hence communities', funds by elected CAPS members. The guide, which has been disseminated to some communities as part of the implementation of a new project, helps communities establish a system of financial record-keeping through its various administrative templates for a users' registry, materials registry, and service shutoff and reconnection requests, among others.

When CAPS succeed in organizational terms to engage residents in water management, this buy-in reflects their local authority and legitimacy. One way to assess CAPS' organizational capacities is through assessing local rule implementation. Rules can be hard to enforce, as accommodations for inability to pay, noted above, make clear. As José Francisco presented to CAPS representatives in Sébaco, the El Zapote CAPS since the late 1990s has organized system beneficiaries into twelve groups to carry out general functions: cleaning, communication, and so forth. This rule-based system, dependent upon residents as volunteers, reflects buy-in of system beneficiaries and ensures broad as well as regular participation on the part of all receiving water service.

Enforcement of rules requiring system beneficiaries to participate in collective choice arrangements, such as users' assemblies, can prove difficult. As Andrew Fuys and Stephan Dohrn contend in regard to customary institutions, "Compliance is more often than not based upon collective respect for local authorities, more than the possibility of punishment for infringements" (2010, 199). However, sometimes compliance requires coercion. José Francisco's CAPS once struggled to get residents to attend communitywide assemblies (interview, May 19, 2010). His committee implemented a risky, albeit ingenious, strategy to increase participation: they cut off the water. José Francisco proclaimed that they no longer had problems with attendance after sending this "message." Notably, breaking one of their own rules (i.e., related to water shutoffs) contributed to improving the effectiveness of another one (i.e., participation in communitywide assemblies).

Like the El Zapote CAPS, Miguel Ángel's La Reina CAPS shared their efforts to limit residents' "free riding" using select incentives (Olson 1965). Confronted with a lack of participation on the part of some system beneficiaries in the community, including, even, some elected CAPS members, CAPS' leaders devised a plan to ensure regularized and rotating participation in system maintenance. Miguel Ángel explains: "When the system needed repairs, the same people went all the time. Most people never contributed to the work because it wasn't paid. So we approved during an assembly a tariff increase from five to ten córdobas, and with those same funds the people doing the maintenance would be paid. It's turned out very well. We don't have problems with leaks" (interview, March 2, 1010). In addition to this formal rule change to pay certain community members for technical repairs, the CAPS has also made changes toward a more effective arrangement for conducting regular cleaning around the water source. For a brief time, the community experimented with a rotation system similar to El Zapote's: one household a month would take responsibility for this work, for a total of twelve different groups each year. However, "in regard to cleaning, not everyone is going to have the same interest, [and] not everyone is going to do the same quality of work," Miguel Ángel explained. Encountering varying levels of interest and wanting to ensure the quality of the work being performed, the water committee decided that elected CAPS members would rotate this responsibility, recruiting several other residents to accompany them at the time of work. This solution to the problem of regularized cleaning and maintenance appeared to work; moreover, this arrangement does not require, as in El Zapote, the engagement of all residents in the "everyday" labors of water management.

One commonly embraced, formal rule *not* implemented across the board, yet often reflective of CAPS members' local legitimacy, is that of regular turnover of CAPS members. Francisco, member of the San Esteban 2 CAPS in Jinotega, had served as coordinator since the water system's founding in 2000. He explained his continued reelection as the result of community members trusting him as a leader. The CAPS appeared to be highly successful along different dimensions: residents paid their water service fees on time, there was secure ownership of the water source, and the CAPS had full membership (i.e., all elected positions filled) and met regularly (interview, August 23, 2008). Although Francisco lacked a clear vision of how to transfer the responsibilities of heading the committee to a different community member, the "strategy" of not overturning the full committee in one election could be seen as contributing to organizational effectiveness. For example, blind adherence to bylaws that encourage annual elections and leadership turnover may leave a water committee ill equipped in terms of knowledge and capacities to function well.[9] With the ability to elect new CAPS members via formal rules, residents' reelection of certain leaders may speak to trusted or effective leadership—however defined—and legitimacy in the eyes of residents, as opposed to a CAPS' organizational deficit.

Although most CAPS spoke of the need for participation of system beneficiaries in local water management, some have found that it may only take a "critical mass" (Marwell and Oliver 1993) to ensure access to this critical resource.[10] The La Reina CAPS, for example, had only two active members at the time of the interview, even though it had "complete" membership on paper—that is, persons elected to all five positions: coordinator, vice-coordinator, secretary, treasurer, and *fiscal*.[11] Edwin, the CAPS treasurer, described the nonparticipation of some elected leaders as an organizational challenge to sustaining the water committee: "You form a committee, and in that moment the president says 'yes,' that all are going to work. They work three, four, five, six months and then slowly they start to back out" (interview, March 2, 2010). Edwin explained that only two elected CAPS members have been taking active responsibility for the work. From his perspective, however, "you have to take the lead," reflecting not only his willingness but also his general sense of responsibility, to step up to the tasks falling to elected CAPS members. Even though Edwin emphasized that "it's one or two who remain at the front" of his CAPS, the water management taking place in La Reina has demonstrated the importance of finding solutions and making decisions that support sustaining water service to residents. With water flows arguably constituting the deepest source of a water committee's legitimacy, the ability of two active members to sustain the committee and local water provision allows the organization to survive and remain legitimate in residents' eyes—even while remaining fundamentally weak in terms of elected membership.

Environmental Stewardship Capacities

When asked about the levels of water access in the country, INAA's Gilberto responded, "Here in the country, nobody has died of thirst. Everyone has access to water. . . . The advantage here is that we have a lot of rivers and water basins. It's contaminated, but we have access" (interview, June 2, 2010). Miguel Ángel shared this assessment from his rural, community-based vantage point: "We have water in this country. We're rich in water, but the water we have that's not contaminated is at risk of being contaminated. This is what we're working on" (interview, December 1, 2009). Water resources—including rivers, lakes and lagoons—constitute a striking 10 percent of Nicaragua's surface area. The country has high annual rainfall and twenty-one watersheds, eight of which drain to the Pacific side of the country, where the population is concentrated. Yet the challenge of assuring potable water, or water fit for human consumption, constitutes an important environmental challenge CAPS confront.[12]

The CAPS studied embraced various measures to slow or counter environmentally degrading processes such as contamination of water sources and deforestation, activities that can reinforce CAPS' empowerment and engender legitimacy. These include health and sanitation education (related to human waste disposal and domestic activities, e.g., clothes washing) and cleanup campaigns around water sources. Many CAPS also reforest around water storage tanks to produce shade and to promote better holding of subterraneous water. These locally focused environmental "solutions" may intersect with financial problem-solving as well: one community in Sébaco reforested their water source with fruit trees, and subsequently sells the fruit in local markets to raise money for the CAPS (interview, February 3, 2010). The proactive behavior of CAPS to fulfill the function of environmental stewardship—a set of roles and responsibilities legally assigned to the state—lends legitimacy to these local institutions and also bestows them with public authority (Lund 2006b).

Water committees are not always able to chlorinate water, the most common way communities treat water, because this depends on the availability and affordability of chlorine tablets. Nevertheless, their work to ensure cleaner drinking water is an important component of their resource management, conferring legitimacy and reflecting local leadership. The water systems CAPS maintain constitute improved water sources (i.e., those with at least a minimal process of water purification) and contribute to reduced instances of sickness among residents. Justo Pastor, a CAPS coordinator from the community of

Santa Fe La Peña, Muy Muy, explained that before his community's potable water system was constructed in 2005, "people in this community were living a crisis, drinking all of their water from the rivers. It came through really contaminated, both from animals as well as from human waste. . . . We chlorinate the water, so it comes a bit more treated. Because of this, illnesses in children, in the elderly, are avoided some. These are changes that are reducing illness little by little. We don't want to say entirely, but on average there is less" (interview, August 22, 2008). Improved water quality, and hence health, results in large part from the basic sanitation systems, including chlorination practices and filtration systems, that CAPS and residents construct, manage, and maintain.

The acceleration of global climate change is the Achilles heel in the evolution of CAPS' work as water managers and service providers. The rural, socionatural landscapes in which water committees and small-scale water systems are embedded confront dramatic weather patterns: both droughts and heavy rains affect water availability as well as the ability to plant and harvest beans and other key staple crops.[13] Problems of water quality are compounded by worsening scarcity. According to a study carried out on the UNOM decentralization process in Matagalpa and Jinotega, almost a third (31 percent) of all CAPS interviewed reported that "generally in the summer there is not sufficient water to satisfy community demand" (ENACAL 2003, 26). In February 2010, an article in the national newspaper La Prensa ran with the headline "Water Committees with Less Work due to Drought" (Pérez 2010). This particular drought proved severe enough to nearly dry up the water available to some communities, in effect leaving local CAPS without the means to work as water service providers.

Too much rain may also prove to be detrimental to rural communities' water sources and systems. Flooding can wipe out or severely damage existing water systems or compromise the potability of drinking water. A storm in late 2010 severely damaged the Molino Sur gravity-fed water system, rendering it useless. The government contributed 130,000 of the 170,000 córdobas total that were required to purchase rights to a different water source in the community; the community paid the balance of 40,000 córdobas. Even with strong financial and organizational skills, CAPS are vulnerable to climate-induced emergency situations that can render their "everyday" problem-solving capacities and resources inadequate. Accelerating climate change will continue to compound preexisting problems in Nicaragua related to water quality and seasonal water quantity variations.

Water committee members demonstrated an acute awareness of climate change and its local impacts. An understanding of the relationship between deforestation and climate change, in addition to how deforestation affects watersheds and local water availability, has influenced many communities' emphasis on reforestation and concern about continued logging at a national scale. In addition to mitigation efforts, such as reforestation, to preserve and conserve local water sources, water committees are aware of the basic need to adjust to a changing environment. Committee members also see the limits of an emphasis on adaptation. José Francisco (CAPS secretary and municipal network leader) challenged the pervasiveness of this notion in public discourse around climate change in Nicaragua: "We don't accept adaptation. It's not the solution. We're not just adapting to a new temperature." Referencing his home municipality of San Dionisio he asserted: "It's as hot as Managua" (interview, July 1, 2016). Nicaragua's dry corridor—extending from the western departments of León and Chinandega through the northern highland departments of Estelí, Madriz, Matagalpa, and Nueva Segovia—most acutely experiences the effects of severe drought in Nicaragua. Variable environmental conditions and the crises they set in motion compromise rural water provision and speak to the dire need for rural communities to have outside support and resources to confront what are inherently global problems experienced on a local scale.

Even ostensibly local environmental challenges are difficult to address through community-based interventions. While many CAPS were unaware of what toxins exist in the water of their "potable" drinking water systems, they recognized the significance of nonlocal sources of pollution. Some CAPS expressed frustration that their efforts toward environmental protection and conservation may be undermined by the state's contribution to environmental degradation. For instance, while small-scale campesinos strive to reforest, businesses get permission to continue deforesting for the purpose of expanding agricultural frontiers. During a National CAPS Network meeting, a CAPS member from El Rama, RAAS, lamented ongoing deforestation ("we no longer have forest frontiers") and nearby river water contamination caused by the mines in the neighboring department of Chontales (Mina "La Libertad" and "Santo Domingo"). He asserted that Nicaragua's Cerro Silva, one of the country's natural reserves, and hence supposedly "protected," areas, is still being deforested (November 5, 2009).[14]

In the same National CAPS Network meeting in November 2009, a CAPS member conveyed his perception of "little concern from those governing this country" in regard to environmental protection and conservation. Another referred to the problem of deforestation as "a policy problem of the government that affects us" and suggested the complicity of the Ministry of Farming, Livestock, and Forests (MAGFOR) through the agency's role in neglecting to enforce restrictions on logging and land clearing. Members of CAPS also noted ongoing contamination of freshwater sources from mining—activity that implicates the Ministry of Energy and Mines (MINAS). In sum, CAPS expressed awareness of how rural communities often bear the burden of the decisions and actions of authorities and actors at other scales.

The relationship of state actors to environmentally degrading processes suggests the need to rethink the common property regime design principles, and common property theory more broadly, in regard to its attention to state-society and local-global connections. A more nuanced approach to the relationship between state and nonstate actors, for example, would account for how state actors' role in common property management is significantly more varied and complex than depicted. Beyond merely recognizing local actors "right" to organize (design principle 7), state actors may actively support commons management. Yet, this principle can be fulfilled while state actors simultaneously undermine community efforts. This can be observed in regard to the state's role in environmental degradation affecting rural communities.

Unless pressured, state actors may be unlikely to intervene to ameliorate or help reverse many of the environmentally destructive processes experienced in acute ways by residents in rural areas. Nor are local governmental officials or state agencies necessarily well equipped to support communities during crises. In 1998, many of Nicaragua's rural communities were hit hard by the destructive Hurricane Mitch. The La Reina CAPS in San Ramón received none of the local government support they requested, an outcome Miguel Ángel attributes to the local government not having an interest in "direct support for water and sanitation." Community members spent three days repairing a damaged water system. The residents' rebuilding of the water system after Hurricane Mitch reflects technical capacities internal to the community as well as a willingness to invest personally in the water project. At the same time that state actors' inaction serves to undermine their own authority and legitimacy, the authority and legitimacy of CAPS as nonstate actors are bolstered as they take action to sustain local water access.

Local government officials themselves may promote the idea that the CAPS are better suited to do this work. The local government water and sanitation técnico of San Ramón, Amílcar, asserted that "the water committees have the best opportunities to work protecting the environment." He believes CAPS are better positioned than outside actors to be environmental stewards because water committees can "from the micro-basins, maintain the water sources, protect those areas, reforest, investigate the areas where the tanks are located"; "having water systems," he says, "permits you to work towards improving climactic conditions, towards bettering the environment in your community" (interview, February 26, 2010).

Scholars have cautioned against romanticizing rural residents' knowledge, wisdom, and choices in regard to "local" environmental stewardship (Agarwal and Gibson 2001; Redford 1991). However, perceptions of rural residents' aptness and ability to act as local environmental stewards are in large part grounded in CAPS' experience of *dando respuesta* (responding to) communities' water needs in the absence of outside actors performing this work. Much scholarship supports the general proposition that residents can carry out certain functions more effectively, and at a lower cost, than external agents, including those of regulation and monitoring. And, as noted, communities' internal capacities to confront problems may evolve to be greater than those of local governments. While this fact supports CAPS' legitimacy and authority at the community level, it does not diminish the potential benefits that formal legal recognition or other forms of state backing or resources could confer upon water committees and the communities they serve.

Political and Legal Capacities

Since the 1970s, albeit with more or less support depending on the political regime in power, CAPS have experienced the basic right to organize in their communities (design principle 7). The distinction between the right to organize and *legal rights* conferred via formal government recognition matters, however. As one water sector report explained, "Once the [water] systems are constructed, they are handed over the CAPS, who, lacking legal status, *legally* cannot receive them" (Government of Nicaragua and PAHO 2004, 100; emphasis added). A lack of legal standing challenges various aspects of CAPS' water management, including legal control over water systems and sources and the ability to manage and safeguard financial resources.

For example, lack of legal status directly impacts the options available to water committees for managing income received from users' tariffs. A CAPS member from the community of Compasagüe 2 explained his perceived financial limitations: "Legally we can't take out 500 córdobas collected and go to open a savings account at a bank, because we don't have legal status. This challenge confronts over 1,200,000 people" (interview, August 21, 2008).[15] Some CAPS members open personal bank accounts, which entail potential problems of transparency in management and use of the committees' funds. Some CAPS reported stolen or unauthorized use of funds, as was recounted in the case of the Molino Sur CAPS in Sébaco. These challenges stand in tension with and can undermine efforts to manage resources responsibly.

However, a tenuous relationship to state actors and omission from legal frameworks have granted, unwittingly, the space for water committees to work autonomously and develop solutions to water access and environmental problems. For example, navigation of legal gray areas can develop social and political capacities and shrewdness pertaining to water management. Without legal status as organizations, many CAPS' property "rights" must be grounded in a locally recognized use and access, rather than in formal rights conferred by the state. The La Reina CAPS depends upon its relationship to the local cooperative to uphold its non–legally-binding agreement with a previous landowner to concede the water source to the community. Contrastingly, José Francisco's El Zapote CAPS used community donations to ensure that water piping was laid on public, versus private, property. This allowed the community to avoid potentially tricky negotiations with land owners. In San Esteban 2, Jinotega, community members amassed 10,000 córdobas to purchase access to the water source supplying their gravity-fed systems. Despite the disadvantages of operating in a legal gray area—including tenuous land and water rights—CAPS' negotiated use of local resources to facilitate water access for residents contributes to their legitimacy as local authorities and leaders.

The significance of CAPS' lack of legal rights or status transcends the local through contributing to a sense of political invisibility beyond the communities in which CAPS work. As members frequently expressed in interviews and meetings, "Somos de hecho, no de derecho" (We're de facto, not de jure), conveying water committees' de facto work without legal backing. The CAPS Compasagüe 1 coordinator lamented in 2008, "Now as CAPS we're not recognized. We're nobodies" (interview, August 22, 2008). This sentiment was confirmed in the wake of the National Water Law's (Law 620) passing in 2007, as the law set forth a new legal framework to manage "all existing water resources in the country" without delineating the essential role of CAPS in rural water management. Water committees' glaring absence from the law, except for a brief mention in the regulations, sent the message that CAPS were an afterthought of lawmakers as they worked to modify the legal framework for the water sector.

The Legitimate Authority of Common Property Organizations beyond the Local

How did CAPS' organic empowerment come to bear on political negotiations and policy interventions at extralocal scales? Understanding how legitimacy and authority *transcend* the local matters, in one basic sense, because community responses to state water policies and politics are themselves multiscalar. As CAPS formed networks, they transcended realms of local resource management to engage with state actors and seek involvement in policy processes. Their legitimacy and authority traveled with them.

The transcommunity mobilization of CAPS starting in 2005 reveals the ways in which unofficial resource management regimes have the potential to continue to engender legitimacy beyond grassroots realms of water management—including vis-à-vis state actors and with implications for state legal frameworks. In particular, CAPS' alliances with NGOs and multilateral organizations enabled the formation and use of new networks as platforms to assert locally generated empowerment and legitimacy as CAPS engaged state officials toward achieving legal recognition. As the following chapter details, these multiscalar and multisectoral processes allowed water committees collectively to draw upon their organic empowerment, bond as social actors, and develop a collective voice. Network spaces would also become sites for strengthening CAPS' political and legal knowledge and capacities toward advocating for their formal legal recognition from the state. In fact, while certain political and legal knowledge would have limited import for everyday water management at the grass roots, political learning in network spaces, including about national legal frameworks, was critical for CAPS' multiscalar political activism and advocacy.

THREE

The Role of Allies in Bridging Divides

Children in navy blue and white school uniforms stood leaning against the wood paneled siding of Delia's house. They were observing attentively from afar as water committee members gathered on a large open field in front of the local CAPS treasurer's home. Delia's Molino Sur CAPS was hosting an intercambio *(exchange) with water committee peers from the municipality of Las Sabanas—another highland city in the department of Madriz near the border of Honduras, several hours away by bus. Delia's house was an important hub for her CAPS' work: a small room at the front of her house, with hard-packed dirt floors and a table with a single chair, served as the office where neighbors would come to pay their water bill.*

From my perspective as an observer, the intercambio, *much like the Sébaco municipal network formation, reflected the important ways NGO "allies" were supporting the bringing together of CAPS from different regions in Nicaragua to learn from one another. That day, the Somoto-based NGO Action against Hunger had helped to coordinate the participation of visiting CAPS: twenty-seven members representing six rural water committees. All were seated in rows of colorful plastic chairs facing a projector screen and a table with a microphone under large, white, tented canopies. The purpose of the* intercambio *was to have visiting water committees meet with a "successful" CAPS and learn about its experience. Action against Hunger's staff member Richard said CAPS in Las Sabanas were having problems with organization and water system sustainability. Local CAPS members hosting took turns presenting on different topics: the history of the Molino Sur water system, funded by CARE Canada*

*in 1991; the challenge of sensitizing beneficiaries to new water meters; and the success
with a community greenhouse constructed in 1997, which was currently home to five
thousand plants. Delia presented her meticulous work as treasurer: she showed slides of
her accounting pages that documented her water committee's income and expenditures
and held up the book for participants to see. Delia had a political message too. She
said CAPS were not taken into account as Law 620 was developed, though there has
been significant involvement in the shaping of the CAPS law: "We've even gone to
the National Assembly in Managua."*

*Early on in the event, Richard mentioned to me that one community's CAPS'
members didn't make it because hard rains prevented them from leaving their community. The story resonated. I had previously canceled site visits, including to where
I currently stood in Molino Sur, Sébaco, owing to rains that prohibited local buses
from climbing the steep and muddied dirt roads leading to Delia's community and
those further north. More important, though, the absence of invited CAPS members
reflected the challenge of mobility and participation in events for residents living in
dispersed rural highland communities. Many communities were hard to leave, as well
as to reach. Physical mobility seemed to present a perennial challenge to water committees' achievement of their transcommunity objectives, including their new multiscalar
engagements as activists. During Q and A, a visiting CAPS member asked Delia
how the Molino Sur CAPS became part of the National CAPS Network. They were
"outside" of it. "You're not outside of the network," Delia responded. "We just don't see
each other in meetings." The idea is to represent all CAPS in the national meetings,
she expressed. Delia ended with a reassurance: she would notify them of the next
meeting in Managua.*

In relation to the previous chapter, an important question becomes *how* CAPS'
experiences and capacities as water managers and service providers mattered for
their attempts to influence state legal frameworks. How did rural water committees in Nicaragua transcend their rural localities and responsibilities as water
managers and service providers? In what ways did networks become productive spaces of collaboration and learning for water committees and their allies
from across regions in Nicaragua—as well as platforms for CAPS' engagement
of state actors? Whereas the prior chapter looked inward to examine CAPS'
resource management and service provision within their communities, this
chapter shifts the focus to explore the increasingly dense connections between

and among water committees and their domestic and international allies as they pursued collective goals.

Engaging with theories of social capital, this chapter argues that CAPS' mobilization to form CAPS networks has been fundamentally dependent upon not only their organic empowerment as resource managers and service providers but also their relationship to NGOs and multilateral agencies. As bonded social actors, water committee members shared an empowerment and legitimate authority in their respective communities. Despite being disconnected in geographic and social terms historically, CAPS' relationships and experiences as water managers and service providers became something that rural development organizations recognized and sought to leverage. Bringing CAPS together across communities would engender further bonding social capital among CAPS, and it would support their strengthening as a collective political actor.

In particular, this chapter documents three specific contributions that allies have made toward the formation and functioning of CAPS' transcommunity networks at the municipal, departmental, and national levels. First, allies

FIGURE 10 Member and treasurer of CAPS Delia presenting her accounting system to visiting water committees during a community intercambio in April 2010.

FIGURE 11 Potable Water and Sanitation Committee members from the municipality of Las Sabanas, Madriz, as Delia presents during the intercambio in April 2010.

FIGURE 12 "Welcome to the community of Molino Sur. Water, source of life." Banner hanging to welcome Las Sabanas water committee members to Molino Sur in April 2010.

facilitated water committees' physical mobility *across* geographic regions, supporting a scaling-*up* of their organizations to higher political (e.g., municipal and national) levels. The newfound mobility of CAPS not only afforded the novel opportunity of coming together as bonded social actors from across communities and regions but also enhanced water committees' political visibility and influence as a collective actor in national and subnational politics. Second, allies developed CAPS' legal and political capacities in network spaces. These capacity-building processes included trainings on national laws, including the draft CAPS Law, and served to strengthen water committees' political savvy and knowledge. Third, allies supported access to state actors through creating state-society interfaces in which CAPS' knowledge and experience as water managers, as well as their newfound legal and political knowledge, came to bear. Through facilitating water committees' physical mobility and political visibility, building of political and legal capacities, and obtaining access to state channels of representation, allies have been integral to the emergence as well as functioning of the CAPS networks. Hence, this chapter discusses allies' role both in the formation and operation of new multiscalar CAPS networks.

The CAPS Networks: Social Capital across Scales

One way of understanding CAPS' day-to-day work and respective relationships in their communities is as a form of bonding social capital shared between and among rural residents. Indeed, this chapter's theorizing is based upon empirical observations of community-based water managers in Nicaragua as bonded social actors in that they share bonding social capital as friends, neighbors, colleagues, and family members. This social capital manifests as familiarity, a sense of solidarity and camaraderie, and shared trust and local networks of support—all of which undergird the daily endeavor to secure potable water for residents in their communities.

Bonding social capital has purported "risks." For instance, because bonding social capital reflects relationships among socially similar actors, it can reflect or promote exclusion of *different* actors. Bonding social capital has also been characterized as having the potential to "become a basis for the pursuit of narrow sectarian interests" (Woolcock and Narayan 2000, 230). It is not a given that the risks of social exclusion and narrow interests will play out, however. In fact, the transcommunity mobilization of water committees in Nicaragua reveal bonding social capital *not* to be an impediment to bridging among different social actors, for example, NGO and multilateral agency staff. In fact, the locally grounded and unique shared experience of managing water within rural communities—reflected in CAPS' bonding social capital—is what *prompted* NGOs to seek to engage water committees in political activism as the national government turned its attention to reshaping the legal framework for freshwater management. In the view of NGO staff, the work of rural residents in managing water resources and service across decades in Nicaragua merited the government's formal legal recognition.

This chapter promotes a dual theoretical argument: first, rather than solely reinforcing exclusive identities and in-group loyalty, bonding social capital can undergird the creation of bridging social capital in the form of collective mobilization across sectoral and other divides. The empowerment of CAPS to manage water and distribute water as a critical resource, and the legitimacy derived from this work, served as an important precondition for their effective political engagements *beyond* the grass roots. Bonding social capital "is good for undergirding specific reciprocity and mobilizing solidarity" (Putnam 2000, 22–23); in fact, relations of trust and reciprocity at the most local levels may increase the likelihood of engaging in collective action beyond the grass roots (Larsen et al. 2004). Nongovernmental organizations and multilateral agencies' engagement of rural water committees in processes of network formation gave CAPS the opportunity to leverage a latent collective empowerment—in other words, "to protect and pursue their collective interests" through bridging social capital or new kinds of relationships with "external institutions and organizations that might help them resist threats to their well-being" (Larsen et al. 2004, 65). CAPS' collaboration across geographic, rural-urban, and sectoral divides thus raises the question: under what conditions does bonding social capital, and the positive synergies among the people who share it, transcend the geographic, social, and political boundaries of these "tight-knit" groups?

The second theoretical argument supported here is that bridging social capital facilitates the spread of bonding social capital. Ties between different social actors reflected in CAPS networks at the municipal, departmental, and national levels also created new ties between and among CAPS as *similar* social actors. Once previously disconnected in social and geographic terms, water committees' convergence in network spaces granted the opportunity to develop new social solidarities among CAPS from diverse regions. In other words, CAPS, as similar social actors at the grass roots, were able to *engender* new bonding social capital once previously disconnected water committees met each other and collaborated via new networks. From another angle, processes of collaboration both between and among CAPS and their allies in network spaces reveal the significance of water committees' organic empowerment as resource managers and service providers. Specifically, rural residents' shared, locally grounded experiences in their respective communities scaled up with them into network spaces convened by NGO and multilateral agency allies. This empowerment supported how network spaces were able to become productive sites of engagement as CAPS could cultivate a shared *collective* identity as "CAPS" and articulate goals that would guide their activism.

CAPS' Domestic and International Allies

As state and primarily urban-based societal actors collaborated to design the National Water Law (Law 620), passed in 2007, NGO and multilateral agency staff seized upon an opportunity to engage water committees in contesting their exclusion from legal processes underway in the water sector. The Coalition for the Right to Water (CODA) sought to support CAPS' pursuit of legal recognition in part through drawing rural social actors into public debates around water use and access. In so doing, the coalition demonstrated a commitment to its objectives of encouraging dialogue, debate, and political mobilization related to water. Water committees did not have to be convinced to contest their substantive exclusion from a law elaborating a more comprehensive framework for the development, use, and protection of water resources in Nicaragua. As CAPS coordinator Antonio in the municipality of Muy Muy explained in 2008, "We're not really in agreement with [Law 620], because it doesn't take us into account" (interview, August 21, 2008). Relationships between CAPS and allies must be viewed as reciprocal. As CAPS received support from professional-sector and urban-based allies, NGOs and multilateral allies benefited from engaging with water committees toward fulfilling their organizational missions.

Starting in the mid-2000s, financial and organizational support came from various domestic NGOs and international agencies to support CAPS network formation (see box 3). Member organizations of the CODA adjusted their work plans to include this more overtly political and advocacy-oriented work with rural-based CAPS. Akin to the work of the NGOs ODESAR and

---

Box 3 Potable Water and Sanitation Committee Domestic and
International Allies

Nongovernmental (NGO) Allies
- Organization for Economic and Social Development in Urban and Rural Areas
  (ODESAR)
- La Cuculmeca
- Latin American Information Service for Sustainable Agriculture (SIMAS)
- Group Promoting Agroecology (GPAE)
- Center for Information and Consulting Services (CISAS)
- Association for the Development of the North (ADEMNORTE)

Multilateral Allies
- AVINA Foundation
- Swiss Agency for Development and Cooperation (COSUDE)
- Development and Ecology Foundation (ECODES)
- Pan American Health Organization (PAHO)
- Norwegian People's Aid (APN)
- SWISSAID
- United Nations International Emergency Children's Fund (UNICEF)
- World Bank Water and Sanitation Program

This box indicates the primary allies working with the National CAPS Network and the
municipal-level networks discussed in this book. It is not reflective of all the domestic and
international organizations and agencies that have supported CAPS' political mobilization and
networking or those who have made financial contributions to the sector over time.

ADEMNORTE in the department of Matagalpa, La Cuculmeca served as
an important ally of CAPS within the department of Jinotega. As a CODA
member, La Cuculmeca was involved in early conversations about fomenting
water committees' policy advocacy at municipal and national levels. Of note,
the organization did not work directly with communities on water and sanitation projects prior to lending their support to water committees for municipal
CAPS networks formation in Jinotega starting in 2009. According to staff
member Harmhel, La Cuculmeca received human and organizational support
from ODESAR toward building their internal capacity to work with rural communities explicitly in the area of water and sanitation.

At the national level, funding from multilateral agencies such as APN was channeled through domestic NGOs, including CODA member organizations such as SIMAS. Since 1986, APN had donated financial and technological resources for water projects in Nicaragua through the domestic NGO Environment Nicaragua. In the early 2000s, after Environment Nicaragua dissolved, the multilateral agency began channeling funds through SIMAS. As a part of this change, APN's funding in the sector began to include supporting advocacy related to water rights, helping to set in motion novel transcommunity bridging among CAPS and between CAPS and urban-based actors as new networks were formed at regional and national scales.

Multilateral agency resources also supported the contributions of two individuals to serve in coordination, facilitation, and capacity-building roles with the National CAPS Network. Eduardo, who had previously worked at SIMAS, and Denis, previously a staff member at CISAS, coordinated with domestic NGO staff and emerging water committee leaders to convene CAPS from across regions for national-level meetings typically hosted in Managua, but rotating through other departments of the country as well. Numerous national-level meetings of CAPS and their allies followed after the first group of CAPS, NGOs, and multilateral agency staff convened in Managua in January 2007. Across four National CAPS Network meetings from 2009 to 2010, the average number of water committee members in attendance was fifty. The number of municipalities represented by those CAPS in attendance ranged from thirteen to forty-one. In addition to playing key roles in the organization of National CAPS Network meetings, Eduardo and Denis served as policy and legal experts within network spaces, providing training on national legislation and supporting participating CAPS in articulating collective goals.[1]

As of 2011, over thirty municipal networks in ten departments had formed around the country, and over eighty municipalities (out of 153 total) had sent CAPS members to participate as representatives in meetings of the National CAPS Network. By 2014, the National CAPS Network had garnered the participation of an estimated 1,900 CAPS (interview, Edgard Bermúdez, Fundación Avina, July 24, 2015). In addition to being the site of a vibrant departmental network, Matagalpa saw the formation of eight municipal-level networks in the cities of Ciudad Darío, El Tuma–La Dalia, Muy Muy, Esquipulas, San Dionisio, Matagalpa, Sébaco, and San Ramón.[2] Working with La Cuculmeca, CAPS in the department of Jinotega formed networks in eight municipalities,

COLORADO COLLEGE LIBRARY
COLORADO SPRINGS, COLORADO

FIGURE 13 Water committees in the National CAPS Network elect their first leadership council in May 2010 in Matagalpa. Thirteen women and thirty-one men participate in the vote.

FIGURE 14 First elected leadership council of the National CAPS Network, May 2010, from left to right: Juan de Dios (Nueva Segovia), José Francisco (Matagalpa), Janeth, (Matagalpa), Francisco (Masaya), Elia (Jinotega), and Leonel (Masaya). Not pictured: Esperanza (Matagalpa).

including El Cuá-Bocay, Jinotega, La Concordia, San Rafael del Norte, San Sabastián de Yalí, Santa María de Pantasma, and Wiwilí.

CAPS Networks: Bonding through Bridging

Once formed, CAPS networks served as spaces bridging actors and organizations across political jurisdictions, partisan loyalties, and geographic regions. The explicitly multisectoral nature of collective action enabled the mobility and effective political interventions of CAPS: as rural and community-based organizations, CAPS benefited from the relationships and resources afforded by urban-based, domestic and international, NGOs and multilateral agencies. The following sections examine three specific contributions allies made toward helping CAPS mobilize across communities and develop new capacities as a collective actor in water governance. These contributions include facilitating water committees' (1) physical mobility and political visibility, (2) political and legal capacity building, and (3) access to public officials. Together, these contributions reflect how bridging social capital (as new relationships between CAPS and their allies) promoted CAPS' efficacy as political activists. Moreover, these dynamics reveal how bridging social capital engendered bonding social capital: connecting across diverse regions for the first time, water committees were able to cultivate positive synergies, based upon shared knowledge and experiences at the grass roots, which informed their goals and empowered them as collective actors vis-à-vis state officials.

Physical Mobility and Political Visibility

Arguably, allies' financing of CAPS' physical mobility constitutes the single most important contribution they have made toward water committees' transcommunity mobilization. In a basic sense, regional travel is prohibitively expensive for many rural residents. Financial resources from NGOs and multilateral organizations were necessary to bring rural water managers into contact with each other from across communities and to facilitate a collective political engagement in water governance. Put another way, financial contributions toward physical mobility enabled both *bridging* water committees and their NGO and multilateral allies and supported *bonding* among previously disconnected CAPS from geographically diverse regions.

It would not be an exaggeration to claim that without resources donated for the purpose of mobilizing water committees, municipal, departmental, and national-level CAPS networks would not have formed. Municipal network formation in Sébaco in December 2009 revealed this dynamic. Participating in the network's formative meeting were roughly thirty CAPS representatives, who convened in a school auditorium in the city's urban center. The committees worked hand in hand with ADEMNORTE to organize the event. The Managua-based NGO SIMAS contributed US$400 to the event for invitations, transportation, food, and printing. Handouts included copies of the National Water Law (Law 620), CAPS' collective action platform, and National CAPS Network pronouncements on climate change and Law 620.

According to network facilitator Eduardo, who spoke of the National CAPS Network, "if we hadn't had initial resources, we wouldn't have gotten it off the ground, unfortunately. But that's how it is" (interview, June 28, 2010). Eduardo shared that it easily cost US$15,000 to cover the costs of 120 individuals to attend a two-day, national-level meeting in the capital, Managua. One meeting, then, constituted 37.5 percent of the US$40,000 (2009) total amount APN contributed to the National CAPS Network in 2009. Some rural community members would travel for three days to reach Managua, via multiple modes

FIGURE 15 Water committee members in Sébaco, Matagalpa, getting sworn in as the elected leadership council of the new municipal CAPS network in April 2010.

of transportation, to attend national-level meetings. This mobility would not have been feasible without allies providing reimbursement for buses, taxis, and lodging.[3]

As community-based organizations, CAPS had engaged in collective action to manage resources at the grass roots across several decades in Nicaragua. However, CAPS networks served to facilitate the transcendence of territorial divides toward pursuing new, and explicitly political, collective goals. As a CAPS member from San Dionisio elaborated: "Before 2005, each CAPS worked individually. Each community looked out for its own CAPS. No one proposed forming an organization. . . . Until Law 620 appeared, and the idea of privatizing water, that's when we started to come together. . . . But we weren't organized. And no one was interested in building our capacities" (June 5, 2010). As the first instances of transcommunity organizing among CAPS, municipal and national-level networks constituted an opportunity for water committees to scale up the trust and ties facilitating their grassroots water management. Networks, reflecting new bridging social capital, became opportunities to cultivate new bonding social capital among CAPS as water managers and service providers.

The lack of previous linkages among water committees made the transformational potential of these gatherings greater since they offered the opportunity to construct a set of *shared* of objectives as CAPS. Ally-convened and ally-financed network spaces allowed CAPS to recognize and articulate interests shared *across* their communities. Several prominent outcomes of CAPS' collaborative work with each other and allies at the national level include the articulation of a collective action platform, political pronouncements on national legislation, and creation of radio spots. The National CAPS Network's Plataforma de Lucha (literally, Platform of Struggle) was developed in 2008 and presented CAPS' objectives pertaining to environmental stewardship, water quality, and legal recognition (see box 4). The platform reflected an activist agenda: several items directly pressured the state to be more active in supporting water access and quality via its legally designated functions. For example, point 3 "demand[ed] resources in municipal and national budgets for the construction, expansion, maintenance, and rehabilitation of systems for quality water management." Point 6 called explicitly upon the Ministry of Health (MINSA) to demand "periodic inspections" of water basins in order to "protect water quality" and ensure "the rigorous application of the law against those committing environmental crimes and damaging water sources." Tenuous rights to water sources,

Box 4 National CAPS Network Collective Action Platform
(September 2008)

1. To demand (1) No to the Privatization of Water Resources, in all of its forms, in all instances necessary, and (2) recognition of CAPS as an important national actor.

2. To promote, across all municipalities, municipal government resolutions against privatization and for protection of water resources.

3. To demand resources in municipal and national budgets for the construction, expansion, maintenance, and rehabilitation of systems for quality water management. To demand that municipal resources for water system administration are invested locally to meet needs in the same region.

4. To demand and push for legal support for the movement for the legalization of land where water sources are located, and to demand that local governments declare eminent domain over land where an easement is needed for water systems.

5. To obtain legal status for CAPS. To demand approval of the Special Potable Water and Sanitation Committee Law proposal. This proposal should be backed with signatures of water system beneficiaries. Legal status should help us demand a way to open and manage bank accounts and support management of land around water sources and aqueducts.

6. To demand periodic inspections of MINSA to protect water quality and ensure rigorous application of the law against those committing environmental crimes and damaging water sources. At the same time, MINSA should facilitate access to chlorine tablets to treat water in our systems.

7. To develop resources for training CAPS to increase knowledge in system administration and maintenance. To establish alliances with institutions, including ENACAL, that can help us with trainings and technical assistance.

8. To promote our participation and involvement in all municipal, watershed, and national bodies involved in water management, especially those created by Law 620. It's necessary that CAPS form part of the Municipal Development Committees, Municipal Environment Councils, Municipal Forest Councils, Watershed Committees, and the National Water Resources Council.

9. To agitate and pressure municipal authorities to have CAPS participate in and be consulted about permit authorization for irrigation water, logging, and mining concessions.

(continued)

Box 4 (*continued*)

10. To seek support for undertaking municipal watershed diagnostics, including assessments of aquifer capacities and recharge areas, that would allow for creating a map of water sources.

11. There should be an effective opening of the Citizens' Association Books at the municipal level so we can inscribe in accordance with the Law of Citizen Participation.

12. To promote municipal governments' learning related to water. To promote awareness campaigns with urban and rural residents to advocate against burning of organic material and water privatization.

13. To promote reforestation and the declaration of protected and recharge areas around water sources on the part of municipal governments and the national government in order to protect water sources. Institutions should not give permits to farm owners who exploit natural reserve areas.

14. To promote alliances with environmental institutions to take action together, especially coordinated work to raise awareness and disseminate information toward fulfillment of the Environment and Natural Resources Law.

15. To pressure local governments to prohibit via municipal ordinances the use of agrochemicals in water recharge zones and around water sources.

16. To promote incentivizing of payments for environmental services such as forest conservation and reforestation, soil conservation, use of organic fertilizers, and natural regeneration among producers. Municipal governments should promote, vis-à-vis the national government, incentives for property owners who conserve forest and sanctions for those who destroy it.

17. To advance CAPS' organization at the municipal, departmental, and watershed levels to increase their engagement as a national network in all bodies and spaces defined by the National Water Law. To collect information about our structures, including departmental and municipal networks, needs and capacities. To promote the creation of departmental CAPS networks that function with their own statutes and regulations, with the goal of monitoring the implementation and application of Law 620, the National Water Law.

18. To promote coordinated meetings and work between indigenous communities and other institutions or people working on the environment, considering the importance of the former in water resources management.

19. To promote meetings and exchanges among CAPS where we can share and establish common ground and agreements about our work agenda.

20. To publish material with useful information like laws, municipal ordinances, or work experiences, strengthening their dissemination through media outlets.

costly maintenance and replacement of deteriorating water systems, and uphill battles against water contamination and land degradation discussed in network meetings formed bases for new social and political solidarities among water committees.

While bridging social capital supported, in a physical sense, CAPS' mobility, connections between water committees and allies simultaneously enabled CAPS to achieve greater visibility as rural social actors and political agents. Allies supported, for example, disseminating and projecting CAPS' collective action platform, letters to public officials, and political pronouncements, including one expressing concern about climate change developed in November 2009 (see chapter 4, box 5). These processes supported awareness of water committees, including their work and calls for change, on the part of urban and rural residents, NGOs, and state officials in Nicaragua. For example, with organizational support from the Coalition for the Right to Water and financing from Norwegian People's Aid, an abbreviated version of CAPS' twenty-point collective action platform was published in 2008 in the popular journal *Enlace*, published by SIMAS. In total, ninety-five hundred copies were published as a free issue focusing solely on CAPS' water management and their history of administering rural water systems (Enlace 2008).

Financed by allies, CAPS began to participate collectively in public events and forums, and, in the process, became increasingly visible to urban publics as a distinct actor and stakeholder in the water sector. The collective showing by CAPS at the National Land Fair—an annual public event showcasing the work and services of agricultural, environmental, and community development organizations—saw the participation of roughly sixty CAPS members from around the country when it was held in Matagalpa at the National Autonomous University of Nicaragua in 2010. Various allies made possible CAPS' presence and participation in the Land Fair. Norwegian People's Aid contributed US$10,000 for water committees' transportation, food, and lodging—a fourth of the US$40,000 total the agency devoted to CAPS' organizational efforts in 2010. Water committees convened around the booth of ODESAR, the local host the day of the fair, where meals were served and from where black baseball caps with "Nicaraguan CAPS Network" printed in bright blue were distributed. Water committee members and NGO staff wore T-shirts bearing "CAPS Network Nicaragua" on the front and "Achieving Integrated Water Management" on the back. Beyond increasing CAPS' public visibility, the event facilitated water committees' direct participation in policy discussions. On a

FIGURE 16 Members of CAPS and National CAPS Network facilitator Denis (second from right) at the National Land Fair in Matagalpa in 2010. The front of CAPS' T-shirts read, "CAPS Network Nicaragua."

FIGURE 17 José Francisco of San Dionisio, Matagalpa, and CAPS members attend a panel on rural water management at the National Land Fair in June 2010.

FIGURE 18 President-elect of the National CAPS Network Juan de Dios speaking on the rural water management panel at the National Land Fair in June 2010. To the far left sits the director of the Department of Rural Aqueducts within the national regulatory agency for water (INAA) and to the right, AVINA Foundation staff member Edgard.

FIGURE 19 Schoolchildren visit the booth of Matagalpa-based NGO ODESAR during the Land Fair in June 2010.

panel session devoted solely to the rural water sector, the elected president of the National CAPS Network, Juan de Dios, participated alongside NGO staff and government officials.

As growing networks fostered ties and a sense of solidarity among CAPS from different communities, many water committee members participating in network spaces expressed recognition that the majority of CAPS nationally had not achieved direct participation in new transcommunity mobilization processes. Indeed, some CAPS' novel inclusion in public debates and policy processes necessarily meant others' exclusion from the same processes. Water committee members interviewed and observed expressed the importance of incorporating greater numbers in CAPS networks as organizations and promoted the idea that networks represented "all" CAPS. During a municipal-level CAPS assembly in Sébaco, member Marbelly shared her vision for the network: "Now that we're organized as a municipal network . . . it's going to represent all CAPS in the municipality of Sébaco, which I imagine are many, and we still don't all know each other. They're going to be able to count upon a directorate that represents them in many events, that speaks for them, and that brings help to those CAPS that need it" (December 12, 2009). Issues of inclusion and exclusion are likely unavoidable in cases of representative organizations and spaces of engagement such as CAPS networks. Notably, however, municipal-level engagement increases the likelihood that a participant will scale up to the national level given the information and invitations circulating in municipal-network spaces. As a result, social capital begets more social capital: participation in municipal events becomes an opportunity for further bridging with dissimilar actors and increased connections among bonded actors—in this case, water committees from diverse regions. Hence, although analytically distinct, both bridging and bonding social capital go hand in hand toward promoting CAPS networks' broad collective base and collective efficacy.

Political and Legal Capacity Building

As rural water managers and service providers, CAPS depended upon the resources of NGOs and multilateral agencies to connect across communities and act collectively at more encompassing geographic, as well as higher political, scales. Once in network spaces, CAPS' shared experiences across diverse regions translated into bases for constructing and pursuing collective political goals pertaining to rural water management and service provision. Developing and articulating collective goals, however, was facilitated in important ways by ally-led capacity-building processes that supported water committees' knowledge, awareness, and defense of their legal rights.

Having occupied roles in research, policy formation, and advocacy within the water sector, NGO and multilateral agency staff contributed information and experience that supported the political education of water committees (Hyman 2002). In this way, bridging social capital played an important role in politically empowering CAPS as grassroots water managers. Starting in the mid-2000s, much of allies' capacity building centered upon three laws: the National Water Law (620), the Law of Citizen Participation (475),[4] and, as it was being developed and after its passing in 2010, the Special CAPS Law (722). Ally-led training on legislation in network spaces afforded CAPS the opportunity to examine and assess policies, work that became the basis for collective political pronouncements that were disseminated to lawmakers. Training focused on reviewing provisions most relevant to CAPS in terms of policy implementation and advocacy vis-à-vis elected officials.

To address Law 620, SIMAS, CISAS, and ODESAR staff spent time in municipal and national-level network meetings primarily on three articles water committees perceived as threats to their organizations and water systems. These included the aforementioned Article 4, which asserted that water service would not be privatized, leaving out reference to the country's water resources. Other provisions on which allies focused CAPS' attention included Article 49, stating that all potable water distribution networks are "property of the state, represented by ENACAL [the state water company]," and Article 75, which asserted that small-scale rural water systems, while administered by "Potable Water Committees," are to be "under the supervision and control of ENACAL." Water committees reacted strongly to new legal provisions that not only ignored the degree to which they had operated independently over time at the grass roots but also challenged their long-standing autonomy as community organizations. As Isabel of the municipal CAPS network in Sébaco expressed in reference to Article 75, "We, the communities, can't allow these systems to pass to the government, because they belong to the community. . . . This is one of the objectives [of the CAPS networks]. To protect the systems and to protect ourselves" (interview, February 24, 2010). Through systematic study of Law 620, CAPS came to embrace an additional provision, Article 150, which they saw as supporting holding government officials accountable to rural communities because it asserted that municipal governments "are obliged to prioritize potable water, sewerage, and sanitation projects above all other projects" in order to reduce residents' "vulnerability" in regard to water access.

Ally-led examination of the draft CAPS Law (Law 722) in network meetings centered upon several provisions. These included CAPS' process of registering with local governments and the national regulatory water agency, the Nicaraguan Water and Sanitation Institute (INAA) (Articles 11–14; 30–33); the establishment of differentiated energy tariffs for those CAPS whose water systems utilize electric pumps (Article 25); and the process through which local governments could declare inputs (e.g., freshwater sources) of "public use" (akin to eminent domain) if private ownership obstructs local water access needs (Article 4). To facilitate review and discussion, allies printed two thousand copies of the draft law in the name of the National CAPS Network, enabling water committees to study the law in network spaces and propose revisions.

In practice, water committees' awareness of legal provisions translated into advocacy on behalf of their organizations and communities vis-à-vis state actors. As Silvio Prado, of the Center for Political Research and Analysis, asserted, "[Laws 620 and 722] allowed CAPS to diversify their contacts and

FIGURE 20 Water committees studying the National Water Law (Law 620) during a municipal assembly of CAPS in Ciudad Darío, Matagalpa, in 2010.

FIGURE 21 Committees studying the recently passed Special CAPS Law (Law 722) in Ocotal, Nueva Segovia, in June 2010.

strengthen the capacity for discussion around something concrete. The laws were their banners, which they grabbed hold of and used to make a forceful entry into the field of political advocacy. These two laws have enabled the CAPS to be what they are now with respect to advocacy" (cited in Kreimann 2010, 26). Across municipalities in Matagalpa, CAPS members shared experiences of legal empowerment and how it informed their activism. Delia of Sébaco, her CAPS' treasurer, recounted how knowing the laws served as a foundation for her advocacy in regard to state officials:

The first time I went to the mayor's office, he had a complete lack of knowledge that we had elected national representatives [to the national network], that there was a CAPS law being developed, and he even suggested that I just return to my community. I brought magazines, because we had contributed twice to the magazine *Enlace*, I brought the National Water Law, I brought the draft water committee law. I said, "look, Don Luis, here is article 150, an article specific to the mayor's offices." I opened the page, and the law says that the mayors are obliged

[to prioritize water-related investments]—it's not just if they want to or not. . . .
Water is fundamental and it's an obligation. (interview, February 24, 2010)

The ability of CAPS to articulate specific demands related to national legislation
was the product of ally-led capacity-building processes. Moreover, "knowing the
laws" has been a means of educating public officials on national laws—a boon
for water governance if this education can be seen as positively impacting the
implementation of laws supporting equitable and sustainable water governance.

Indeed, CAPS in several municipalities leveraged new legal knowledge about
local governments' prescribed role in the rural water sector as a means to garner
greater state resources in line with Law 620's provision requiring local governments to support rural water supply. In the municipality of Esquipulas,
Matagalpa, CAPS succeeded with a request for funding from the local government: 100,000 córdobas, or roughly US$4,760, was awarded in 2009 to reha-
bilitate a water system (interview, June 5, 2010). In Jalapa, Nueva Segovia, the
local government supported the municipal CAPS network with an office space

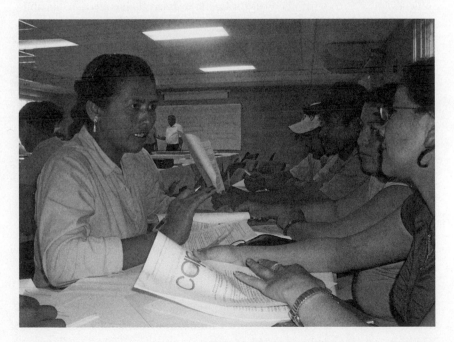

FIGURE 22   CAPS members Jessenia (left), Elia (right), and others discuss draft statutes for the National CAPS Network's application to form a nonprofit association during
the network's meeting in November 2009 in Managua.

(interview, May 25, 2010). In Muy Muy, Matagalpa, local government contributed US$690 for the municipal network's functioning in 2016, and similar financial support was received by the municipal network in San Ramón (interview, July 4, 2016). This direct financial support not only reflects an important state contribution to rural water access in terms of supporting water systems infrastructure; it must also be viewed as the outcome of bridging social capital: water committees' relationship with allies increased their political and legal knowledge and sense of efficacy as water managers in a way that supported their advocacy for greater distribution of resources to rural communities.

Access to State Officials and Channels of Representation

How did CAPS gain access to state officials at the national level in order to leverage their organic empowerment in addition to newly cultivated legal and political knowledge? Beyond facilitating physical mobility and visibility, NGO and multilateral allies played a critical role in creating CAPS' access to public officials—in other words, channels for CAPS to assert their collective demands. Carmen María of APN stressed the importance of allies' personal and professional linkages in order to facilitate the opening of space for CAPS within government and to create new state-society linkages where they have not previously existed (interview, June 30, 2010). She emphasized her relationships with members of government because of the time she spent working with the revolutionary government in the 1980s; the primary facilitator of the National CAPS Network, Eduardo, also worked for the Sandinista government in this era. These relationships with political elites and elected officials, also developed through work in the NGO and international aid sectors that required direct coordination with government actors, enabled allies to facilitate communication between and among CAPS, lawmakers, and state water agency officials.

Collaborating with NGOs, including SIMAS and ODESAR, the national government hosted a series of regional forums in 2007, attended by water committees from across municipalities. The Matagalpa "A Toast to Life" water forum was the beginning of what would be a series of water committee consultations with state authorities through to the passing of the CAPS Law in May 2010. This forum in September 2007 brought together roughly a hundred CAPS members in addition to NGO staff and government officials. The director of INAA's Department of Rural Aqueducts, Gilberto, characterized the departmental forums as an explicit opportunity to solicit feedback on national legislation: "Various CAPS leaders were invited to get to know the draft [CAPS] law. That was part of the consultation. I was collecting CAPS leaders' opinions to better the law" (interview, June 2, 2010). Those CAPS in attendance used the event to interrogate their exclusion from consultations on Law 620 as well as to assert demands regarding the law's implementation.

Notably, owing to novel bridging between CAPS and their allies that supported building water committees' legal and political capacities, those CAPS participating appeared more versed in Law 620's content than National Assembly lawmakers in attendance. During a question and answer period with FLSN lawmakers, CAPS member and municipal network coordinator José Francisco solicited comments from the elected officials on Article 4 of the law, which proscribes privatization but only of "water service." José Francisco also drew lawmakers' attention to articles specifically outlining procedures for granting water extraction and use rights to private individuals or entities. Lawmakers searched through the text of the law to locate and read the article before responding, giving the impression that José Francisco's familiarity with and knowledge of

FIGURE 23 José Francisco speaking at the Matagalpa water forum, "A Toast to Life," at the National Autonomous University in September 2007.

the law surpassed that of the government officials who passed the law. This dynamic, here in regard to national-level state actors, reinforces the notion that water committees' knowledge and capacities in the sector can exceed those of government officials.

Alongside water committee representatives at the forum, NGO allies actively contested CAPS' exclusion from policy consultations, defending rural water managers' right to participate in the formulation of water laws. As National CAPS Network facilitator Eduardo asserted during the forum: as a "network with a national dimension," CAPS are "not being taken into account in the processes of defining the country's water policies." Furthermore, water committees' access to state officials during the event evinced how bridging social capital served as an antidote to CAPS' historical exclusion from water policy discussions and debates.

In addition to face-to-face meetings, allies helped to place CAPS' political pronouncements directly in the hands of elected officials. The National CAPS Network's first pronouncement elaborating recommendations for a CAPS Law had been developed in response to Sandinista deputies' draft version of the law presented at the 2007 Matagalpa water forum. Water committees crafted recommendations based on the draft during an ally-facilitated workshop the same year. Studying the draft law with ODESAR, CAPS in the Matagalpa departmental network sought to "correct" what were deemed to be inappropriate provisions. Javier, an ODESAR staff member, asserted that the original draft "didn't recognize the needs of water committees." For example, "the first draft of the document said that a committee could have access to being legal after functioning for five years. Committee members said no. That it was illogical. That each committee should be able to access legality after one year of operating. And that's how it was written" (interview, June 21, 2010). Water committees and their NGO allies also recommended not excluding as "Potable Water and Sanitation Committees" those organizations managing water systems with fewer than fifty taps. "There are small CAPS that are very well-organized, and there are big ones that are a disaster," Javier emphasized. Water system size did not correlate with levels of water committee organization, and, hence, the potential benefits of legal recognition through a CAPS law should extend to all water committees. In October 2007, the National CAPS Network sent a letter presenting collectively produced feedback and ideas to the president of the National Assembly's Commission of Environment and Natural Resources.

Water committees had direct impacts on the final CAPS Law passed in 2010. Their role in shaping the legislation contributed to how it would viewed as a bottom-up "win" with symbolic importance for water committees in Nicaragua, regardless of its practical implications. Reflecting on how CAPS' feedback had been taken into account by lawmakers, CAPS leader Esperanza asserted, "The law has practically been elaborated by CAPS. It hasn't been a law that's come from above, but rather one from below. It's we who have been elaborating the law, working with some lawmakers in the National Assembly's Natural Resources Commission. We have an activity at the end of September to look over some things: how the law is going [and] how it will look when it's presented to the commission" (interview, September 21, 2008). In late 2007, FSLN deputies had submitted a complete draft of the CAPS Law along with a "presentation of rationale" to the president of Nicaragua's National Assembly. It also became a draft CAPS would study in network spaces. While Law 620 ignored the CAPS as community-based actors in the sector, this document asserted that a CAPS law would serve to "institutionalize over thirty years' experience of community participation" in Nicaragua. Legislators referenced CAPS' decades of work as resource managers, serving as a public recognition of rural residents' contributions to the sector that for decades had not been recognized formally in state legal frameworks.

Some face-to-face consultations between CAPS and state actors on the CAPS Law proved more contentious than those observed during the Matagalpa water forum in 2007. Nevertheless, they revealed dynamics of learning and exchange on the part of national and local government authorities, NGOs, multilateral agency staff, and CAPS. In November 2009, Carmen María of Norwegian People's Aid coordinated a meeting of CAPS, national lawmakers, and state water company staff, describing it as a "triumph," given that CAPS members were granted access to the National Assembly and had the opportunity to assert their interests and demands to national officials (interview, June 30, 2010). The meeting demonstrated how CAPS' direct engagement with lawmakers served as an opportunity to contest and correct what they perceived to be inaccurate characterizations of their work as resource managers and service providers; moreover, CAPS' face-to-face engagements with state actors revealed how bridging social capital can "play a critical role in terms of generating bargaining power" with public officials—a collective form of empowerment that grassroots actors frequently lack in the absence of horizontal ties between "base groups" (Fox and Gershman, 2006, 209).[5]

One concrete feature of the Special CAPS Law upon which negotiation centered concerned CAPS' name. The draft CAPS law to date referred to the Comités de Agua Potable, or CAPs, omitting the "S" for "sanitation" as had been done in the Regulations of Law 620. Water committees' negotiations with state actors revealed the "S" to hold not only symbolic importance but also potential material and financial significance for water management. Sébaco's Delia recounted ENACAL's assertion that CAPS "didn't do sanitation," which according to ENACAL included constructing waste storage tanks: "We said to the deputies that maybe we didn't do that, but we were chlorinating water in our communities and examining sanitation practices, seeing that people don't burn trash, that they don't allow water to pool. That yes, it wasn't the sanitization that they provide, but yet, it was a basic sanitation. How are we going to make waste storage tanks?" (interview, July 14, 2010). The testimony of Jessenia of Nueva Segovia revealed further potential implications of a formally articulated responsibility for sanitation in relation to state institutions: "I think the bottom line for ENACAL was the budget. They said that if the CAPS took responsibility for sanitation, we would take half of their national-level budget. They wanted sanitation for themselves, because sanitation brings money, even from the international organizations. That was the other key. We fought and fought in our second session in the National Assembly, until the "S" remained" (interview, June 4, 2010).

As part of their organic empowerment, CAPS have taken provisions to ensure sanitation locally. In water committees' view, taking away their "S" would have overlooked as well as undermined the important sanitation work they perform in their communities. According to Delia, the ENACAL representative at the meeting consulted with the company's president, Ruth Selma Herrera, over the phone and "left angrily" at the end of the meeting, stating a desire to engage ENACAL's lawyers in the debate (interview, July 14, 2010). Sandinista lawmakers, however, ultimately agreed to leave the "S" in the final version of the law.

Allies' Role in Augmenting Inclusion in Water Governance

"ODESAR has always accompanied us, trained us, mobilized us." José Francisco's assertion synthesized the important ways allies were supporting CAPS' transcommunity mobilization and political learning toward engagement in national politics (interview, May 19, 2010). Combined with newfound physical mobility and knowledge of national laws, CAPS' access to state officials enabled a multiscalar political strategy in the pursuit of collective goals, including their formal recognition as water managers and service providers. The experience that CAPS had mobilizing to form transcommunity networks reveals that bonding social capital is not an inherent impediment to broader political participation and networking; in fact, similar experiences at the grass roots provided the groundwork for establishing new bonds and a sense of collective solidarity among previously disconnected CAPS from across regions in Nicaragua. Moreover, the multisectoral collaborations evident in new CAPS networks provide evidence that the limits on potential synergy beyond the grass roots and with different actors "seem to be set less by the initial density of trust and ties at the micro level" or, in this case, by CAPS' bonding social capital. Rather, what must be overcome are "the difficulties involved in 'scaling up' micro-level social capital to generate solidary ties and social action" at other scales (Evans 1996, 1124). That is, locally grounded, materially resource–poor, bonded actors often must *bridge* with different (and differently endowed) actors in order to gain mobility, access new spaces of engagement, and increase their political efficacy.

As water committees developed a collective presence beyond the community level, their legitimacy as resource managers and service providers was enhanced by their collective voice. That is, CAPS' discourses of water governance—to which the next chapter turns—served to heighten awareness and understanding of rural residents' experiences in the sector. Ally-supported projection of CAPS' voices, including through opportunities for water committees to speak directly with public officials and elected leaders, contributed to state actors' basis for knowing and understanding *who* CAPS were and *what* work they performed in rural areas. This expanded knowledge and awareness influenced public officials' perceptions of CAPS as having legitimate authority in the water sector and, consequently, as meriting formal recognition.

FOUR

Shaping Politics through Discourse

We've had our potable water system for eleven years. We've been working to be responsive to the community, to their demands, so people have access to water. To date we've maintained ourselves well. Thank God, sometimes we crawl along, little by little, working so that our water system keeps developing and meeting the needs of everyone. Because everyone has to drink water.

I'm clear that every water committee needs to be reelected every one or two years. We have to work well together, united. But, there are times when a community leader has earned the great confidence of the community, they love him like a brother, like an important person. Building others' capacities in workshops, seminars—the community cares for you. I've been a community leader and coordinator of our [system] for eleven years. September 18 we gave the community an opportunity to elect a new leadership board. Not because we didn't want to work, but because our bylaws require it. You have to give space and opportunities to others. But the community said, "No, you all are going to work for us because the mini-aqueduct is doing well, we've never had problems with the funds that you manage . . ." I wanted to leave. You know how we work. Milking cows, wielding a machete—we do it all. Sometimes you devote more time to serving the community than to doing other things. The majority of community leaders, those working with love for our community, for our municipality, the majority live in poverty. We're the volunteer army of the community.

—LUIS ADOLFO, CAPS SAN FRANCISCO,
SAN LORENZO, BOACO (FEBRUARY 17, 2010)

How CAPS talk about their work and organizations reflects having achieved a way of understanding and describing their work that arose from on-the-ground experiences in rural water management. The testimony, above, of CAPS coordinator Luis Adolfo, was shared with me during a February 2010 National CAPS Network meeting in Managua. Luis Adolfo emphasized his committees' development of water management capacities that ensured a well-functioning water system and sound management of the community's funds. Moreover, his CAPS' capacities had engendered the trust and support of system beneficiaries. This buy-in contributed to how Luis Adolfo and other leaders were embraced as legitimate authorities at the grass roots.

This chapter sheds light on the discursive dimensions of CAPS' organizing and activism: a third and distinct factor supporting their successful transcommunity and multisectoral mobilization. The chapter builds on the previous two to document, first, how CAPS' collective discourses reflect their locally grounded work as resource managers and service providers in Nicaragua. In important ways, then, CAPS' discourses reflect their organic empowerment (chapter 2). Second, the chapter argues that CAPS' discourses served to mediate their collective engagements with state officials as allies supported their scaling up to form networks and engage in national-level politics (chapter 3). Three interconnected discourses examined in the chapter include CAPS' (1) claims to ownership over water systems and autonomy vis-à-vis the state; (2) description of their work in terms of legally prescribed state responsibilities in the water and sanitation sector; and (3) emphasis on collective problem-solving across rural-urban, state-society, and partisan divides.

Water committees' collective discourses emerged in municipal, departmental, and national network spaces as CAPS from across communities and regions engaged in dialogue. Water committees' collective story, or how they talked about themselves and their work, also entered the public sphere through their collective action platform, political pronouncements, participation in public events, and use of media outlets—including billboards and radio spots. The committees' discourses, akin to collective action frames as examined in the social movements literature, furthermore showed up and informed the character of CAPS' exchanges and negotiations with state actors around the Special CAPS Law. As both a reflection and an assertion of grassroots rural water management over time, these discourses proved salient and effective toward promoting water committees' goals of legal recognition and political inclusion as consequential actors in water governance.

Discursive Representations of Community-Based Water Governance

As mentioned above, discourses of water governance are akin to collective action frames as explored in the vast literature on social movements. This chapter builds upon the social movement scholarship's conception of framing in order to account for the distinctive and crucial role that collective discourses, much like movement frames, play in promoting movement objectives. As "the collective processes of interpretation, attribution, and social construction" (McAdam, McCarthy, and Zald 1996, 2), framing has been cast as a "dynamic, negotiated, and often contested" process (Johnston and Noakes 2005, 206). The frames that result from collective processes of interpretation reflect shared ideas and meanings among movement participants.

How does a collective action frame influence social movement trajectories and achievement of movement goals? In practice, collective action frames "mediate between opportunity and action" (McAdam, McCarthy, and Zald 1996, 5). Not surprisingly, grassroots conceptions and experiences of water governance intersect, and may come into conflict with, extralocal or top-down representations of water governance, including those outlined in state policy. States' adoption of "one size fits all" legal characterizations of grassroots organizations, for example, can effectively deprive communities of water management prerogatives or responsibilities via the imposition of culturally or politically inappropriate rules or decision-making bodies. Communities of water users and managers may respond.

In the Nicaraguan case, a *lack* of explicit inclusion in formal policy frameworks not only prompted a response on the part of CAPS but also may have facilitated more effective political interventions. That is, the state's failure to articulate the contours of rural water management in national laws gave CAPS a discursive space to shape their public representation as water managers and service providers. This kind of legal representation by omission, as opposed to an imposed articulation of CBWM in Nicaragua, may have unwittingly supported water committees' ability to frame their work in the public sphere as they mobilized. Like other water users' associations in Latin America (see, e.g., Boelens, Hoogesteger, and Baud 2015; Perreault 2006; Roth, Boelens, and Zwarteveen 2005), CAPS' self-representations of their community-based organizations and socioenvironmental landscapes were leveraged to contest top-down water policies in which they were overlooked. Discursive representations of their organizations and work also supported achieving the objectives of shaping public opinion, persuading decision makers (including elected officials), and mobilizing a base of supporters.

Framing is often qualified as strategic in the social movement literature.[1] However, CAPS' discourses can best be understood as instrumental, though not intentionally strategic, projected understandings of water governance. In other words, CAPS' discourses reflect and convey the social and material experiences of water management at the grass roots. Rather than reflect the outcome of collective *strategizing*, the language CAPS used to describe their work and frame their demands for recognition mirrored their everyday, historical and contemporary, experience as water managers and service providers. It is notable that water committees were effective in garnering the support of the media and state actors, as shown by how these actors adopted water committees' language in their own public discourses. The buy-in of state actors is all the more counterintuitive since state actors were also the principal *targets* of CAPS' political and policy interventions, and were characterized by water committees as shirking their roles as public officials.

Yet, from another angle, state actors' contesting of CAPS' discursive frames ultimately would not have been politically advantageous. Doing so would have also meant contesting, and in effect *denying*, CAPS' claims. These included that CAPS do the work that they do with little state support, that the state is the legally responsible guarantor of basic services such as water, and that more state support to rural communities in the endeavor of water management is valid and important. The purpose of examining CAPS discourses—and the claims within—is not to ascertain their "truth." Rather, it is to understand "how such claims to truth are being used in practice, how they shape perceptions of reality and also define socionatural reality itself" (Boelens 2014, 240). As CAPS engaged with urban and rural publics as well as with state actors, they were *perceived* as credible frame articulators who produced characterizations of local water management with a high degree of "empirical credibility" (Benford and Snow 2000). The first collective discourse of autonomy and ownership, discussed below, demonstrates how CAPS sought to leverage their "truths" to pursue their objectives.

Discourse of Autonomy and Ownership: "Aquí somos los dueños" (Here we are the owners)

It is noteworthy that CAPS draw upon their experience of "abandonment" and resulting independence in local water management to assert autonomy vis-à-vis the state. Members of CAPS spoke openly and emphatically about the little support they receive from the government. Referencing her committees' experience participating in the Municipal Development Council prior to formation of the Muy Muy municipal CAPS network in 2005, CAPS coordinator Esperanza explains, "The truth is that before participating, we never had the support of any mayor. And we have been around for a long time" (interview, August 8, 2008). Marbelly likewise emphasized her community's independent work in Sébaco: "We've crawled along by ourselves, with our own money, for our own work. We have never, to this day, had help from a mayor" (interview, December 11, 2009). Rural residents, including CAPS members, invest time, labor, and monetary resources into constructing rural water systems. This social and financial investment fosters a strong sense of ownership over local water systems and related responsibilities and prerogatives.

The acute sense of ownership on the part of CAPS has fostered a willingness and eagerness to articulate claims to water systems publicly using new networks as a platform. A November 2009 National CAPS Network's Pronouncement asserted that CAPS were "concerned" about the National Water Law's implementation. In particular, CAPS referenced a provision referencing ownership over water distribution systems. It read: "In no case . . . will potable water distribution networks be privatized. These, though constructed privately, will be property of the Nicaraguan state, represented by ENACAL" (Law 620, Article 49).[2] Although carrying out work with a public quality and character, CAPS, of course, did not deem themselves part of the state. The National Water Law, while lacking explicit reference to rural water committees, invoked the notion of state ownership over CAPS' "privately" constructed water systems. This was perceived as threatening. Water committees' proclamation to state officials read: "We declare ourselves on alert regarding ENACAL's intentions to take over our potable water systems which can be seen in Article 49 of Law 620 and in different opinions published in media outlets."

Assertions of autonomy and ownership have been made not only in relation to state actors. Misael, CAPS municipal network coordinator of El Tuma–La Dalia, explained during a municipal assembly in Sébaco that a sense of abandonment can generate the perception of a threat—even from, in this case, CAPS leaders visiting from "outside" the community: "Imagine the sense of abandonment the local government gives CAPS in their communities at times. It leaves great repercussions. We arrived at a community where the person who had donated the well [for the community water system] was waiting for us with machete in hand. He told us, 'here the system is mine, the property is mine,' etc., etc. We told him that we were an organization that didn't come to get involved with internal community issues, that our work is social, organizational, moral and we had to present what we do" (December 9, 2009). This story indicates that the work of new CAPS networks has at times been challenged by the legacies of state abandonment. Rural residents not engaged in CAPS' transcommunity networking were skeptical of residents from other communities showing up to discuss water committees' regional and national-level work. Unfortunately, an effort to share local organizational and collaborative efforts among CAPS was perceived as a threat to local land and water ownership.

The 2008, free to the public, special issue of the Nicaraguan magazine *Enlace* captured stories of several water committees from across the country who made assertions of local authority and ownership. Some stories drew attention to the significance of how communities began working as resource managers and service providers. Antonio of Muy Muy asserted: "Look, no one helped us— not in the design or the construction of our water system. We dug the ditches, bought and installed ten kilometers of pipes, and made the water storage tank, which cost us 35,000 córdobas [US$1,842]" (Enlace 2008, 27). María, a CAPS coordinator from the same municipality, expressed, "We are the owners of these resources, and we are the ones who have worked to have water in our homes." Carlos expressed a similar point: "These systems have cost us: we built them, and we administer them. Because of this we're asking that the law protects this autonomy." These statements reflect a strong sense of ownership over and responsibility for local water systems. They also indicate that CAPS' promotion of autonomy and ownership has been influenced historically by a tenuous relationship with state and other outside actors.

Notably, being autonomous in partisan political terms is a prerogative water committees connect to their autonomy as local water managers and service providers. Assertions of independence and autonomy also appeared in CAPS' efforts to limit the influence or interference of government officials whose partisan agendas may be divisive. As CAPS member Antonio of Muy Muy expressed: "What's political is political. Here we don't allow those things to mix, the political with the social. Partisan politics, that is. *We're autonomous*" (interview, August 21, 2008; emphasis added). Just weeks before the 2008 municipal elections, Antonio explained his water committees' approach to an upcoming meeting with municipal government candidates:

> By chance, the eighth [of August] we're going to a meeting with all the candidates so they can know everything that has to do with the water projects as well as avoid ending up using those projects for political purposes, because this isn't

political; the only politics we embrace is that of people needing to have water to satisfy their needs. This is not something political. That's what we try to avoid. And because of that we're building the capacity of our members, the same users who have to know everything that's happening so no one fools us along the way. (interview, August 21, 2008)

Luis Adolfo of Boaco recounted a direct interaction he had with his municipality's mayor, wherein he objected to the mayor's attempt to put local water systems in the hands of the Citizen Power Councils: "I said to the mayor, 'One moment, here in the community we are the owners and *señores* of this water system.'" Luis Adolfo explained to the mayor that the previous mayor had purchased the land containing the water system and source and had subsequently donated it to the community (interview, February 17, 2010). He expressed concern about what appeared to be an effort to force water committees to cede control of potable water systems to the Citizen Power Councils—organizations he and others perceived as partisan.

Beyond concerns about partisan influence, how the water committees' name would be represented in a new Special CAPS Law prompted claims to ownership within rural water governance. The draft law to which CAPS were introduced referred to Comités de Agua Potable, or CAPs, omitting CAPS' "S." Yet, CAPS' "S," as discussed in the previous chapter, represents a collective identity and speaks to tangible dimensions of what CAPS consider to be their rightful prerogatives within the water and sanitation sector.

In November 2009, CAPS leaders from the National CAPS Network met with representatives of ENACAL and the National Assembly's Commission of Environment and Natural Resources to discuss the law, including CAPS' capacity to provide for basic sanitation in their communities. Jessenia from Ocotal recalled the ENACAL representative questioning the capacity of CAPS, yet following with the acknowledgment that their company has not had sufficient coverage in rural areas. She recounts her subsequent intervention that addressed ENACAL staff directly:

So that's when I asked to speak and I said: "You're telling us that we're incompetent. Excuse me but we—the water committees—are more competent than ENACAL. Because, yes, we have entered into rural communities and you haven't been able to. And there we are. We're getting people water. You think that we're not capable of providing sanitation but we're already doing so. We chlorinate water, we do sanitation campaigns. If we haven't constructed drainage systems, latrines, or hygienic services, it's because we haven't had the legality to do so." (November 5, 2009)

Via their national network, CAPS members fiercely contested losing the prerogative of local sanitation—here represented by having their name altered within impending national legislation. "Winning" the struggle over the S, at once discursive and material, depended upon CAPS' articulations of their independent contributions to sanitation at the community level. National lawmakers' ultimate siding with CAPS and in opposition to the state water company demonstrates that CAPS were perceived as legitimate and credible when representing their rural work.

Some of the contention characterizing CAPS' meetings with public officials appeared linked to state actors' ignorance of rural water management and service provision. When state officials began to interact with CAPS in the mid-2000s owing to the coordinating work of allies, CAPS had the opportunity to contest what they deemed to be state actors' misunderstandings of their experiences as water managers and service providers. One such example occurred after the passing of the National Water Law (Law 620) in 2007: CAPS member José Francisco of San Dionisio participated in a workshop hosted and led by the Nitlapán Research Center (Central American University) on the implications of Law 620 and how it would be implemented. The only CAPS member participating in the event, José Francisco found himself in the company of representatives of state institutions such as the Ministry of Energy and Mines and domestic NGOs such as ODESAR and Action against Hunger. He recounted an exchange with a government official from the Ministry of the Environment and Natural Resources (MARENA): "I was the one there representing CAPS, so I spoke as a CAPS. Someone from MARENA comes and she tells me that the CAPS aren't anything, that they don't know anything. 'What?' I tell her. 'One moment. The CAPS—there are five thousand of us and we serve 200,000 people across the country. And no one gives us anything. If you don't know us now, you're going to get to know us'" (interview, March 19, 2010). José Francisco hence strongly countered the government authority's discounting of CAPS in terms of their knowledge and, implicitly, contributions to water management at a national scale. With increasing inclusion via networks in spaces of dialogue with public officials, CAPS leveraged new opportunities to assert themselves vis-à-vis state actors and shape public understandings of their work.

Discourse of Stateness: "Un trabajo que corresponde al estado" (Work that corresponds to the state)

Water committee members frequently invoked the state in defending their local water management and service provision. They did so in part to establish that they worked with very little state resources and support, lending sympathy to their cause. Like water users elsewhere in Latin America (e.g., Boelens 2008; Hoogesteger, Boelens, and Baud 2017), CAPS encouraged and promoted an *augmented* role of the state in rural water management at the same time that they asserted autonomy. The way that CAPS discursively juxtaposed their state-like work with the state's shirking of its legal responsibilities—and those that are a part of popular imaginaries of the state—bolstered water committees' demands for political recognition.

The water governance discourses of CAPS called attention to the state's failures in supporting water access, including state neglect of environmental conservation responsibilities. The 1987 Nicaraguan Constitution makes the state responsible for basic services, citing "an obligation of the State to promote, facilitate and regulate provision of basic public services." The Constitution affirms that "access to these," including water, "is an inalienable right of the population" (Art. 105). The preamble to Law 620 confirmed the state's role in securing water access: "Water is a finite and vulnerable resource essential for life and development . . . whose access is a right associated with life and human health that should be guaranteed by the State." Water committee members demonstrated an awareness of the state's legally ascribed responsibility for water provision. As Sébaco CAPS member Marbelly expressed:

> From 2007 to the present . . . I've been in the CAPS' struggle in which we're aspiring to a law that supports us. Now we've realized, from Article 150 in Law 620, that it's an obligation of the local government to look after water systems. And they've never done it. Of course, as we didn't know the law, we never went to knock on their door. NGOs, yes, because we would go to them to ask for backing. But I tell you, the only thing [the government] has done is give a signature so [NGOs] could work in the community. (interview, December 11, 2009)

Local governments were not the only entity CAPS referenced when speaking about a lack of involvement on the part of state actors. Many CAPS members reported that the state health agency, MINSA, did not take regular water samples from rural water systems. In practice, many CAPS were unaware of the actual quality, including potability, of the water flowing through their "potable water" systems.

The water management and environmental stewardship undertaken by CAPS may be actively undermined by national-level state actors as well. In some cases, the results of MINSA's tests were not shared with water committees and residents (Enlace 2008). Some NGO staff cast this as a way to avoid dealing with serious issues of water quality. Members of CAPS also spoke of state actors as complicit in the destabilization of community-based conservation efforts through insufficient regulation and a failure to regulate companies or landowners for breaching the law. One CAPS member pointed out during a 2009 National CAPS Network meeting that as campesinos they do not receive "payments for environmental services" from the government, but in practice they are the ones fulfilling the role of stewards of forests and water sources.

National media outlets took up the work of sharing experiences emanating from CAPS networks, demonstrating their ascribing of legitimacy to rural water committees. Published articles from both major newspapers, *El Nuevo Diario* and *La Prensa*, emphasized the state's legal duties in the sector while simultaneously projecting an image of water committees as the de facto guarantors of potable water in rural areas. According to one article: "The CAPS are practically the only ones who enable the provision of potable water in rural areas, given that the Nicaraguan Water and Sewerage Company (ENACAL) only covers urban areas, although not all. Where ENACAL is not, you'll find the CAPS" (Pérez 2010). This article portrayed CAPS, much as they portrayed themselves, as "filling in gaps" left by the state in rural areas. The other national newspaper similarly asserted that water committees were working where ENACAL "doesn't offer public service" (García 2008b), and it cited Law 620's provision requiring local governments to prioritize urban and rural water projects above all public investments (García 2008a). The journalist Francisco Mendoza quoted a CAPS member from Muy Muy to draw attention to Article 66, specifying that the government must prioritize allocation of water for human consumption before all other uses: "This article provides an important tool for municipal authorities to prioritize water for the population" (2008, n.p.). The media's adoption of CAPS' discourses not only reflected the perceived empirical credibility of CAPS but also supported *elevating* CAPS as legitimate and consequential actors in national water governance.

Reformers in the state advocating for CAPS' recognition likewise adopted a discourse recognizing the state's shirking of its legally assigned role of assuring water and sanitation to the population. In early 2010, the bipartisan Environment and Natural Resources Commission submitted to the president of the National Assembly an introductory report entitled "The Potable Water and Sanitation Committee Law Project." According to the report, CAPS "are just groups of voluntarily organized people at the community level, in charge of the maintenance and sustainability of potable water and sanitation projects. Said in few words, [CAPS are] taking actions that correspond to the state to assure the population's access to water in the country's [rural] zones." Characterizing CAPS' work as legally assigned to the state, lawmakers demonstrated the bottom-up effects water committees had on national policy discourses. Notably, elected officials further sanctioned CAPS' demands for legal recognition through paraphrasing the voices of water committees they heard during consultations on the proposed law: "One expression we gathered during the consultations was the following: 'In passing this law, it would hardly be a cancellation of one of the many debts the government and the deputies have with us, given that we've been doing the work of the government without receiving anything in return; better said, we've made sacrifices through paying high prices for the materials that we buy. In general, we have been abandoned by the government and the municipalities'" (Rodríguez et al. 2008). Perhaps counterintuitively, rather than be contested, CAPS' discursive representations of their organizations and work become reflected in the public policy discourse of state officials. These confirmations of CAPS' autonomy and their capacities as resource managers and service providers, or their organic empowerment, reflected how state actors perceived CAPS as legitimate and credible actors in water governance. Ultimately, lawmakers' integration of CAPS' discourses into their policy making reveals how language emerging from the grassroots can be instrumental toward advancing movement goals.

In May 2010, the Special Potable Water and Sanitation Committee Law (Law 722) passed unanimously in the National Assembly. The law conferred the official recognition that water committees had pursued since the formation of the first CAPS network in 2005. In a basic sense, the law also served as state actors' formal recognition that CAPS exist. *La Prensa*, referencing an interview with Sandinista member of the National Assembly, Edwin Castro, contended that the CAPS Law assured "the more than five thousand, four hundred CAPS who exist at a national level will have specific rights that are going to guarantee them a legal framework" (Morales 2010). The law codified state actors' recognition that CAPS were doing work that left them, in a sense, off the hook for rural water provision: the beginning section of the law, presenting its rationale, asserted, "It's important to point out that thanks to the work CAPS do in their communities, the government does not incur the costs of rural water infrastructure maintenance; system administration, operation, and maintenance fall on the community." The law went beyond recognizing CAPS' work, though, to codify new ways in which state institutions should support rural water provision. Chapter 7 of the law outlined how various entities—including the national water regulatory agency (INAA), the Ministry of Health (MINSA), and the Emergency Social Investment Fund (FISE), among others—would support CAPS via consulting, oversight, and training on topics such as system administration and maintenance, water quality, and environmental protection.

Why would state actors pass such a law, especially one that delineates an expansion of state responsibilities and accountability to the rural sector after decades of neglect? The state's contesting of CAPS' assertions of autonomy, ownership, and fulfilling of state roles in the sector would have meant contesting the empirical "truthfulness" of CAPS' discourses. From one perspective, this may have been politically (and administratively) disadvantageous given rural residents' decades of experience in the sector. From another angle, denying the "truth" of these claims could have impacted the state's own legitimacy. The 2006 election of President Ortega, representing the Sandinistas' return to power at the national level, lends credence to this interpretation when considering the party's citizen participation and empowerment agenda. That is, recognizing CAPS in national legal frameworks dovetailed with national agendas seeking to reshape the state's relationship to organized sectors. State actors may have deemed the public and political value of this recognition all the more important given the crisis of legitimacy Ortega has faced, given claims of electoral fraud and undermining of representative institutions (Chamorro, Jarquín, and Bendaña 2009; Ética y Transparencia 2008; Prado 2010). When confronting conflicts over water, "the State and its legal system face the need to incorporate local fairness constructs and solve normative conflicts in order not to lose legitimacy and discursive power in the eyes of its citizens" (Boelens 2009, 315).

Discourse of Collective Problem-Solving

In the government-issued press release on Law 722, Sandinista lawmaker Agustín Jarquín declared that "CAPS demonstrate that . . . organized citizens, assuming control and the power of their community, resolve their problems"

(Ramírez 2010, n.p.). The lawmaker's claim reflected a view that CAPS themselves held about their work—in short, that they were engaging in necessarily collaborative work to ensure water access in their communities. Water committees' discourse of collective problem-solving stood in contrast to the more clearly "us vs. them" framework characterizing CAPS' assertion of water systems ownership and autonomy vis-à-vis the state.

In descriptions of their local work, CAPS expressed the importance of collaboration, including with state actors, to address day-to-day environmental challenges and water access issues. The efforts of CAPS to work across state-society, partisan, and territorial divides to problem-solve reflect an understanding of the complexities of water governance in practical terms. For example, as resource managers and service providers, CAPS have significant community-based experiences with land degradation, water contamination, and changing water availability. These experiences, and the state-society interdependencies they entail, influenced CAPS' calls for a more active state role in rural water governance.

Water committee members frequently vocalized concerns around climate change, which they framed as requiring problem-solving in collaboration with outside actors and institutions. Like land degradation and water quality, the issue of climate change transcends rural communities' environmental stewardship efforts. For example, while CAPS notice lowering water tables in their communities, they also recognize their limitations as unofficial, nonstate actors in curbing these potentially detrimental changes. In the view of some CAPS members, a lack of legality and formal political authority compromised their ability to ensure effective environmental protection and conservation. As CAPS member Carlos of Muy Muy asserted, "[Global warming] can be confronted. But that's where we have a problem of legality. If the owner upstream decides to clear land for pasture, it's his property. In that case it's only the [government] authority that can go and say, 'Look, below is a water source that serves this many people, if you deforest there and make a pasture, you're going to lower the water table, because this is a water recharge area.' We can't do that as a water committee, the authority has to do it" (interview, August 21, 2009).

Climate change was an explicit agenda item during the November 2009 National CAPS Network meeting, and resulted in a new network pronouncement. During the meeting, an NGO representative presented national and global climate change data, including the assertion on the part of the Intergovernmental Panel on Climate Change (IPCC) that globally Nicaragua was the third-most-vulnerable country to the risk factors associated with climate change, after Honduras and Bangladesh.[3] As one CAPS member present expressed: "This responsibility should touch each one of us" (November 9, 2009). Concerns articulated about environmental degradation and climate change had notable temporal dimensions. As another CAPS member articulated in the same meeting: "The water levels are lowering each day. . . . What are we going to do for the coming years? For the next generations?" The vocal recognition by CAPS of actual and impending water shortages engendered a sense of urgency for problem-solving that transcended rural communities in geographic and social terms, and, of importance, that sought to draw in state actors. In their November 5, 2009, pronouncement, CAPS expressed concern "about the effects of climate change which will impact the population, water availability especially." The substance of the pronouncement, directed to "our authorities," continued by encouraging several actions across state and society divides (see box 5).

As an additional example, CAPS' anti–water privatization stance conveyed the importance of acting collectively across urban-rural and sectoral divides because of what CAPS perceived to be the potential multiscalar implications of this policy shift affecting the state water company, ENACAL. During and in the wake of the anti-privatization social movement (2000–2007), CAPS spoke of their perceived connection to a broad community of water users who would potentially be affected by water privatization. Specifically, their discursive framing of privatization reveals their perception that this kind of policy prescription would affect people across geographic, including urban-rural, divides, and thus requires transcending these divides to confront. As a member of the Muy Muy CAPS municipal network, water committee coordinator Justo Pastor, expressed: "We saw the need to form a municipal-level water network to focus on the problematic of water privatization. Before we saw this problem as only affecting Muy Muy. But after some time we understood that not only Muy Muy was going to be affected'" (interview, August 21, 2008). Particularly for the small number of CAPS in Matagalpa who engaged in anti-privatization organizing, the threat of privatization was one of the primary reasons for forming municipal CAPS networks: "When people were talking about privatization, we formed the network," explains José Francisco of San Dionisio (interview, November 5, 2009). The multiscalar, including transcommunity, organizational strategy of CAPS reflects their understanding of this potential national policy as having implications for not only urban but also rural Nicaraguans at a national scale.

The Potable Water and Sanitation Committees networks discursively projected their stance on water privatization via several means. A set of declarations

Box 5 Potable Water and Sanitation Committee Climate Change Pronouncement (November 2009)

We, the below signers, members of the coordinating commission of the National Network of Potable Water and Sanitation Committees, in our role as municipal CAPS leaders, meeting in Managua the fifth of November 2009, worried about the effects of climate change which will impact the population, especially through water availability, encourage our authorities

1. To enforce the law to avoid deforestation, contamination of water sources, and natural resource concessions.
2. To support positions for humanity's defense and actions for mitigation and adaptation that the poorest countries [should] demand in the next [United Nations Framework Convention on Climate Change] meeting in Copenhagen.
3. To take on the National Climate Change Strategy and assign economic and human resources to it.
4. To work for food and nutritional security for the population.
5. To hasten changes to the energy matrix of the country.
6. To develop with urgency the Law for Environmental Water Services mandated by Law 620, the National Water Law.
7. To apply Law 620 through strengthening watershed management.
8. To promote sustainable agriculture, reducing agrochemical use and establishing programs for organic practices, such as no organic burns and preservation of native seeds.
9. To promote adequate treatment of trash, reducing contamination at all levels.

coming out of a September 2008 National CAPS Network meeting (published with funding from Norwegian People's Aid) voiced demands for the government to fulfill its legal imperative to prioritize water and sanitation projects at the municipal level. Additionally, CAPS asserted a demand to participate in national-level committees devoted to freshwater resources management. Each declaration concluded with the following statement: "The right to water access is a human right essential for life, the privatization of this resource is a social crime." Moreover, the National CAPS Network's collective action platform stated its objective to "Promote anti–water privatization and water resource protection resolutions in all municipalities," making explicit the notion that local government policies must work in concert with other, including CAPS' community-based, environmental protection efforts. Notably, CAPS were excluded from government consultations on the National Water Law, passed in 2007, which brought national-level anti-privatization organizing to a close; nevertheless, CAPS continued to embrace an anti-privatization stance publicly as a unifying construct of their transcommunity mobilization.

Discourse's Democratizing Effects

Within CAPS network spaces and beyond, water committees' collective discourses of water governance emphasized autonomy and ownership, state roles and responsibilities in the water sector, and collective problem-solving across state-society and partisan divides. For CAPS, being resource managers and service providers encompasses processes of identity formation emerging out of "everyday" water management practices at the grass roots. Their discourses, not surprisingly, reflect a strong sense of identity as resource managers and service providers. They also reflect empirical "realities" concerning CAPS' position within the political economy of water governance in Nicaragua. That is, as legitimate authorities in water management at the grass roots, CAPS exercise a great degree of control over water flows and local political economies that regulate water use and access. The limited contributions of state actors over time to rural water management and provision not only produced the *imperative* for rural residents to develop water management capacities; these also have engendered a keen sense of ownership over water sources and systems.

Media and state actors' adoption of language similar to that CAPS use to describe their own work is evidence of the empirical credibility of CAPS' as community-based water managers and service providers. The salience of CAPS' stories about their work and organizations also suggests that water committees and their allies benefited from a relatively blank discursive terrain in terms of Nicaragua's existing legal framework prior to the passing of the Special CAPS Law. Mobilized CAPS and their NGO and multilateral allies did not have to *reinterpret* or challenge existing characterizations of rural water management, because these scarcely existed.

This discursive landscape's reflection of a "representation by omission" in national legal frameworks reveals how the absence of conflicting characterizations may lend social movements leverage in constructing representations of themselves and their demands. Additionally, the experiences described in this chapter demonstrate how language functions as a distinct variable in social mobilization. In the Nicaraguan case, CAPS' language also had democratizing effects in terms of promoting political inclusion. When lawmakers passed the Special CAPS Law (Law 722) in May 2010, it recognized CAPS as autonomous water management organizations, with a commitment to problem-solving in their communities and who merited recognition for having carried out "the state's work" for decades. The law, reflecting a significant outcome of water committees' transcommunity and multisectoral mobilization, made CAPS *visible* in state legal frameworks. The next chapter turns to an initial assessment of Law 722 for water committees in Nicaragua.

FIVE

Assessing Water Policies
in Practice

On May 7, 2010, a meeting of twenty-six CAPS members began with a prayer: the group stood, and CAPS secretary and municipal network coordinator José Francisco read from a typed note. He expressed thanks to God for water, for food, for resources. For the water flowing through rivers that were once dry. Representatives of thirteen water committees had gathered for a municipal water committee assembly in San Dionisio, Matagalpa, in the local office space of ODESAR. José Francisco wore a bright orange, collared shirt with "ODESAR" embroidered above the right breast. A big banner hung on the wall: "Let's construct relationships of love, trust, equity, and respect. March 8th, International Women's Day." A key agenda item of the meeting— among others including water system status updates, discussion of the National CAPS Network, and a plan for organizational assessments of local CAPS—was the Special CAPS Law. Handing out pieces of flip-chart paper and copies of the yet-to-be-passed CAPS Law, ODESAR staff member Diego told the group they would read the law and "analyze it," starting with writing down notes and observations.

As the meeting progressed, participants' reflections on the law yielded critical, pointed questions. Ears perked up, and bodies leaned in, when someone started reading from Chapter 3 of the law: after registering with local government, CAPS were to seek final approval for their legalization in Managua with the state regulatory agency for urban and rural water systems, the Nicaraguan Water and Sanitation Institute (INAA). Water committee members perceived several potential risks of submitting detailed paperwork to the government: Travel is expensive—how will we get to Managua to submit our paperwork? Could we be hurt or lose autonomy by handing over our statutes and bylaws to the government? Would being in municipal and national registries mean we would have to pay taxes? If some CAPS cannot register, what will happen to them when left outside of the law? The CAPS networks were actively working in support of water committees' learning about the new law. José Francisco and Diego did their best to field questions, though the meeting revealed numerous uncertainties surrounding the law's implementation and its potential effects two weeks before its passing.

Five years later, in July 2015, I sat with a group of six water committee members from different municipalities in Matagalpa to talk to them about the effects of the CAPS Law to date. When I asked about the benefits of the new law, CAPS president and municipal network leader Esperanza replied energetically: "One, you have a legal status, and two, you can make use of the benefits the law gives you. For example, tax exonerations, or opening a bank account without a lot of red tape. . . . With legality I can do things on my own without needing to go to through the local government. I can go [directly] to an embassy or an NGO because the law gives me a legal status. For me this is important because before we weren't recognized as CAPS. We existed de facto, but not in law. . . . For me it's been very important because it gives me autonomy. . . . With legality many of us have been able to buy land in the CAPS' name. They are little things, but they've served us. Now everyone knows that CAPS are legal."

When the Special Potable Water and Sanitation Committee Law (Law 722) passed on May 19, 2010, water committees had achieved one of the primary objectives of their transcommunity mobilization: formal recognition in state legal frameworks. Law 722 recognized CAPS' work as resource managers and service providers. It even reflected CAPS' own strong assertions of autonomy as community-based organizations, referring to "respect and defense of their autonomy and independence" as one of CAPS' governing principles. Notably, as the questions on the part of CAPS in San Dionisio reflected, the content of Law 722 raised some concerns as it was nearing passage. In particular, CAPS expressed apprehension about the process outlined in the law to register with local and national government; becoming "legalized" as individual CAPS appeared to increase the potential for state actors to exercise control over water committees. Given the historical legacies and ongoing realities of water committees' work at the grass roots, these concerns were not surprising. CAPS were accustomed to the imperative of working and problem-solving independently in their communities and would seek to avoid unnecessary financial and other risks to their organizations and rural water systems.

As of 2015, almost 30 percent of CAPS nationally had been registered at both the local (i.e., municipal) and national levels of government in Nicaragua (INAA interview, July 25, 2015).[1] In the northern highlands of Matagalpa, home to San Dionisio's CAPS and Esperanza's community of El Chompipe, Muy Muy, CAPS were pursuing legalization vigorously in coordination with local governments and the Matagalpa-based NGO, ODESAR. As a local CAPS coordinator and CAPS network leader at the municipal and departmental level, Esperanza was a vocal advocate of the new law. She was well versed in the law in terms of new prerogatives, such as tax exonerations for large system purchases, afforded to CAPS. She also heralded the political benefits of the law in terms of the autonomy and recognition she experienced it as conferring. Esperanza's assertions reflected that in her experience, the tension between formal state recognition and autonomy had been reconciled.

FIGURE 24   In ODESAR's office in San Dionisio, Matagalpa, CAPS members gather before the start of a municipal assembly in May 2010.

Five years in, what were some of the initial assessments of Law 722 from the perspective of water committees, NGOs, and state officials? Much of the scholarship on recognition policies in Latin America remains critical of attempts to legalize, or "formalize," community-based water management regimes, in part related to how these have been viewed as assertions of state control over rural communities. This chapter contributes to these assessments through documenting some of the initial benefits and limitations associated with the CAPS Law in Nicaragua. The chapter's primary contention is that the law has functioned as a double-edged sword, and in some ways a blunt sword in terms of having very little impact, in relation to water committees and their work. While benefits accruing to CAPS have included financial and legal prerogatives and enhanced political recognition, there have also been limitations in terms of the challenges of legal compliance and the potential risk of some CAPS remaining "outside" of the law. Of importance, several ostensible benefits and limitations of the CAPS Law are not *fully* attributable to the new legal framework. Hence, transcending an analysis bounded by Law 722's legal provisions matters for understanding how the on-the-ground contours of water management continue to evolve.

This chapter begins with a look at how scholars have assessed policies legalizing or formalizing community-based water management in Latin America. Particular attention is drawn to an issue not addressed in the scholarship: variance across drinking water and irrigation sectors and respective legal frameworks. Next, the chapter turns to an overview of Law 722 in Nicaragua, followed by a discussion of some of the primary financial, legal, and political implications of the law several years after its passing. Ultimately, the Nicaraguan case confirms that legalization policies for community-based water management regimes, while not panaceas for many of the perennial challenges of grassroots water management, are not inherent threats to autonomy. Moreover, policies such as the CAPS Law are necessary, but not sufficient, ingredients for supporting and sustaining community-based water management into the future.

Assessing Formalization Policies in Latin America

Regionally in Latin America, a convergence of from-above and from-below dynamics has produced efforts to formalize community-based water management (CBWM) regimes through state policy. From above, the policy trend of decentralization has provided some of the impetus for national states to integrate grassroots organizations into legal frameworks (Dobbin and Sarathy 2015; Ribot and Larson 2005). In important ways, recognition and formalization policies such as the CAPS Law in Nicaragua are distinct from conventional decentralization policies that devolve national decision-making authority to subnational actors. In part, this is because they reflect integration of *preexisting* grassroots authorities into new legal frameworks. The CAPS Law and similar policies serve largely to recognize, and sometimes alter, an already existing division of labor in the sector as opposed to transfer authority from higher to lower levels of government (and governance).

The impetus for the formalization of community-based water management regimes has also come from below, as water users and managers have sought to address persistent challenges to their work at the grass roots. These may include, as in Nicaragua, issues of political marginalization and exclusion. Not all instances of political mobilization and claim making center upon demands for legal recognition as a mechanism for achieving goals. In theory, though, recognition or formalization policies can strengthen the financial, legal, and political foundations upon which nonstate actors carry out their work. And in practice, many water users' associations have viewed having a *personería jurídica* (legal status) as a potentially useful strategy toward achieving greater levels of organization, access to funding, and political clout. Formalization has been assessed, for example, as a "strategy" for garnering greater material resources from the state since it can entitle grassroots organizations "to public monies and to the right not to be excluded" (Perera, cited in Llano-Arias 2015, 79).[2] Access to public resources, titles to property, and the ability to open a bank account constitute some of the potential benefits water users' associations gain from formalizing by way of the state.

Legalization or formalization also carries risks. For instance, the great diversity of rules and norms characterizing community-based irrigation regimes in the Andes has led several scholars to caution against legalization policies (see, e.g., findings in Boelens 2009; Llano-Arias 2015; Roth, Boelens, and Zwarteveen 2015; Seemann 2016). One reason given relates to how state water policies can undermine community-based norms, values, and discourses surrounding water use and management. This can be the case when policies reflect fundamentally different ideas about water and how it should be managed, including at the most local levels. Modern water laws and the water sectors in which they emerge have been informed, for example, by neoliberalism and its emphasis on the economic valuing of resources (Van Koppen, Giordano, and Butterworth 2007; see also Boelens 2009).[3] In Nicaragua, a *monetary* valuing of water service is something that rural residents, including CAPS, have learned through a process of socialization and that aligns with the 2007 National Water Law and other policies. However, rural communities who have not worked with government actors, NGOs, or multilateral agencies on water projects may find the notion of paying for water service offensive or unreasonable given community norms and values (LaVanchy, Romano, and Taylor 2017). In such circumstances, grassroots water managers may resist what they perceive as top-down water policies threatening their local regimes. An additional caution against recognition or formalization policies includes how new legal frameworks, and potentially new rules, might render some grassroots water users' practices—or even their organizations— illegal (Seemann 2016).

The Importance of Disaggregating Policy Assessments along Sectoral Lines

Since the majority of scholarship assessing the impacts of formalization policies focuses on community-based *irrigation* regimes, there is a need to consider what may be different about these policies when applied to drinking water regimes. This is in part because formalization or legalization policies appear to vary along sectoral lines in terms of content and outcomes (see table 3). Most analyses of community-based irrigation water management in the Andes have documented the impacts of legislation that recognizes specific rights to water sources and regulates water use—including allocation. Laws codifying rights to water sources or certain quantities of water, such as the National Water Law of 1969 in Peru, are *qualitatively different* from laws such as the CAPS Law in Nicaragua. The CAPS Law did not seek to regulate or alter water use and distribution. Rather, the law constituted primarily a form of political recognition of existing organizations for managing drinking water in rural areas of the country. This is just one example of how state policies integrating water users' associations into legal frameworks may differ along sectoral lines (e.g., drinking/ irrigation) and thus will likely produce varied assessments in terms of impacts.

The divergent histories of community-based drinking water and irrigation water management, respectively, help to explain why legal frameworks have evolved differently in substantive terms. For one, small-scale drinking water systems in rural areas in Latin America have been the result of relatively recent international and domestic investment patterns. In contrast, the origins of some irrigation systems trace back centuries, with many groups of users depending upon local *usos y costumbres* (customary practices).[4] Moreover, irrigation systems in Latin America have been heavily influenced by national states: irrigation water management has been fundamentally tied to state policy and regulation because of its relevance to national political economies of development. Colonial-era bestowing of recognition and "rights" on local users have been documented, for example, as water grabs *from* indigenous communities in order to recognize and confer rights *upon* private water owners and users in order to advance national economic development. One result of states' historical and modern-day role in shaping irrigation regimes through policy is that modern-day irrigation water users—simultaneously agricultural producers—are very diverse in terms of size, wealth, and political power. It is not surprising that we see a critical bent in the literature pertaining to community-based irrigators' associations given marked disparities in terms of who benefits and who loses from recognition and legalization policies.

Rural drinking water regimes, in contrast, do not share this historical relationship to industry or state- and private-sector visions of regional economic development. Instead, community-based drinking water regimes emerged much more recently as a result of international and domestic attention to water as a part of broader public health and human rights concerns. Because of these and other differences, the practical and symbolic implications of state formalization or recognition policies have the potential to diverge along sectoral lines.[5] Drinking water is in many ways unique from not only irrigation but also from other basic services. For instance, many states have a constitutional provision referencing the state's role in facilitating access to water; moreover, a fundamental distinction with relevance for shaping and assessing formalization or recognition policies is that "everyone" needs access to drinking water. This fact undergirds global frameworks specifying water as a human right, and it is one of the reasons many countries have seen vibrant opposition to water privatization when it has threatened the costs of drinking water and access to water for domestic use. Access to irrigation water is similarly essential for everyone in terms of local, regional, and global food production and consumption. However, when considering irrigation water management, it is possible to see that there are *certain* water users, in some cases, entire communities of users, for whom irrigation access facilitates productive work in a for-profit sector. This distinction is not to imply that irrigation water has lesser importance;[6] rather, it is to recognize that

TABLE 3 Community–Based Water Management: Comparing Irrigation and Drinking Water Regimes[a]

	Irrigation	Drinking and Domestic Use
Historical origins	• In Andean region, some systems are pre–Inca Empire. • Primarily self-organizing, but some evidence of a transition from state-run to farmer-managed systems in the 1980s.	• Most have emerged since the late 1970s with a significant funding role of NGOs and international development organizations. • Small minority self-organized and funded.
Community-based rules, norms, and rights	• Locally developed by users. • Locally grounded regimes that resemble common property regimes (Ostrom 1990).	• Locally developed by users, often in collaboration with NGOs or other funding agencies. • Locally grounded regimes that resemble common property regimes (Ostrom 1990).
Relationship to state legal frameworks	• State policies reflect government regulation of irrigation in support of agricultural sectors and national production. • Integration into legal frameworks may be demanded from below, as in Bolivia. • Integration into state legal frameworks has also been imposed from above, as in Peru. • Water users and managers may play role in shaping policy frameworks.	• State policies reflect government responsibility for drinking-water access. • Variation in regard to degree of legal recognition, for example, "legalized" in Costa Rica, Nicaragua, Honduras, and "unofficial" in Chile and Guatemala.[b] • Integration into legal frameworks demanded from below. • Water users and managers may play role in shaping policy frameworks.
Content/intent of legalization and/or recognition policies	• Delineation of rights to water sources and amounts of water. • Recognition of water users' associations, including local *usos y costumbres*. • Improved water security. • State control over water resources and their allocation.	• Legal backing to water users' associations. • Political recognition of water users' association fulfillment of "state-like" drinking water service provision roles.

Sources: Boelens 2009; Dobbin and Sarathy 2015; FANCA 2006; Hoogesteger 2013; Ostrom 1990; Perreault 2008; Romano 2012; Roth, Boelens, and Zwarteveen 2015; Schouten and Moriarty 2003; Seemann 2016; Van Koppen, Giordano, and Butterworth 2007.

[a]This table seeks to distinguish between water systems and respective community-based regimes in terms of their primary *intended* use. The table thus overlooks the ways in which water sources and systems often have overlapping uses in practice.

[b]This unofficial status is akin to what CAPS in Nicaragua experienced prior to the passing of the CAPS Law.

the political economies of different sectors motivate and require different legal frameworks toward achieving the most equitable and just outcomes.

The Special CAPS Law (Law 722)

Prior to Law 722's passing, water committees in Nicaragua had pinned their hopes to its ability to constitute a political and legal tool for their organizations and respective water management and service provision responsibilities. Not only did water committees vigorously pursue legal and political recognition, but, owing to their working relationship with various domestic and international allies, they also played a key role in shaping the CAPS Law's content.

What did the Special CAPS Law purport to do? In broad strokes, Law 722 assigned official rights and responsibilities to CAPS, as well as outlined specific roles and responsibilities of state actors in relation to CAPS and rural communities (see box 6). Similar to the Costa Rican ASADAS' "formal delegation agreement with the state" (Dobbin and Sarathy 2015, 391), Law 722 officially delegated water management and service provision in the country's rural areas to CAPS. The law also presented a path for legalization for individual CAPS via a process of registering with local and national government. This two-step process requires CAPS, first, to present their charter, bylaws, and regulations to the local government in order to obtain a Certificate of Municipal Registry. Second, CAPS seek inscription with the Central Registry of Water and Sanitation Service Providers managed by INAA in Managua through presenting the above documents. Successfully adhering to this process affords CAPS a "Certificate of Registration" as evidence of their legal status as an individual water committee (Chapter IV, Article 11).[7]

The law also elaborated specific roles and responsibilities of state actors in relation to CAPS and rural communities. In so doing, the law reflected an "institutional remapping granting new roles to old actors" (Novo and Garrido 2010, v). For example, the law established that "it's an obligation of the State to guarantee and promote [CAPS'] advancement and development"—the first delineation of the Nicaraguan state's responsibilities to rural water committees within legal frameworks. Additionally, Article 12 of the law's regulations established that water committees are subject to regulation by the Nicaraguan Water and Sanitation Institute (INAA)—the state agency charged with implementing the CAPS Law. Since INAA had been the state regulatory agency for the urban and rural water sectors since its creation in 1979, this was a preexisting role.

Box 6 Potable Water and Sanitation Committee Roles, Prerogatives, and Obligations Outlined in Law 722

Chapter 5, Article 15: Powers and authority

a. To acquire goods necessary for the construction, rehabilitation, expansion, improvement, conservation, development, and maintenance of potable water systems.

b. To rehabilitate, maintain, and expand works and necessary services for the operation and maintenance of potable water systems.

c. To prevent and control water contamination localized within the municipality where the CAPS is located.

d. To guarantee potable water distribution to communities in line with technical service capacities and sanitation norms.

e. To adequately manage and administer funds resulting from water distribution tariffs, entailing use of these solely for water service administration and system maintenance.

f. To sign collaborative agreements with respective municipalities or other state or nonstate, national or international, entities for the elaboration, development, financing, and execution of potable water and sanitation projects.

g. To arrange with the respective authorities the services, assistance, and equipment needed for better development of CAPS' activities.

h. To promote and participate in programs of formation and capacity building for CAPS members and leaders in the areas of organization, technical training, and others which support community-level problem-solving.

i. To partner with other legal entities in a way that does not compromise or transfer CAPS' benefits, privileges, and exemptions.

j. To partner with other CAPS for service provision to communities within one or more municipal territories.

Chapter 5, Article 17: Functions and obligations

a. To comply with the norms and regulations of the Nicaraguan Water and Sanitation Institute (INAA) pertaining to the administration, operation, and maintenance of rural aqueducts.

b. To convene meetings with community members to address issues relevant to the water system.

c. To strive for strong service functioning, executing work as needed for service conservation and betterment, with INAA's supervision.

(*continued*)

Box 6 (*continued*)

d. To authorize or suspend in-home services in accordance with the CAPS'
    regulations.
e. To collect and administer funds resulting from water service tariffs in addition
    to any additional contributions (e.g., from raffles and social events) that result
    from efforts to increase the CAPS' resources.
f. To collaborate with INAA, mayors, and the Health Ministry [MINSA] in
    campaigns for promoting community sanitation relative to water usage.
g. To promote adequate water system usage, controlling periodically for water loss
    and improper use (e.g., irrigation) that is not authorized by INAA.
h. To guard and protect the water sources feeding into the system, avoiding their
    contamination and helping to protect the micro-watersheds serving as water
    sources.
i. To contract personnel services as needed for the operation and maintenance of
    the community's water system.
j. To keep records of the CAPS' functioning in accordance with the community's
    regulations, statutes, and norms.
k. To comply with water quality norms established by INAA and the Health
    Ministry.

Source: *Ley Especial de Comités de Agua Potable y
Saneamiento*, Chapter V, Articles 15 and 17.

However, it is one that had been implemented unevenly across communities
and time in Nicaragua given limited human and financial capacities. Of importance, the pathway to legalization for individual CAPS established by Law 722
constitutes one of the most significant ways that state actors and institutions
would become immediately drawn into CAPS' own attempts to implement the
new law: the law charged not only the national-level agency, INAA, but also
local governments, with creating registries of legalized CAPS.

Prerogatives and Benefits of Law 722

What are the main prerogatives and benefits conferred by the CAPS Law,
according to CAPS, NGOs, and state officials? One of the primary benefits of

the law assured to CAPS are new financial prerogatives: CAPS registered with the government are eligible for exemptions from national and local taxes (Art. 22), a differentiated energy tariff for CAPS managing wells with electric pumps (Art. 25), and an exemption from paying the water extraction tax (Art. 25). There is evidence of these benefits being received in practice. The Nicaraguan Institute of Aqueducts and Sanitation's Department of Rural Aqueducts reported that CAPS with electric pumps have been paying 3–5 percent less, on average, than they would have otherwise for the costs associated with operating their systems (interview, July 30 2015). Committees in Sébaco reported that the community of El Caracol was in the process of constructing a water system that would use an electric pump: "If their bill came to 4,000 córdobas [US$160] they would only have to pay half of that" (interview, July 17, 2015). Moreover, as CAPS member Esperanza emphasized, achieving legal status via Law 722 facilitates the opening of a bank account, helping to resolve issues of theft and financial mismanagement at the community level. While the law indicates CAPS must *rendir cuentas* (keep account) of their spending activities, opening a bank account in a CAPS name appears to be a financial benefit not directly cited in the law yet facilitated by obtaining an official legal status. Similarly, purchasing land as a water committee and in a CAPS' name is an additional prerogative of having a legal status as organizations.

Legalization, additionally, provides potentially greater access to outside financial and technical support for CAPS and water system management. As the INAA lawyer managing the national CAPS registry suggested, it is "better" for CAPS to register with the government because of the possibility of receiving external funding in the future (interview, July 25, 2015). The director of INAA's new Department of Rural Aqueducts, Gilberto, expressed that "CAPS need to be legalized to receive technical assistance" or, minimally, to be prioritized by local government for assistance (interview, June 13, 2014). This interpretation of the law was shared by the Matagalpa local government's director of environment (interview, June 10, 2014). If this particular benefit of the law plays out, it would confirm findings of other studies in Latin America that legalizing in accordance with state policy can be beneficial in terms of eligibility for and receipt of state funding for water projects.

In practice, Law 722 reveals an intertwining of both practical and symbolic political and legal benefits for CAPS. Symbolically, the new law was an important recognition that rural residents had "taken on the responsibilities of the state for years," as asserted by CAPS member Delia (interview, July 14, 2010). In

FIGURE 25   A San Juan del Río Coco, Madriz, local government staff member (left) in the Nicaraguan Water and Sanitation Institute (INAA) office in Managua in July 2015, who had arrived to submit paperwork for the legalization of several water committees in his municipality. He stood next to the director of the newly established Department of Rural Aqueducts, Gilberto, who has worked with INAA since the 1980s in Nicaragua.

more practical terms, water committee members referenced being "invited" to meetings by public officials, as well as perceptions of a heightened awareness of their rural water management organizations, which served to ease interactions with governmental authorities. As a result of the law, CAPS have both garnered greater attention from state officials and become empowered to act autonomously in taking proactive steps to support water management and service provision. Referencing a newfound political power, Esperanza asserted: "The judge in Muy Muy trembles when we arrive" (interview, July 28, 2015). Backed by legalization documents and following a formal denunciation, her CAPS prompted a ruling to fine a landowner for illegal deforestation around the community's water source. Codifying CAPS' "autonomy and independence" via legal backing to registered CAPS has affected their members' ability and willingness to wield new political power as water managers and service providers.

   An interesting caveat to positive assessments of the CAPS Law is that not all touted benefits should be understood solely as the result of the new law. For example, water committees' history in Nicaragua demonstrates that legalization—including formal integration into state legal frameworks—is not a necessary condition for CAPS to be empowered to fulfill much of their day-to-day work. For highly functioning CAPS (for example, those discussed in chapter 2), becoming legalized via Law 722 serves merely to reinforce many water committees' organic empowerment—including the financial, technical, organizational, and other skills cultivated at the grass roots over time in the absence of official legal status. As the president of the National CAPS Network, Andrés, explained in regard to his CAPS in Tipitapa, Managua: "If you think about it, Law 722 was passed just about five years ago and we've been working without the law, without the legal framework, for thirty-five years, that now gives us much more backing. . . . Now we have rights given to us by Law 722, and that is something good" (interview, July 31, 2015). It matters that CAPS attribute benefits such as legal backing and new financial and political prerogatives to Law 722—and, many water committees have the potential to be strengthened as organizations as a result. It must also be recognized, however, that much of CAPS' work reflected a high degree of capacities as empowered and autonomous water managers and service providers prior to their recognition in formal legal terms.

What about CAPS who have not—and will not—register with the government? Although national officials implied that CAPS who failed to register with local and national government would not be eligible or prioritized for the same direct support as would legalized water committees, there was no evidence to substantiate this claim. In part, this relates to an active working relationship between and among CAPS, NGOs, multilateral agencies, and government actors as the law is being implemented. Although limited to four Managua-based staff devoted to rural areas, INAA staff have conducted trainings at the subnational level for CAPS and local government officials. The funding for conducting trainings has come from multilateral agencies including the UN International Emergency Children's Fund (UNICEF) and the Swiss Agency for Development and Cooperation (COSUDE). Moreover, within Matagalpa, the local government's environment division was actively working with ODE-SAR staff and CAPS leaders to generate awareness of Law 722 and to support CAPS' legalization in the department. Within the environment division, local government official Juana—as part of a seven-member team—was charged with working with rural communities to assist with the registration process. Juana explained that her office helps CAPS with setting up email accounts and making CAPS' financial declarations of income online and in person with the General Revenue Management Office (interview, June 10, 2014). In some cases, local government officials have taken on the work of physically submitting individual CAPS' paperwork to INAA's office in Managua given the financial constraints on rural residents' mobility.

Rather than *excluding* some CAPS from outside assistance, the CAPS Law appears to be drawing CAPS and government actors together in new ways to support water committees. Seeking to implement the CAPS Law is serving to grow state actors' involvement in the sector in service to CAPS and rural communities. For example, the law successfully mandated the creation of the Department of Rural Aqueducts within INAA, which entailed the hiring of new staff and devoting the work of a lawyer to manage a new CAPS registry at the national level. The Nicaraguan Water and Sanitation Institute, lacking regional delegations at the subnational level, also adopted a strategy of coordination with local environmental departments and regional delegations of the National Water Authority (ANA)—a new state institution mandated by the National Water Law. The institutional expansion and new state-society synergy in the water sector prompted by the CAPS Law are, in important ways, "mobilizing the state" toward greater involvement in the water and sanitation sector and in the process improving "the state's ability to serve the public interest" (Abers and Keck 2009, 294). As was asserted in 2010 by the director of the Department of Rural Aqueducts, Gilberto: "this law is going to strengthen state institutions given that it promotes participation and coordination in order to help build CAPS' capacities for administration, sustainability, service operation, water quality control, [and] environmental care and protection" (interview, June 2, 2010). Through organizational support to CAPS and assistance with legalization, the law has the potential to move the state closer to fulfilling its constitutional provision "to promote, facilitate and regulate" water service nationally.

Drawbacks and Limitations of Law 722

The generalized and important political benefits of the law aside, the financial benefits of the CAPS Law are not always easily obtained nor have they thus far made significant impacts on the "everyday" work of water committees who have legalized. Furthermore, a key limitation of the law moving forward is state actors' capacity and, in cases, willingness, to implement the law. This has and will affect the extent to which Law 722 will have significant or discernable impact at a national scale for grassroots water management and service provision.

In cases of legalized CAPS, there is some evidence that decreases in CAPS' financial obligations have been minimal or nonexistent. Sales tax exemptions apply to large, and hence infrequent, material purchases at specific businesses only, and energy tariff reductions mirror those given to for-profit, large-scale industries such as rice farming. As the 2015 president of the National CAPS Network, Andrés of Tipitapa, declared: "The [state revenue agency] treats us like a private company and doesn't give us preferential treatment like the CAPS we are" (interview, July 31, 2015). In short, several provisions of the law do not reflect tailoring to CAPS' financial needs and circumstances as grassroots, small-scale, and "not-for-profit" water service providers.

One financial provision mentioned across interviews as particularly burdensome for CAPS is Law 722's requirement of declaring any income to the government's revenue agency. Local government official Juana explained that many CAPS do not have access to the Internet in their communities to ease monthly reporting. She elaborated, "These communities are so simple that they don't have a computer, neither do they know how to use one; there are people that don't even know how to read" (interview, June 10, 2014). Staff from ODE-SAR echoed this fact (interview, July 28, 2015). Limited financial resources, in addition to low levels of education, can affect compliance with the law and have the potential to result in CAPS receiving government fines. One CAPS in Sébaco even hired an accountant from the city of Matagalpa to support its income declaration. In Marbelly's words,

> The only problem that we have is with the [General Revenue Management Office]. The law says that CAPS can look for an accountant to work for the committee. In our case, we as treasurers [of our CAPS] have capacities in our community work. But to get online and access the online portal is really difficult for us, so we did have to look for an accountant. . . . She's from Matagalpa, an accountant referred by [Matagalpa-based] ADEMNORTE, the NGO that rehabilitated our system in 2006. . . . She does the work for us because we couldn't. . . . It's one of the worst aspects of the law. . . . The rules [of the General Revenue Management Office] didn't change to be easier for CAPS. (interview, July 17, 2015)

Marbelly's CAPS reported paying the accountant almost US$50 a month, including her transportation, to help the community fulfill this provision of the CAPS Law.

In addition to inadequate tailoring of income reporting requirements for water committees, a major financial drawback of the CAPS Law is its mandate that CAPS will be self-sufficient in economic terms. The law asserts that water committees "will obtain their principal income from the payment of tariffs or fixed fees for water consumption" (regulations article 23). CAPS might find ways to leverage their legality to receive new financial resources; however, this provision of the law serves to reproduce the tenuous financial circumstances of many CAPS. For example, when flooding destroyed Delia's Molino Sur, Sébaco, system in 2010, roughly US$17,500 was need for repairs. This is one example of how environmental change can swiftly and powerfully increase the costs of water management and provision—to prohibitive levels even for the most effective and well-functioning CAPS. With monthly fees for water service ranging from $0.23 and $2.85 per household, the effects of extreme storms and flooding on drinking water systems can make their maintenance prohibitively expensive for rural communities.

In political terms, greater recognition and attention from state actors can prove a double-edged sword. While CAPS from Muy Muy and San Ramón spoke of productive working relationships with government officials, CAPS in Sébaco criticized what they perceived to be a creeping in of partisan politicization in their municipality. As CAPS member Delia described the changing political landscape: before the law, "no one knew that we existed in our communities." When her CAPS sought their municipal certificate with the Sébaco local government, they were initially turned away; a local government official said that their request was not valid because no one from the government office had attended the recent community assembly where new CAPS members were elected.

Implicitly raised across interviews is the question of how obtainable legalization is for individual CAPS. Not all CAPS perceive an easy path to legalization, given financial and other constraints. The feasibility of legalization matters, among other reasons, because completing the formal registration process is a prerequisite for tax exemptions and other financial benefits outlined in the law. Like in Sébaco, Matagalpa, CAPS in other regions have encountered political barriers to registering their organizations: CAPS members in the community of Gigante, Tola, in the department of Rivas, reported that the local government had not wanted to spend the resources necessary to help the CAPS complete its registration with INAA in the capital (interview, May 3, 2014). In June 2010, soon after Law 722's passing, an ODESAR staff member in Matagalpa commented that "not all CAPS are going to achieve legal status, regardless of the fact that the law is approved" (interview, June 21, 2010). He attributed the potential failure of some CAPS to legalize to the financial costs of travel for filing paperwork with government. Nevertheless, potential political barriers remain relevant too.

Although 70 percent of CAPS nationally had not achieved a legal status as organizations as of 2015, for some not legalizing is by choice. While no interviewees expressed this sentiment personally, many referenced a secondhand understanding of why some water committees are shying away from the process. These included a mistrust of state institutions, fear of water privatization, fear of private companies or state actors taking over water committees, and fear of higher water prices.[8] According to an ODESAR staff member, a rumor had circulated in Matagalpa after the law's passing that "legalized water committees were going to fall into the government's hands and lose their autonomy" (interview, July 28, 2015). Such rumors have the potential to affect whether or not CAPS will seek to register with the government.

Government actors' capacity and political will to implement the law also matter for assessing *access* to legalization for individual CAPS. Nicaraguans often express that their country "has good laws." But, laws often fail to be implemented. An experience with the National Water Law proves illustrative in this respect. Despite Law 620's mandate that water sources be declared for "public utility" in order to provide water access for residents (Art. 19), local governments risk alienating private property owners if they follow through with this provision. In one rather infamous unfolding of events, the president of the state water company, ENACAL, appointed by President Ortega, refused to cede access to a stream on her property in accordance with Law 620 so local residents could use the water source for a new gravity-fed system and source of drinking water. This case was also particularly ironic since the landowner was, before her appointment within ENACAL, the director of the National Consumers' Defense Network and a leader in the 2000–2007 anti–water privatization social movement in Nicaragua. Residents of the community of La Chocolata, San Ramón, worked with a local NGO, ADEMNORTE, to measure the water source on Herrera's property and to coordinate a protest at the mayor's office in San Ramón and at the departmental government office in Matagalpa. In the end, the San Ramón mayor failed to work out an agreement with Herrera.

Like the National Water Law (Law 620), Law 722 promotes greater engagement of the state in the water sector in ways that could develop state capacity (and, in the best-case scenario, political will) over time. Water committees, NGOs, and multilateral agencies in the sector were highly critical of the insufficient public funding allocated to implementing Law 620. Politics also slowed the law's effective implementation. For example, the law mandated the creation of ANA, the National Water Authority, as the highest state institutional authority in the water sector, but disagreements among national lawmakers regarding who would head the new body contributed to a lag time of three years before the government appointed someone to direct the new institution, in June 2010.

Issues pertaining to state knowledge and capacities, financial resources, and politics have the potential to impact negatively the implementation of Law 722 as well. The law gives both INAA and local governments roles in the creation of water committee registries at the national and municipal levels, respectively. These registries require both financial and human resources for creation and maintenance. Since working with one staff member devoted to rural areas prior to the law's passing, INAA has grown its personnel capacities to four since the CAPS Law passed. Yet, it is in ways shocking that the national agency charged with regulating rural water systems and implementing the CAPS Law has such a small number of staff devoted to rural areas to attend a population of over 2.5 million (40 percent of the total population of Nicaragua). To draw a contrast: the local government in Matagalpa has a seven-person environment team, including a staff person devoted to CAPS, just for the region. The director of the Department of Rural Aqueducts also reported that funds to carry out their national level work remain insufficient, as they were prior to the CAPS Law.

The ability of local governments to fulfill provisions of the CAPS Law— including registry creation—will be uneven across municipalities. In part, this will arise from insufficient local resources to create and maintain a registry of CAPS.[9] There are knowledge gaps as well. Some local government offices, including those of decentralized state agencies, have been slow to learn about the law in relation to CAPS' eagerness to seek legalization. The knowledge gap was evident in the experience CAPS in Matagalpa had when visiting the General Revenue Management Office for the first time: government staff did not know who or what a CAPS was and were also completely unaware that there was a new law to which they were integral. Matagalpa local government official Juana expressed that the General Revenue Management Office "told us that they didn't understand the law. They didn't understand 'Potable Water Committees'" (interview, June 10, 2014). Urban-based state actors' limited familiarity with CAPS as organizations directly affected, at least early on,

Law 722's implementation. Another perennial issue affecting state knowledge and capacities at the local level is frequent staff turnover. Taken together, these kinds of issues and dysfunctions will continue to have tangible implications for implementation of the CAPS Law.

For some legalized CAPS, the law is proving to be a "blunt sword" in that it is having little impact. In Sébaco, CAPS reported that aside from being exempt from certain taxes, similar to a legal provision applied to agricultural cooperatives in Nicaragua, their organizations and work had not been affected greatly by the CAPS Law (interview, July 15, 2015). The CAPS Law will also, likely, be rendered a blunt sword in terms of its direct impacts on water committees' work for CAPS who will not register (i.e., become legalized) on an individual basis. For the immediate term, the CAPS Law does nothing to fundamentally change CAPS' independent water management and service provision at the grass roots. Future potential inequities between legalized and nonlegalized CAPS merit study. However, the CAPS Law as a recognition policy may do little to alter, either positively or negatively, the "everyday" water management and service provision in many rural communities across Nicaragua.

The law also has notable *gaps*. For example, Law 722 passed without a provision pertaining to the legalization of water sources in relation to the legalized water committees that use them, leaving water source rights tenuous for CAPS and the rural communities they serve. Additionally, the law does not address climate change, despite the ways this accelerating phenomenon will continue to compound preexisting problems in Nicaragua related to water quality and seasonal water quantity variations, and hence potable water access and management.[10] Furthermore, in asserting that CAPS are to be self-sustaining financially, the law reflects a significant gap in terms of not assuring a kind of government fiscal transfer to their organizations—much like would be expected with conventional decentralized service provision.

Following from some of the law's perceived shortcomings, CAPS, NGOs, and national and subnational government actors began discussing potential legal reforms to Law 722 soon after its passing. Reforms that would ease the reporting and accounting requirements via the General Revenue Management Office emerged as salient across interviews. The committees have also indicated interest in reforms that would address issues such as conflict mediation and property rights over water sources, not currently addressed in the law, at the local level. As José Francisco asserted in a June 2014 regional CAPS leaders' meeting in Matagalpa: "the law doesn't protect CAPS" when it comes to resolving local water-related conflicts (June 11, 2014). In the meeting, CAPS voiced that in some cases it is best not to engage state officials—for example, police officers—in local level conflicts because they do not know or understand community dynamics in the way that CAPS, as members of a community, do. Because conflict mediation is a blind spot in Law 722, the law leaves questions pertaining to local-level conflicts around, for example, water sources and access, inadequately addressed.

The Benefits and Limits of Legalization

Five years after its passing, the CAPS Law was generating tangible and symbolic benefits as well as challenges to water committees in Nicaragua. Implementation of the CAPS Law did not appear, as some rural residents feared, to be compromising CAPS' independence as community organizations. Yet, because the CAPS Law means water committees now *derived* some of their legitimacy directly from the state, the new law did not fully resolve the basic tension that characterized CAPS' demands as they mobilized—that is, the tension between desiring autonomy *and* state recognition. Moreover, from the perspective of CAPS avoiding legalization out of fear of greater state control, a recognition policy such as the CAPS Law will continue to be perceived as a threat to local autonomy and water systems. However, rather than compromising CAPS' independence as organizations, the evidence to date points to how the law has served as a formal confirmation of CAPS' asserted autonomy and ownership in rural water management.

Public policies recognizing nonstate freshwater managers must be a part of addressing issues of local water use, access, and conservation. In fact, these policies are necessary ingredients of a context that will politically and financially support and sustain grassroots nonstate water managers. Drinking water management does not lend itself to *complete* decentralization to residents in part because of the financial resources and, in some respects, technical expertise required (see also Dobbin and Sarathy 2015). In this sense, it is beneficial that the CAPS Law calls on state actors to extend greater assistance to rural communities and that the law has produced some institutional growth to facilitate these ends.

Although necessary in terms of providing a legal backing to grassroots organizations and opening pathways that ease seeking outside resources, policies such as the CAPS Law are not *sufficient* ingredients for supporting and sustaining community-based water management into the future. This in part has to do with the law in substantive terms, as resolving complex issues of water use, access, and conservation are unlikely to be found in legal frameworks that fundamentally constitute a *recognition* of certain actors in water governance. Adequate support of community-based water management and service provision requires not only formal recognition but also a much more comprehensive set of actions and policies. Owing to their experience and expertise, grassroots water managers and service providers should be engaged in national debates and policy processes pertaining to freshwater and environmental governance. The concluding chapter turns to a discussion of this point in addition to other takeaways from this book.

Conclusion

Confronting and Creating Change from the Grass Roots

Across diverse political regimes since the 1970s, Potable Water and Sanitation Committees (CAPS) in Nicaragua have endeavored to secure potable water access to their neighbors in rural and semirural areas of the country. Since some of the first rural water systems were constructed with international assistance during the Somoza era, CAPS have grown to work at an impressive scale: CAPS-managed water systems ensure water for drinking and domestic use to over one million residents across the country, about one-sixth of the country's population.

Despite the large scale at which they worked, CAPS were not visible as a collective political actor in anti–water privatization policy consultations and debates in the early 2000s. Water committees' political invisibility in national water politics mirrored their marginalization in legal frameworks, since for decades, CAPS had operated below the radar of formal policies. "Somos de hecho, no de derecho" (We're de facto, not de jure) became a defining refrain of water committee members reflecting upon their neglect as water managers and service providers. When anti–water privatization organizing propelled the designing and 2007 passage of the National Water Law, it quelled the primarily urban-based social movement. Yet, the law reproduced the status quo of omitting CAPS as resource managers and service providers from legal frameworks, including those explicitly for freshwater management. More troubling to CAPS was the law's insinuation that rural water projects fell under the domain of the state water company, ENACAL—an institution with little relevance for CAPS' everyday community-based work.

From the grass roots, CAPS confronted what they perceived to be threats to their organizations and work: water privatization and potential co-optation of their organizations and water systems. From the start of their transcommunity organizing in 2005, CAPS embraced a dual and paradoxical objective. This included demanding recognition and greater resources from the state and protecting the autonomy of their organizations and water systems. The committees were also seeking to *create* change from the grass roots. They mobilized not only to contest their political exclusion and legal marginalization but also to rectify their exclusion through forming multiscalar advocacy networks and gaining legal recognition. The 2010 Special CAPS Law (Law 722) constituted evidence that state actors deemed CAPS as meriting a legal backing. Moreover, it reflected acknowledgment that CAPS existed. As CAPS member and network leader José Francisco asserted, "We've done a job that corresponds to the state—to ENACAL and INAA. . . . Now the state knows that we exist" (Managua, May 7, 2010).

This book undertook, first, to examine how rural water committees became politically activated in Nicaragua. Second, it addressed the question: *What factors explained CAPS' successful transcommunity mobilization to achieve a national collective presence and, ultimately, legal recognition from the state?* In so doing, the book traced the process of how water committees in Nicaragua transcended their rural localities and roles as water managers and service providers to engage in fundamentally new forms of political activism and advocacy vis-à-vis the state. The book documented three interconnected factors that proved fundamental to water committees' transformation from engaging in local resource management to collective political activism. These include CAPS' (1) de facto empowerment as rural water managers and service providers and their resulting legitimate authority in the water sector, (2) alliances with domestic and international organizations, and (3) collective discourses that describe and outwardly project their locally grounded understanding of water governance.

The remainder of this concluding chapter begins with a section summarizing the main argument, findings, and theoretical contributions pertaining to chapters 2–4, the chapters of the book addressing the main research question. The second part of the conclusion turns to discussion of several practical and policy implications of CAPS' story of resource management and political activism. In particular, I draw attention to the challenges of rural water management and service provision in the Global South, the increasingly critical intersection between water and climate change, and the important role of activism for promoting more equitable and sustainable water governance.

Summary of Arguments and Contributions to Literature

Three interconnected factors proved crucial to explaining CAPS' process of political activation, mobilization, and ultimate achievement of legal recognition. These included (1) water committees' de facto empowerment as community-based water managers and service providers and their legitimate authority in the water sector as a result, (2) their alliances with domestic and international NGO and multilateral allies, and (3) their publicly projected discourses of water governance. At a theoretical level, this book lends new insight into how politically marginalized and impoverished social actors gain greater political inclusion, including within democratic decision-making processes.

Cultivating a Bottom-Up, "Organic" Empowerment

The Nicaraguan case confirms the importance of nonstate actors' empowerment as a precondition for resource management and service provision. Yet, this book challenges the idea that empowerment must be conferred from above to grassroots actors. The 2010 Special Law of Potable Water and Sanitation Committees (Law 722) carried significant weight in terms of constituting formal recognition of over five thousand rural water committees. However, the law was an ex post facto decentralization policy: rural residents, for decades, had engaged in water management and service provision in their communities. What explained CAPS' effectiveness in providing water access despite not being "properly empowered" in terms of their legality?

An important finding of this book is that rural water management regimes are not dependent on the state in order to be empowered to manage resources. Empowerment may be either a formally conferred or de facto access to and control over local resources. Most drinking water users' associations in Nicaragua and elsewhere in the Global South benefit from outside support for water system construction; this establishes an initial moment of empowerment in terms of taking over rural water infrastructure, but this process is usually not accompanied by communities' receipt of legal status for organizations formed to manage new infrastructure. Nevertheless, an *organic* empowerment is one that evolves at the grass roots from this initial moment of empowerment, through the day-to-day labors of resource management and service provision. In the absence of formal state delegation of water management roles and responsibilities, CAPS' work has entailed cultivating financial, organizational, and other capacities that have undergirded their maintenance and administration of water systems. In turn, CAPS' work has generated *legitimacy* vis-à-vis their neighbors (i.e., community members) who benefit from water service. Local legitimacy and expressions of authority are important social and relational dimensions of CAPS' local work that promoted state actors' perception of CAPS as legitimate authorities in the water sector once they mobilized beyond their communities.

This book accounts theoretically for CAPS' processes of empowerment and cultivation of legitimate authority through drawing together the scholarship on common property regimes and decentralized natural resource management. Common property scholars have principally focused on microlevel institutional dynamics of rule creation and change, stopping short of explaining how resource users and managers engage at higher political scales in ways that draw upon grounded experiences within common property regimes. Moreover, although the common property scholarship overlooks legitimacy relative to its emphasis on institutional design, this relational component propels and sustains community-based commons management. The organic empowerment of CAPS also requires that we consider alternative, nonstate sources of empowerment and legitimacy within studies of decentralized natural resource management. Expanding decentralization frameworks allows for granting explicit attention to how state policies and decision making overlap with unofficial, nonstate actors in resource governance, including how nonlegally sanctioned water users' associations assert their legitimate authority to promote their recognition and inclusion in legal frameworks.

Bridging and Bonding via Alliances

The transcommunity mobilization of CAPS was successful in large part because it was *multisectoral*: new CAPS networks linked grassroots, rural water managers with professional, urban-based NGO and multilateral agency staff. Water committees' relationship to these domestic and international allies was of paramount importance to the ability of CAPS as rural social actors to engage in collective action beyond the communities in which they worked and toward pursuing collective goals.

First, NGO and multilateral agency allies supported CAPS' physical mobility. In a simple but important sense, allies' financing of water committees' travel across regions created the collective encounters necessary for forming new CAPS networks at the municipal, departmental, and national levels. In network spaces, previously disconnected CAPS from across regions in Nicaragua had the opportunity to develop a collective voice and set of shared goals that would guide their activism. The second major contribution allies made to CAPS' transcommunity mobilization and pursuit of collective goals was legal and political capacity-building processes. Within CAPS network spaces, NGO allies led training on national legislation and facilitated processes wherein CAPS could articulate collective pronouncements on issues and laws affecting them (e.g., climate change and the National Water Law, respectively). Last, allies facilitated water committees' direct connection to public officials, including national lawmakers and staff at state agencies. Most important, allies arranged face-to-face meetings between CAPS and lawmakers—engagements in which CAPS' enhanced political savvy and growing legal knowledge informed their demands for legal recognition.

In conceptual and theoretical terms, the bridging social capital reflected in CAPS' relationship with allies served to generate bonding social capital, or new connections and relationships between and among "bonded" social actors. These dynamics demonstrate the importance of bridging social capital in helping rural social actors with limited financial resources overcome barriers to physical mobility that otherwise would have impeded connections across communities. Thus, in contrast to its negative characterization in the literature as impeding social mobility and connecting, bonding social capital in fact functions as a *precondition* for collection action and civic engagement at other scales. It also has the potential to interact positively with bridging social capital toward enhancing the mobility, capacities, and political efficacy of bonded social actors with limited resources.

The Role of Discourse in Shaping Politics

The conditions under which CAPS managed water at the grass roots over time not only contributed to their evolving empowerment as resource managers and service providers but also shaped the ways they *talked about* and advocated for their work and organizations beyond their communities. Three central discourses emerged out of CAPS' transcommunity mobilization. These included water committees' (1) claims to ownership over water systems and autonomy vis-à-vis the state, (2) description of their work in terms of legally prescribed state responsibilities in the water and sanitation sector, and (3) emphasis on collective problem-solving across rural-urban, state-society, and partisan divides. Akin to collective action frames in the social movement scholarship, collective discourses served as an important means of communicating about rural water governance from CAPS' unique vantage point as water managers and service providers.

The role of CAPS' discourses in their transcommunity mobilization has relevance for the social movement scholarship in three senses. First, in contrast to the scholarship's depictions of frames as highly contested, CAPS' descriptions of their work became mirrored, counterintuitively, in the policy discourse of state officials—the principal "targets" of water committees' activism. Second, though not intentionally *strategic*, CAPS were credible frame articulators and their discourses had high empirical validity because of how they reflected the "everyday," historical and contemporary, experience of water management at the grass roots. The discourses of CAPS also implicated the state as the ultimate guarantor of drinking water in law; this contributed to their instrumentality in prompting state actors to support water committees' political and policy goals. Third, lacking recognition in legal frameworks, CAPS did not have to challenge preexisting legal delineations of their organizations. This representation by omission in Nicaragua's legal frameworks unwittingly supported water committees' ability to inform the content of a new law. Being relatively unknown among urban-based state actors also contributed discursive space to grassroots actors to shape characterizations of their organizations and work in the public sphere as they mobilized.

What are the practical and policy implications of CAPS' story of grassroots water management, service provision, and transcommunity activism to achieve recognition? The following section discusses some of the implications of this book, drawing attention to the challenges of rural water management and service provision in the Global South, the increasingly critical intersection between water and climate change, and important role of activism for promoting more equitable and sustainable water governance.

The Challenge and Promise of
Rural Water Governance

In the twenty-first century, the challenges of rural water access and management are significant and growing. Deteriorating infrastructure, water contamination, and "competing" urban demands on water sources are just a few of the challenges growing more acute in national contexts of population growth and accelerating global climate change. This is one major takeaway for readers of this book: we must better understand the challenges of rural water management and the promise that it holds in terms of securing livelihoods and promoting well-being in both rural and urban populations globally.

Despite significant urbanization trends, part of the promise of attention to rural water governance is that sustainable and equitable management of water in rural areas fundamentally affects the lives and well-being of growing urban populations. For instance, much water for urban uses and residents is sourced from rivers, lakes, and aquifers located in rural areas. As urban water scarcity increases, there is potential for cities to rely increasingly on sourcing water from nonurban watersheds. *Urban* water users and uses are not the only reason for scholars, policy makers, and others to focus on *rural* water governance, however. Significant portions of the Global South countries' populations remain rural. As a result, issues of water use, access, and conservation primarily affecting rural residents merit attention notwithstanding rural-urban interconnections and interdependencies. Roughly 40 percent of Nicaraguans live in rural areas; yet, only an estimated 33 percent of rural residents have access to piped water compared to 95 percent of urban residents—a 62 percent disparity between rural and urban areas (World Health Organization and United Nations Children's Fund 2017). This inequity in terms of water access disparities reflects social and environmental injustice as limited access to water for drinking and domestic use disproportionately impacts rural sectors.

Both urban and rural areas in the Global South face serious issues of water quality and quality. However, the dispersion of rural residents and the infeasibility of economies of scale make a high number of small-scale water systems an expensive undertaking. For these reasons, among others such as insufficient political will, national and subnational governments have not undertaken large-scale water provision in rural areas. Moreover, drinking water provision arrangements in impoverished rural areas are just not profitable in contexts where residents have little to pay or, in some cases, refuse to pay. As a result, rural water delivery is difficult to privatize. The state's (and private sector's) opting out of rural water management and provision has left a "gap" that has been partially filled by NGOs and multilateral agencies that help build rural water systems infrastructure.

In the absence of other entities willing or able to do the work of day-to-day water and environmental management, some promise can be found in nonstate, community-based water managers. In Latin America alone, roughly eighty thousand community-based groups engage in the management and provision of drinking water to an estimated forty to seventy million rural and semirural residents. In Central America, CAPS are part of a regional phenomenon of an estimated twenty-four thousand water committees who provide water service to a quarter of the isthmus's population. The committees and their counterparts thus fulfill the "state-like" and largely state-assigned role of water management and service provision in their communities. As water committees in Nicaragua attest, this work is often done with little outside material, organizational, or moral support.

Even though many rural water users' associations carry out their work largely independent of outside support or resources, this approach is increasingly less viable. For one, all small-scale water systems at some point need major over-hauls or replacement—an expensive and sometimes highly technical undertak-ing. Many water systems built in the 1980s and 1990s are reaching the end of their *vida útil* (useful life). Additionally, environmental change is compounding pressures on grassroots actors tasked with managing water resources. Even as rural water users' associations in Latin America are seeking to increase their internal and outward capacities as organizations, global environmental change is working in the "opposite" direction in terms of how it undermines sustainable water use and management. Accelerating climate change is the Achilles heel of sustainable water management, both urban and rural.

A second takeaway from this book is that laws can and should play a role in supporting and bolstering grassroots water managers and service providers as part of an overall strategy to improve rural water governance. Laws are an important component of water *governance*—that is, the multiscalar realm of people, institutions, and policies that make and enact decisions about water, and, consequently, shape the distribution of benefits and harms. Laws, of course, are not panaceas for many of the everyday water management issues users' asso-ciations face. In Nicaragua, even the most successful water committees will continue to confront issues the CAPS Law may not be effective in mediating, such as intra- or intercommunity conflicts around water sources. And to reiterate, the CAPS Law does not address nor even reference climate change in its delineation of CAPS' work despite this phenomenon's negative impacts on water quality and quantity.

Moreover, laws are often implemented unevenly and have uneven effects across communities and regions. The distribution of risks and benefits results not only from where and how authorities, both official and "unofficial," implement the law but also from how preexisting factors filter the effects of the law. Geographic, financial, socioorganizational, and other axes of variation will mediate what impacts the law will have in a given context—including whether or not some water committees will obtain or even seek "legalization." In practice, a legal benefit to one water user may be a disadvantage to another. Laws can thus be highly fraught in terms of their substance on paper and their varied, including contradictory, effects. Nevertheless, policy makers can strive to get the policies "right," through reforming existing laws or developing new ones.

Despite the caveats discussed above and in the previous chapter, policies recognizing rural water users and managers are a necessary, albeit insufficient, ingredient to more equitable and sustainable rural water governance. Of course, it is paradoxical to assert, as this book has, that nonstate water users and managers want state recognition while at the same time wanting to preserve their independent and nonstate character. Indeed, CAPS and other water users' associations in Latin America fiercely defend their work while simultaneously engaging the state as a potential source of resources and protection. Residents are highly invested in their community-based work and do not want to cede it to other actors, a fact that complicates neoliberal narratives of state retrenchment and individual responsibility. That is, not only were national states never doing this work to begin with, but also it would be misguided to see rural residents as manipulated into being the owners and managers of their potable water systems.

Facing perceived threats such as water privatization and the impacts of top-down state policies, water users' associations have determined they *need* the state in various ways. In the case of rural drinking water, this counterintuitively may include needing the state in order to secure legal autonomy as nonstate organizations. An unofficial legal status rendered CAPS in Nicaragua particularly vulnerable in political, legal, and financial terms. Moreover, legal backing of the state is necessary to open the door to direct access to state and nonstate financial resources, legal titles to water sources and land, access to organizational bank accounts, and other prerogatives. While not a *necessary* condition for certain forms of political empowerment and inclusion into policy processes, official legal recognition vis-à-vis the state can *enhance* a sense of empowerment and the right to be included.

This relates to a third takeaway from CAPS' story: nonstate rural water managers and service providers are sectoral experts who should participate in the formal aspects of governance, including policy design. Participation in policy processes could be cast as a time- and resource-related burden for rural residents whose primary role is managing water resources. However, what matters is that members of water users' associations want to engage in these processes. This is not surprising. In Nicaragua, water committees contributed to the development of a more comprehensive legal and political framework for the governance of the country's freshwater resources. From CAPS' vantage point, the passing of the CAPS Law served as a corrective of sorts given water committees' blatant omission from previous legal frameworks. In practical terms, beyond bestowing new legal, financial, and political prerogatives upon CAPS, Law 722 provides an important foundation for grassroots actors to hold state agencies and officials accountable to rural communities. In these ways and more, the engagement of water users and managers in public policy design can be a boon to water governance.

A fourth takeaway from this book is the power and importance of collective action, including collaborative approaches to political activism. In the case of rural water users' associations, certain kinds of political activism may not be possible *without* collaboration. In Nicaragua, CAPS' transcommunity mobilization was not fully "autonomous." Rather, it was possible owing to multisectoral collaboration and relations of interdependence with domestic and international allies. There are risks inherent in collaborative, multisectoral social change strategies when these entail high-resource differentials on the part of participants. For instance, if certain NGOs or multilateral organizations were to lose funding or shift their priorities, this would have a detrimental impact on the physical mobility of rural social actors. This might be an inescapable risk of collaboration, though, and one that goes two ways since any collaborator could choose to step back from collective efforts. Notably, in 2010, leaders of the National CAPS Network called directly upon NGO allies *not* to distance themselves from the network *because* of its dependence on their particular contributions. The first elected president of the National CAPS Network asserted that CAPS' allies are a "part" of the network and "cannot unglue themselves" (Matagalpa, May 25, 2010).

The activism of grassroots water users and managers is another feature of rural water governance holding *promise* for increased equity within this consequential realm of political decision-making. Indeed, claims that "the era of top-down water policy formulation and implementation has surely ended" (Boelens, Getches, and Guevara-Gil 2010, 4) rest upon evidence that popular-sector organizations, including nonstate water users and managers, have mounted effective challenges to elite-led shaping of rural and urban water sectors. Examples of such water struggles are numerous and extend beyond Latin America to diverse national contexts including South Africa, Indonesia, and the United States (Belanyá et al. 2005; Hall and Goudriaan 1999; Hall, Lobina, and De La Motte 2005).

Across contexts globally, decentralization, privatization, and other policy trends will continue to affect the politics of inclusion and exclusion within the governance of water and other sectors. Policy shifts from above as well as pushes for new and different policies from below create the imperative to study how locally grounded actors and organizations are affected by and articulate with actors, institutions, and policies at other scales. This necessarily includes cases wherein certain social movement participants enjoy a kind of grounded expertise informing their activism and potential contributions to policy. For example, nurses protesting the privatization of health care in El Salvador, teachers and students resisting the privatization of education in Chile, and indigenous communities opposing new mining operations in Peru reflect the mobilization of stakeholders with unique expertise formed through on-the-ground experiences. This mobilization reflects a transcendence of everyday roles and responsibilities into realms of activism that draw on locally grounded knowledge and experience. When this activism informs public policy processes, we not only create more inclusive governance but also the potential for greater social and environmental justice.

Notes

Preface

1. In Latin America, departments refer to territorial delineations similar to provinces. Each department is home to several cities, or municipalities, which have local government structures including mayors and city councils. Unlike countries with federal systems, such as Mexico and Colombia, Nicaragua's departments do not have governors or elected officials.

Introduction

1. In 2000, massive protests in Cochabamba, Bolivia, resulted in overturning of the government's contract with Aguas del Tunari (a subsidiary of Bechtel Corporation) to lease the municipal water supply system. The Cochabamba "water wars" quickly became recognized globally as a case of overturned water privatization, and more broadly as evidence of strong resistance to neoliberal economic policies in the Global South (see Assies 2003; Romano 2012).
2. As Boelens elaborates: "[Notwithstanding] their often contradictory objectives, it would be mistaken to suggest that local user organizations try to avoid interaction with the state or development institutions to defend their autonomy. Actual practice proves the contrary. For instance, both the state and the users try to achieve the most favorable ratio of investment versus control for their purposes, where local user groups try to gain more access to state resources and international funding without handing over local normative power" (2008, 62).
3. The World Bank (2018) provides estimates of rural populations.
4. While this book uses the language of foreign and international "investment," this refers not to loans, but rather donations to the rural water and sanitation sector via

direct financing of water systems and sanitation infrastructure. In addition, these investments reference foreign funding to domestic NGOs who carry out rural water and sanitation projects with communities.

5. Needless to say, some political leaders' actions matter more than others in terms of impacting global greenhouse gas emissions. The Nicaraguan government did not initially sign the Paris Climate Accords emerging from the United Nations Framework Convention on Climate Change Conference of Parties (COP 21) in 2015. This initial decision related, in part, to the extremely marginal contributions to climate change on the part of Nicaragua relative to major greenhouse gas emitters such as China and the United States. As of 2018, all countries had signed on to the accords, though President Donald Trump announced the intention of the United States to withdraw in 2017—the same year Nicaragua and Syria signed on to the agreement. Per the rules of the Paris Accords, the United States cannot formally withdraw until November 2020.

6. See, for example, Schouten and Moriarty (2003) and the vast scholarships on common property regimes and resource users' associations.

7. Bridging social capital conceptually subsumes "weak ties," or those ties among people who do not know each other very well, as well as "cross-cutting ties," which Narayan defines as "linkages between social groups" (1999, 13).

8. While I conducted interviews with the coordinator of the municipal CAPS network in Muy Muy, I did not conduct a group interview with the network's board of directors.

9. According to *New York Times* reporting, this reduced payout reflected an increase in the amount being spent toward covering beneficiaries' medical costs.

10. See, for example, the government's May 31, 2018, press release, Gobierno de Reconciliación y Unidad Nacional (2018).

11. "The GIEI-Nicaragua's report also states that the Nicaraguan authorities have used practically all the state apparatus, including the National Police, the Prosecutor's Office and the judicial system, as well as pro-government armed groups, to kill, imprison, ill-treat, torture and persecute those people who oppose their policies or are perceived as such. The Nicaraguan government announced the temporary suspension of the presence and visits of the Inter-American Commission on Human Rights (IACHR) and its Special Monitoring Mechanism for Nicaragua (MESENI), as well as the end of the GIEI's mandate prior to the presentation of their final report" (Amnesty International 2018).

Chapter One

1. This section focuses primarily on the development of the rural water and sanitation sector under the Somoza dictatorship. For a broader overview and discussion of the Somoza era in Nicaragua, as well as the sources drawn upon in this section, see Baumeister 1985; Bugajski 1990; Clark 1992; Diederich 2007; Gould 1987, 1990; Mande 1994; Millet 1977; Solaún 2005; and Vanden and Prevost 1993.

2. Booth (1982) outlines five factors affecting capital concentration during the Somoza era: "(1) the greatly increased land concentration in the coffee and cotton industries; (2) the coffee and cotton price increases (and the cotton cultivation boom) beginning in the late 1940s; (3) the expanded ties of Nicaraguan capitalists to U.S. banks and investors; (4) the political peace purchased by Somoza through permitting Conservative faction participation in the government; and (5) the growing role of Somoza and his family in the economy" (66).

3. Descriptive and evaluative data on historical and international initiatives to promote community health in Nicaragua are scarce. For example, the Nicaragua country profile on the USAID website references water sector collaborations beginning only in 1990; archived "success stories" are not available before this date. Nevertheless, available evidence indicates that these bilateral programs and collaborations prompted the construction of potable water systems and latrines and the development of vaccination programs in the country's rural areas where they had not existed previously.

4. Unless otherwise noted, estimates of rural water systems within this chapter reflect data within SINAS, which includes estimates through part of 2004 only.

5. This section draws upon the following authors: Bossert 1982; Booth 1982; Coraggio and Irvin 1985; Enríquez 1985; Gilbert 1988; Harris and Vilas 1985; Horton 1999; Langlois 1996; Luciak 1995, 2001; Martínez and González 1981; Ortega 1990; Prevost and Vanden 1999; Reding 1991; Ruchwarger 1987; Serra 1982, 1991; Smith 1996; and Trask 1993.

6. See also Donahue (1989) on the effects of the war on the Sandinistas' social agenda.

7. The U.S.-funded Contra War sought the political and economic undermining of the Sandinista regime in Nicaragua. This proxy war against the Sandinistas involved both military aggression (funded by the U.S. government, including the CIA) and economic sanctions (including a full U.S. economic embargo by 1985) (Smith 1996). The estimated death toll for all Sandinista military, Contra, and civilians (by 1989) was 30,865, with many more seriously wounded, left orphaned, or without homes (Kornbluh 1991, 344). For further reading on the Contra War, see Harris and Villas 1985; Prevost and Vanden 1999; Smith 1996; and Trask 1993.

8. For a more comprehensive discussion of the political, economic, and social outcomes of the Revolution, including a more nuanced discussion of the mass organizations, see Gilbert 1988; Luciak 1990, 2001; Prevost and Vanden 1999; Serra 1982; and Vanden and Prevost 1993.

9. Serra's (1982) estimate of seventy thousand participants in the Literary Crusade contrasts with Ruchwarger's (1987, 111) estimate of fifty thousand.

10. Writing in 1987, Ruchwarger notes the potential conflict of interest: "It remains to be seen whether FSLN delegates who are also mass organization leaders will be able to effectively represent their memberships" (147).

11. Two qualitative accounts the author found of this role include Medrano et al. (2007) and RRAS-CA (1998).

12. Ostensibly, these estimates do not take into account the monetary value that the labor communities provide during and after project implementation.

13.   Municipalities that did not have municipal UNOM—including Sébaco, Esquipulas, and San Isidrio—remained dependent on the technical support and assistance of the regional, or centralized, Office of Rural Aqueduct offices.

14.   Several NGOs that formed during this era in Nicaragua—including various agricultural, community, and rural development organizations—would later become the political and social allies of CAPS in the mid-2000s as water committees started to organize across communities. NGO alliances with CAPS are discussed in detail in chapter 3.

15.   The delineated project cycle includes the following phases: (1) policy development, sector planning, and program formulation; (2) identification of programs and projects; (3) preparation of programs and projects; (4) evaluation and approval of programs and projects; (5) implementation and monitoring; (6) operation and monitoring; (7) extensions or next phases of the programs; and (8) evaluation (Department for International Development 1998).

16.   This loan was part of the IADB's Program to Modernize the Management of Water and Sewerage Services, and also included US$5.9 million in cofinancing from the Organization for Petroleum Exporting Countries (OPEC) and US$2.1 million in Nicaraguan counterpart funds.

17.   Ortega, who held the presidency during the Sandinista Revolution from 1985 to 1990, was also returning to power.

18.   As one study found based on focus groups with active participants of the Citizen Power bodies, "All of the internal dynamics of Citizen Power (work agenda, relationships and alliances, formation process) are defined by the FSLN agenda and are applied through public institutions" (Chaguaceda and Stuart 2011, 15).

19.   Increased government prioritization of water and sanitation in terms of spending should not be seen as necessarily correlated with greater government *capacity* in the water sector. For example, state institutional capacity continued to decline after the passage of Law 620, when the last DAR offices shut down, coinciding with the expiration of financial support from UNICEF for capacity building and technical support at the municipal level.

20.   It is unlikely that lawmakers intended "users' organizations" in the law to refer to rural water committees; rather, these likely referred to the National Consumers' Defense Organization (RNDC) and other NGOs that participated actively in shaping the law at the time.

Chapter Two

1.   *Vida útil* literally means "useful life," and is the language water committees and development organizations use to refer to the number of years for which a water system was technically designed to function.

2.   Several scholars have discussed how water rights, or de facto "authorized" use of water within a local system of rules and norms, oftentimes develop at the grass

roots in the absence of state authorization (Boelens and Doornbos 2002; Boelens and Hoogendam 2002; Hoogesteger 2013).

3. The National Information System of Rural Water and Sanitation (SINAS), a database created by the Nicaraguan government and international donors in the mid-1990s to document project implementation, reflects water system constructed through part of 2004 only. In the absence of comprehensive documentation of CAPS and water systems nationally, efforts to conduct representative research prove challenging.

4. A 2003 report of the state water company found that "very few new CAPS members receive a (formal or informal) training from a UNOM [National Operation and Maintenance Unit] (Regional or Municipal) promoter" (ENACAL 2003, 28).

5. In one Kenyan district, Narayan found that the local government "instituted a legal transfer of hand pump ownership to communities when they found that, *despite training, communities expected the government to repair pumps*" (1994, 11). This is relevant to the Nicaraguan case in that it suggests that where governments or other "external" actors have helped to implement projects, there may be an initial expectation on the part of beneficiaries (i.e., rural residents) that continued support will be forthcoming.

6. This commitment to meeting basic needs in many cases also reflects the prioritization of community over individual needs and thus stands in contrast to liberal notions of equity that inform state-supported systems of individual property and resource rights and market-guided systems of resource allocation (see Anderson 1994; Boelens 2009).

7. Interestingly, despite cases of financial remuneration, many CAPS members consider themselves fundamentally community volunteers.

8. Expenditures such as stipends to committee members may go against the recommendations of some NGO staff, who advise CAPS to use the funds generated from users' tariffs for reinvesting into the water system. As ADEMNORTE's Mirna expressed, funds provide a safety net. Spending them as water committee income is, according to her, "not right because when an emergency arises they don't have a means to respond" (interview, April 10, 2010). The financial situation and spending strategies of individual CAPS would have to be further investigated to determine whether or not they compromise current or future water provision work.

9. This finding of nonturnover in leadership is similar to that of Tendler et al. (1983) in their research on Bolivian cooperatives: although "[leadership] and management positions usually rotated among the same few persons," hence not conforming to researchers' "vision of coops as participatory and democratic" (5), these organizations may still be highly successful. Tendler et al. found that cooperatives with exclusionary and nonparticipatory decision-making structures still could provide members and even nonmembers with many benefits, including better prices for goods, lower transportation costs, and availability of credit.

10.   "It is not whether it is possible to mobilize everyone who would be willing to be mobilized. It is not even whether all the members of some organization or social network can be mobilized. Rather, the issue is whether there is some social mechanism that connects enough people who have the appropriate interests and resources so that they can act. It is whether there is an organization or social network that has a subset of individuals who are interested and resourceful enough to provide the good when they act in concert and whether they have sufficient social organization among themselves to act together" (Marwell and Oliver 1993, 54).

11.   *Fiscal* refers to the person in charge of general oversight to ensure transparent functioning of the committee, including its use of funds. Some CAPS incorporate other positions as well, including individuals in charge of environmental protection (in some cases, "reforestation") and public relations.

12.   The problem of water contamination in Nicaragua is both human induced and naturally occurring. A 2003 investigation conducted by UNICEF with funding from the Swiss government concluded that an estimated 5.7 percent of freshwater sources nationally had levels of arsenic higher than those deemed safe for human consumption (Barrangne-Bigot 2004). Both lead and arsenic as naturally occurring contaminants have the potential to enter a water supply when wells are dug.

13.   An estimated 92.3 percent of rural Nicaraguan households carry out some form of productive agricultural or forest-based activity (Gómez, Ravnborg, and Rivas 2007).

14.   These dynamics extend beyond Nicaragua. Examining case studies from across Africa, Asia, Europe, and Latin America, Fuys and Dohrn present instances in which "state-led conservation efforts have increased conflicts over natural resources and undermined existing systems to manage resources as common property, such as through the creation of national parks and forest reserves" (2010, 203).

15.   Here the CAPS member cites the number of estimated rural beneficiaries nationally of CAPS-managed water systems, per documentation in SINAS (see note 3, above).

Chapter Three

1.   As of 2017, only Eduardo continued to work directly with the National CAPS Network. However, both individuals worked extensively to plan, coordinate, and facilitate the formation of the National CAPS Network in the mid-2000s.

2.   The author's selection of five municipal network cases was drawn from this pool of CAPS networks within Matagalpa.

3.   As a CAPS member from San Ramón, Matagalpa, expressed, "To go from the north to Managua is expensive for us. . . . Just the cost of travel is 45 córdobas [US$2]" (interview, April 20, 2010). It is important to note that this kind of travel entails additional "costs," such as losing time away from family and productive activities.

4. Law 475 passed in 2003, establishing provisions for citizen participation in law development, including participation in consultations on proposed legislation.
5. The benefits of scaling horizontally and vertically to form networks may not be limited to resource-poor actors: Bebbington et al. (1971, 2006) found bonding social capital, reflecting horizontal relationships, to have significant benefits for both elites and the poor in Indonesian villages: while elites could use it maintain power in local institutions, the poor could use it to offset livelihood insecurities. Similarly, bridging social capital, reflecting vertical forms of integration, increased villagers' capacity to address livelihood and village governance issues.

Chapter Four

1. "There is widespread agreement among movement framing researchers that the development, generation, and elaboration of collective action frames are contested processes" (Benford and Snow 2000, 625).
2. An additional provision of concern to CAPS, and one explicitly referencing their organizations, was Article 75 in the law's regulations: "In communities where the service provider [ENACAL] does not have coverage, systems will be administered by the community, specifically the Potable Water Committees, who will guarantee service to the community, all below the supervision and control of ENACAL." Although the vast majority of ENACAL's investments have been in urban areas, Law 276 creating the institution does specify the state company's prerogative to "investigate, explore, develop and exploit the water resources necessary" to provide service in rural areas.
3. Noted risk factors included displacement, crop destruction, spread of diseases, and species extinction.

Chapter Five

1. Nicaraguan Water and Sanitation Institute (INAA) staff declined to share data indicating which CAPS and where had registered.
2. "'Becoming formal' is now a strategy for the poor to defend their right to water commons gained by being in place over time and through entrenched patterns of appropriation and material and emotional investment. Given their recognition in several pieces of legislation as legitimate providers of water, 'becoming formal' entitles them to public monies and to the right not to be excluded" (Perera, cited in Llano-Arias 2015, 79).
3. Modern legal frameworks for water also tend to prioritize the technical over the social dimensions of resource management. This means that those individuals and institutions deemed technical "experts" are often assigned greater formal responsibility in the sector than communities of users. According to Seemann, Peru's General Water Law of 1969 "made the Ministry of Health responsible for water quality and the preservation of resources and declared the Ministry of Agriculture

the main water authority in charge of water allocation and distribution of water use rights. This ignored the traditional water authorities and regulations to assign water rights, replacing them by engineers and technicians" (2016, 55).

4. "*Usos y costumbres*, as applied to campesino irrigation, are the mutually agreed-on norms of water rights and management practices that govern communal irrigation systems" (Perreault 2008, 835).

5. Notably, Perreault's assessment of the 2004 irrigation law in Bolivia (Promotion and Assistance of the Irrigation Sector, or Law 2878) is similar to how CAPS in Nicaragua have perceived the CAPS Law: "With the passage of this law, irrigators at last had achieved legal recognition and protection for their *usos y costumbres* regarding water rights and management practices" (Perreault 2008, 845).

6. Indeed, we can consider it problematic that water for irrigation has been underemphasized in global rights frameworks, national constitutions, and public policies as a right or as a public good the same way drinking water has. The food sovereignty movement that exists in part to assert "the right to be a farmer" is instructive here in the context of global industrialization of food and agricultural production (Claeys 2015).

7. I use the language of "legalization" since this is the language both CAPS and other state and nonstate stakeholders used in interviews to describe the outcome of registering with the government.

8. These echo many of the concerns Seemann (2016) found in her research on water users' association formalization in Peru.

9. According to INAA staff: "the local government makes a registry and afterwards they send this registry to INAA so we can issue certifications. But there are local governments that are poor and that don't have a technical person who can take charge of making the registry" (interview, June 2, 2010).

10. As a legal framework, the law outlines CAPS' "responsibilities" regarding environmental stewardship, but it does not contain provisions relevant to rural residents' urgent need to confront and adjust to a changing environment.

References

Abers, R., and M. E. Keck. 2009. "Mobilizing the State: The Erratic Partner in Brazil's Participatory Water Policy." *Politics and Society* 37(2): 289–314.

Adler, P. S., and S. Kwon. 2002. "Social Capital: Prospects for a New Concept." *Academy of Management Review* 27(1): 17–40.

Agarwal, A. 2005. *Environmentality: Technologies of Government and the Making of Subjects*. Durham, N.C.: Duke University Press Books.

Agarwal, A., and C. Gibson. 2001. *Communities and the Environment: Ethnicity, Gender, and the State in Community-Based Conservation*. New Brunswick, N.J.: Rutgers University Press.

Agarwal, A., and K. Gupta. 2005. "Decentralization and Participation: The Governance of Common Pool Resources in Nepal's Terai." *World Development* 33(7): 1101–14.

Agarwal, A., and J. Ribot. 1999. "Accountability in Decentralization: A Framework with South Asian and West African Cases." *Journal of Developing Areas* 33(4): 473–502.

Amnesty International. 2018. "Nicaragua: Report Affirms the Government of President Ortega Has Committed Crimes against Humanity." February 21. https://www.amnesty usa.org/press-releases/nicaragua-report-by-independent-experts-affirms-that-the -government-of-president-ortega-has-committed-crimes-against-humanity/.

Anderson, L. E. 1994. *The Political Ecology of the Modern Peasant: Calculation and Community*. Baltimore, Md.: Johns Hopkins University Press.

Anderson, L. E. 2010a. *Social Capital in Developing Democracies: Nicaragua and Argentina Compared*. New York: Cambridge University Press.

Anderson, L. E. 2010b. "Poverty and Political Empowerment: Local Citizen Participation as a Path toward Social Justice in Nicaragua." *Forum on Public Policy* 4: 1–19.

Anderson, L. E., and L. C. Dodd. 2005. *Learning Democracy: Citizen Engagement and Electoral Choice in Nicaragua, 1990–2001*. Chicago: University of Chicago Press.

Anderson, L. E., and L. C. Dodd. 2009. "Nicaragua: Progress amid Regress?" *Journal of Democracy* 20(3): 153–67.

Assies, W. 2003. "David versus Goliath in Cochabamba: Water Rights, Neoliberalism, and the Revival of Social Protest in Bolivia." *Latin American Perspectives* 30(3): 14–36.

Baltodano, F., and J. Olmedo. 2008. "Evaluación de la decentralización de la UNOM en comunidades de los Departamentos de Matagalpa y Jinotega." Managua: Universidad Nacional Autónoma de Nicaragua.

Barrangne-Bigot, P. 2004. *Contribución al estudio de cinco zonas contaminadas naturalmente por arsénico en Nicaragua.* Managua: UNICEF.

Baumeister, E. 1995. "Farmers' Organisations and Agrarian Transformation in Nicaragua." In *The New Politics of Survival: Grassroots Movement in Central America*, ed. A. Criquillon, 209–37. New York: Monthly Review Press.

Beach, D. 2017. "Process-Tracing Methods in Social Science." *Oxford Research Encyclopedia.* DOI: 10.1093/acrefore/9780190228637.013.176.

Bebbington, A., J. H. Carrasco, L. Peralbo, G. Ramón, J. Trujillo, and V. Torres. 1993. "Fragile Lands, Fragile Organizations: Indian Organizations and the Politics of Sustainability in Ecuador." *Transactions of the Institute of British Geographers* 18(2): 179–96.

Bebbington, A., L. Dharmawan, E. Fahmi, and S. Guggenheim. 2006. "Local Capacity, Village Governance, and the Political Economy of Rural Development in Indonesia." *World Development* 34(11): 1958–76.

Becker, C. D., and E. Ostrom. 1995. "Human Ecology and Resource Sustainability: The Importance of Institutional Diversity." *Annual Review of Ecology and Systematics* 26: 113–33.

Belanyá, B., B. Brennan, O. Hoedeman, S. Kishimoto, and P. Terhorst, eds. 2005. *Reclaiming Public Water: Achievements, Struggles and Visions from around the World.* Booklet. Transnational Institute and Corporate Europe Observatory.

Benford, R. D., and D. A. Snow. 2000. "Framing Processes and Social Movements: An Overview and Assessment." *Annual Review of Sociology* 26(January 1): 611–39.

Bergh, S. 2004. "Democratic Decentralization and Local Participation: A Review of Recent Research." *Development in Practice* 14(6): 780–90.

Boelens, R. 2002. "Recipes and Resistance: Peasants' Rights Building and Empowerment in the Licto Irrigation System, Ecuador." In *Water Rights and Empowerment*, ed. R. Boelens and P. Hoogendam, 144–72. Assen, Netherlands: Van Gorcum.

Boelens, R. 2008. "Water Rights Arenas in the Andes: Upscaling Networks to Strengthen Local Water Control." *Water Alternatives* 1(1): 48–65.

Boelens, R. 2009. "The Politics of Disciplining Water Rights." *Development and Change* 40(2)(March 1): 307–31.

Boelens, R. 2014. "Cultural Politics and the Hydrosocial Cycle: Water, Power, and Identity in the Andean Highlands." *Geoforum* 57: 234–47.

Boelens, R., and B. Doornbos. 2002. "The Battlefield of Water Rights: Rule-Making and Empowerment in the Arena of Conflicting Normative Frameworks—Irrigation Development in Ceceles, Ecuador." In *Water Rights and Empowerment*, ed. R. Boelens and P. Hoogendam, 217–39. Assen, Netherlands: Van Gorcum.

Boelens, R., D. Getches, and A. Guevara-Gil. 2010. "Water Struggles and the Politics of Identity." In *Out of the Mainstream: Water Rights, Politics and Identity*, ed. R. Boelens, D. Getches, and A. Guevara-Gil, 1–25. London: Earthscan.

Boelens, R., and P. Hoogendam, eds. 2002. *Water Rights and Empowerment*. Assen, Netherlands: Van Gorcum.

Boelens, R., J. Hoogesteger, and M. Baud. 2015. "Water Reform Governmentality in Ecuador: Neoliberalism, Centralization and the Restraining of Polycentric Authority and Community Rulemaking." *Geoforum* 64: 281–91.

Booth, J. A. 1985. *The End and the Beginning: The Nicaraguan Revolution*. Boulder: Westview Press.

Bossert, T. J. 1982. "Health Care in Revolutionary Nicaragua." In *Nicaragua in Revolution*, ed. T. W. Walker, 259–72. New York: Praeger Publishers.

Brown, E., and J. Cloke. 2005. "Neoliberal Reform, Governance and Corruption in Central America: Exploring the Nicaraguan Case." *Political Geography* 24(5): 601–30.

Bugajski, J. 1990. *Sandinista Communism and Rural Nicaragua*. New York: Praeger.

Chaguaceda, A., and R. Stuart. 2011. "Democracia participativa en Nicaragua? Los Consejos de poder ciudadano y el gobierno del FSLN (2006–2011)." *Encuentros* 8(2): 5–22.

Chamorro, C., E. Jarquín, and A. Bendaña. 2009. "Understanding Populism and Political Participation: The Case of Nicaragua." *Woodrow Wilson Center Update on the Americas*, June.

Claeys, P. 2015. *Human Rights and the Food Sovereignty Movement: Reclaiming Control*. New York: Routledge.

Clark, P. C. 1992. *The United States and Somoza, 1933–1956: A Revisionist Look*. New York: Praeger.

Collier, D. 2011. "Understanding Process Tracing." *Political Science and Politics* 44(4): 823–30.

Collins, R. C., J. W. Neal, and Z. P. Neal. 2014. "Transforming Individual Civic Engagement into Community Collective Efficacy: The Role of Bonding Social Capital." *American Journal of Community Psychology* 54(3–4): 328–36.

Coraggio, J. L., and G. Irvin. 1985. "Revolution and Democracy in Nicaragua." *Latin American Perspectives* 12(2): 23–38.

Crook, R. C., and J. Manor. 1998. *Democracy and Decentralisation in South Asia and West Africa: Participation, Accountability, and Performance*. New York: Cambridge University Press.

Department for International Development. 1998. "DFID Guidance Manual on Water Supply and Sanitation Programmes." Department for International Development. https://gsdrc.org/document-library/dfid-guidance-manual-on-water-supply-and -sanitation-programmes/.

Diederich, B. 2007. *Somoza and the Legacy of US Involvement in Central America*. Princeton, N.J.: Markus Wiener Publishers.

Dobbin, K. B., and B. Sarathy. 2015. "Solving Rural Water Exclusion: Challenges and Limits to Co-Management in Costa Rica." *Society and Natural Resources* 28(4): 388–404.

Donahue, J. M. 1983. "The Politics of Health Care in Nicaragua before and after the Revolution of 1979." *Human Organization* 42(3): 264–72.

Donahue, J. M. 1986. *The Nicaraguan Revolution in Health: From Somoza to the Sandinistas.* Hadley, Md.: Bergin and Garvey Publishers.

Donahue, J. M. 1989. "International Organizations, Health Services, and Nation Building in Nicaragua." *Medical Anthropology Quarterly* 3(3): 258–69.

Dupuits, E., and A. Bernal. 2015. "Scaling-Up Water Community Organizations: The Role of Inter-Communities Networks in Multi-Level Water Governance." *Flux* 1(99): 19–31.

ENACAL. 2003. *La decentralización de La Unidad Nacional de Operación y Mantenimiento.* Managua: n.p.

Enlace. 2008. "Comités de Agua Potable: La población organizada para resolver su problema de agua." *Enlace* 18(special issue).

Enríquez, L. J. 1985. "Social Transformation in Latin America: Tensions between Agro-Export Production and Agrarian Reform in Revolutionary Nicaragua." PhD diss., University of California, Santa Cruz.

Ética y Transparencia. 2008. *Informe final elecciones municipales.* Managua: Fundación Grupo Cívico Ética y Transparencia.

Evans, P. 1996. "Government Action, Social Capital and Development: Reviewing the Evidence on Synergy." *World Development* 2(6): 1119–32.

FANCA (Fresh Water Action Network). 2006. *Las Juntas de Agua en Centroamérica.* [Costa Rica?]:Red Centroamericana de Acción del Agua.

Feeny, D., F. Berkes, B. J. McCay, and J. M. Acheson. 1990. "The Tragedy of the Commons: Twenty-Two Years Later." *Human Ecology* 18(March): 1–19.

Fox, J. 1996. "How Does Civil Society Thicken? The Political Construction of Social Capital in Rural Mexico." *World Development* 24(6): 1089–103.

Fox, J., and J. Gershman. 2006. "Enabling Social Capital? Lessons from World Bank Rural Development Projects in Mexico and the Philippines." In *The Search for Empowerment: Social Capital as Idea and Practice at the World Bank*, ed. A. Bebbington, M. Woolcock, S. Guggenheim, and E. Olson, 207–38. Boulder, Colo.: Kumarian Press.

Fuys, A., and S. Dohrn. 2010. "Common Property Regimes: Taking a Closer Look at Resource Access, Authorization, and Legitimacy." In *Beyond the Biophysical: Knowledge, Culture, and Power in Agriculture and Natural Resource Management*, ed. L. German, J. J. Ramisch, and R. Verma, 193–214. New York: Springer.

García, N. 2008a. "Aguadoras comunitarias piden reconocimiento y apoyo oficial." *El Nuevo Diario*, May 29. http://www.elnuevodiario.com.ni/contactoend/17082.

García, N. 2008b. "Iniciativa de Ley de CAPS sale de gaveta y llega a secretaría." *El Nuevo Diario*, October 3. http://www.elnuevodiario.com.ni/contactoend/28648.

Gerlak, A., and M. Wilder. 2012. "Exploring the Textured Landscape of Water Insecurity and the Human Right to Water." *Environment Magazine* 54(2): 4–17.

Gibson, C. C., J. T. Williams, and E. Ostrom. 2005. "Local Enforcement and Better Forests." *World Development* 33(2): 273–84.

Gilbert, D. 1988. *Sandinistas: The Party and the Revolution.* Cambridge: Basil Blackwell.

Gobierno de Reconciliación y Unidad Nacional. 2018. "Nota de Prensa del Gobierno de Reconciliación y Unidad Nacional." *El 19 por Más Victorias*, May 31. https://www.el19digital.com/articulos/ver/titulo:77593-nota-de-prensa-del-gobierno-de-reconciliacion-y-unidad-nacional.

Gould, J. L. 1987. "For an Organized Nicaragua: Somoza and the Labour Movement, 1944–1948." *Journal of Latin American Studies* 19(2): 353–87.

Gould, J. L. 1990. "Notes on Peasant Consciousness and Revolutionary Politics in Nicaragua 1955–1990." *Radical History Review* (48): 65–87.

Government of Nicaragua and PAHO. 2004. *Análisis sectorial de agua potable y saneamiento de Nicaragua*. Managua.

Granovetter, M. 1983. "The Strength of Weak Ties: A Network Theory Revisited." *Sociological Theory* 1(1): 201–33.

Grigsby, W. 2005. "Why So Little Social Mobilization?" *Revista Envío* (July). http://www.envio.org.ni/articulo/2988.

Hall, D., and J. W. Goudriaan. 1999. "Privatization and Democracy." Public Services International Research Unit Report, University of Greenwich.

Hall, D., E. Lobina, and R. De La Motte. 2005. "Public Resistance to Privatization in Water and Energy." *Development in Practice* 15(3–4): 286–301.

Hanemann, U. 2005. *Nicaragua's Literacy Campaign*. Hamburg, Germany: UNESCO Institute for Education.

Hardin, G. 1968. "Tragedy of the Commons." *Science* 162(3859): 1243–48.

Harris, R. L., and C. M. Villas, eds. 1985. *Nicaragua: A Revolution under Siege*. London: Zed Books.

Hoogesteger, J. 2012. "Democratizing Water Governance from the Grassroots: The Development of Interjuntas-Chimborazo in the Ecuadorian Andes." *Human Organization* 71(1): 76–86.

Hoogesteger, J. 2013. "Social Capital in Water User Organizations of the Ecuadorian Highlands." *Human Organization* 72(4): 347–57.

Hoogesteger, J., R. Boelens, and M. Baud. 2017. "Territorial Pluralism: Water Users' Multi-Scalar Struggles against State Ordering in Ecuador's Highlands." *Water International* 41(1): 91–106.

Hoogesteger, J., and A. Verzijl. 2015. "Grassroots Scalar Politics: Insights from Peasant Water Struggles in the Ecuadorian and Peruvian Andes." *Geoforum* 62(June): 13–23.

Horton, L. 1999. *Peasants in Arms: War and Peace in the Mountains of Nicaragua, 1979–1994*. Vol. 30. Athens: Ohio University Press.

Hyman, J. B. 2002. "Exploring Social Capital and Civic Engagement to Create a Framework for Community Building." *Applied Developmental Science* 6(4): 196–202.

INAA. 1989. *Los acueductos rurales en Nicaragua*. Managua: Instituto Nicaragüense de Acueductos y Alcantaril.

Johnston, H., and J. A. Noakes, eds. 2005. *Frames of Protest: Social Movements and the Framing Perspective*. Lanham, Md.: Rowman and Littlefield.

Kaimowitz, D., and J. R. Thome. 1982. "Nicaragua's Agrarian Reform: The First Year (1979–80)." In *Nicaragua in Revolution*, ed. T. W. Walker, 223–40. New York: Praeger.

Kornbluh, P. 1991. "The U.S. Role in the Counterrevolution." In *Revolution and Counterrevolution in Nicaragua*, ed. T. W. Walker, 323–49. Boulder, Colo.: Westview Press.

Kreimann, R. 2009. "Gestión social de un bien común: Los Comités de Agua en Nicaragua, contextos diferenciados periferia urbana y rural." Master's thesis, Centro de Estudios Demográficos, Urbanos y Ambientales.

Kreimann, R. 2010. "The Rural CAPS: Ensuring Community Access to Water." *Revista Envío* 339(June). http://www.envio.org.ni/articulo/4197.

Krishna, A. 2004. "Understanding, Measuring and Utilizing Social Capital: Clarifying Concepts and Presenting a Field Application from India." *Agricultural Systems* 82(3): 291–305.

Kull, C. A. 2002. "Empowering Pyromaniacs in Madagascar: Ideology and Legitimacy in Community-Based Natural Resource Management." *Development and Change* 33(1): 57–78.

Kuzdas, et al. 2015. "Identifying the Potential of Governance Regimes to Aggravate or Mitigate Local Water Conflicts in Regions Threatened by Climate Change." *Local Environment* 21(11): 1387–408.

Langlois, R. 1996. "Becoming a Contra: The Dilemma of Peasants during the Revolution in Nicaragua." *International Journal* 52(4): 695–713.

Larsen, L., S. L. Harlan, B. Bolin, E. J. Hackett, D. Hope, A. Kirby, and S. Wolf. 2004. "Bonding and Bridging: Understanding the Relationship between Social Capital and Civic Action." *Journal of Planning Education and Research* 24(1): 64–77.

Larson, A. 2004. "Formal Decentralisation and the Imperative of Decentralisation 'from Below': A Case Study of Natural Resource Management in Nicaragua." *European Journal of Development Research* 16(1): 55–70.

Larson, A. M., and J. C. Ribot. 2004. "Democratic Decentralisation through a Natural Resource Lens: An Introduction." *European Journal of Development Research* 16(1): 1–25.

LaVanchy, G. T., S. T. Romano, and M. J. Taylor. 2017. "Challenges to Water Security along the 'Emerald Coast': A Political Ecology of Local Water Governance in Nicaragua." *Water* 9(9): 655.

Llano-Arias, V. 2015. "Community Knowledge Sharing and Co-Production of Water Services: Two Cases of Community Aqueduct Associations in Colombia." *Water Alternatives* 8(2): 77–98.

López, R., and A. Váldez. 2000. "Fighting Rural Poverty in Latin America: New Evidence of the Effects of Education, Demographics, and Access to Land." *Economic Development and Cultural Change* 49(1): 197–211.

Luciak, I. A. 1995. *The Sandinista Legacy: Lessons from a Political Economy in Transition*. Gainesville: University Press of Florida.

Luciak, I. A. 2001. *After the Revolution: Gender and Democracy in El Salvador, Nicaragua, and Guatemala*. Baltimore, Md.: Johns Hopkins University Press.

Lund, C. 2006a. "Twilight Institutions: An Introduction." *Development and Change* 37(4) (July 1): 673–84.

Lund, C. 2006b. "Twilight Institutions: Public Authority and Local Politics in Africa." *Development and Change* 37(4) (July 1): 685–705.

Mande, A. G. 1994. "The Somoza Regime: Internal Dynamics of Nicaraguan Politics, 1933–79." Master's thesis, Ohio State University.

Martínez, G., and O. González. 1981. "Primer Seminario Nacional de Agua Potable y Saneamiento." Managua.

Marwell, G., and P. Oliver. 1993. *The Critical Mass in Collective Action: A Micro-Social Theory*. New York: Cambridge University Press.

McAdam, D., J. D. McCarthy, and M. N. Zald. 1996. *Comparative Perspectives on Social Movements: Political Opportunities, Mobilizing Structures, and Cultural Framings*. New York: Cambridge University Press.

McKean, M. A. 1996. "Common Property: What Is It, What Is It Good for, and What Makes It Work." *Forests, Trees, and People Programme*, Phase II Working Paper, IFRI Research Program Studies, 1–26.

Medrano, E., O. Tablada, A. Kome, F. Baltodano, N. Medina, N. Swagemakers, and W. Obando. 2007. *22 años de experiencia recopilada sobre el trabajo de acueductos rurales*. Managua: n.p.

Meinzen-Dick, R., and M. Zwarteveen. 1998. "Gendered Participation in Water Management: Issues and Illustrations from Water Users' Associations in South Asia." *Agriculture and Human Values* 15(4): 337–45.

Mendoza, Francisco. 2008. "Se constituye red defensora del agua y del medio ambiente." *El Nuevo Diario*, August 21. http://www.elnuevodiario.com.ni/departamentales /24759.

Morales, Roberto A. 2010. "Parlamento aprueba ley de los CAPS." *La Prensa*, May 19, 6A.

Morris, C. D. 2018a. "Unexpected Uprising: The Crisis of Democracy in Nicaragua," *NACLA Report on the Americas*. May 14. https://nacla.org/news/2018/05/14 /unexpected-uprising-crisis-democracy-nicaragua.

Morris, C. D. 2018b. "Understanding the Roots of Nicaragua's April 19 movement." https://thisishell.com/interviews/1005-courtney-desiree-morris.

Millet, R. 1977. *Guardians of the Dynasty: A History of the US Created Guardia Nacional de Nicaragua and the Somoza Family*. Maryknoll, N.Y.: Orbis Books.

Murphree, M. W. 2009. "The Strategic Pillars of Communal Natural Resource Management: Benefit, Empowerment and Conservation." *Biodiversity and Conservation* 18(10) (May 22): 2551–62.

Narayan, D. 1994. "Contribution of People's Participation: Evidence from 121 Rural Water Supply Projects." *Environmentally Sustainable Development Occasional Paper Series* (1).

Narayan, D. 1999. *Bonds and Bridges: Social Capital and Poverty*. Policy Research Working Paper Series. Washington, D.C.: World Bank.

Novo, P., and A. Garrido. 2010. "The New Nicaraguan Water Law in Context: Institutions and Challenges for Water Management and Governance." IFPRI Discussion Paper.

ODESAR. 2017. "Misión y visión." www.oedesar.org.ni/?page=inicio?section=2.

Ohmer, M. L. 2010. "How Theory and Research Inform Citizen Participation in Poor Communities: The Ecological Perspective and Theories on Self- and Collective

Efficacy and Sense of Community." *Journal of Human Behavior in the Social Environment* 20(1): 1–19.

O'Kane, T. 1995. "New Autonomy, New Struggle: Labor Unions in Nicaragua." In *The New Politics of Survival: Grassroots Movements in Central America*, ed. M. Sinclair, 183–207. New York: Monthly Review Press.

Ortega, M. 1990. "The State, the Peasantry and the Sandinista Revolution." *Journal of Development Studies* 26(4): 122–42.

Ostrom, E. 1990. *Governing the Commons: The Evolution of Institutions for Collective Action*. New York: Cambridge University Press.

Ostrom, E. 2002. *The Drama of the Commons*. Washington, D.C.: National Academy Press.

Pacheco-Vega, R. 2015a. "Gobernanza del agua residual en Aguascalientes: Captura regulatoria y arreglos institucionales complejos." *Región y sociedad* 27(64): 313–50.

Pacheco-Vega, R. 2015b. "Agua embotellada en México: De la privatización del suministro a la mercantilización de los recursos hídricos." *Espiral* 22(63): 221–63.

Pan American Health Organization (PAHO). 2017. "Nicaragua Country Report." https://www.paho.org/salud-en-las-americas-2017/?page_id=143.

Pahl-Wostl, C. 2009. "A Conceptual Framework for Analysing Adaptive Capacity and Multi-Level Learning Processes in Resource Governance Regimes." *Global Environmental Change* 19(3): 354–65.

Pérez, W. 2010. "Comités de agua con menos trabajo por sequía." *La Prensa*, February 11, Section 8A.

Perreault, T. 2003. "Changing Places: Transnational Networks, Ethnic Politics, and Community Development in the Amazon." *Political Geography* 22: 61–88.

Perreault, T. 2006. "From the Guerra del Agua to the Guerra del Gas: Resource Governance, Neoliberalism and Popular Protest in Bolivia." *Antipode* 38(1): 150–72.

Perreault, T. 2008. "Custom and Contradiction: Rural Water Governance and the Politics of *Usos y Costumbres* in Bolivia's Irrigators' Movement." *Annals of the Association of American Geographers* 98(4): 834–54.

Phillips, T. 2018. "Nicaragua's Sandinista Stronghold Is a City 'at war' with the President." *Guardian*, June 7. https://www.theguardian.com/world/2018/jun/06/nicaragua-daniel-ortega-masaya?CMP=share_btn_fb.

Prado, S. 2010. "Municipal Autonomy Is More Threatened than Ever." *Revista Envío* (349) (August). http://www.envio.org.ni/articulo/4226.

Prevost, G. 1999. "The Status of the Sandinista Revolutionary Project." In *The Undermining of the Sandinista Revolution*, ed. G. Vanden and H. E. Vanden, 9–44. London: Macmillan Press.

Prevost, G., and H. E. Vanden, eds. 1999. *The Undermining of the Sandinista Revolution*. London: Macmillan Press.

Putnam, R. D. 2000. *Bowling Alone: The Collapse and Revival of American Community*. New York: Simon and Schuster.

Quandt, Midge. 1995. "Unbinding the Ties That Bind: The FSLN and the Popular Organizations." In *The New Politics of Survival: Grassroots Movements in Central America*, ed. M. Sinclair, 265–91. New York: Monthly Review Press.

Ramírez, Pedro O. 2010. "Ley de Comités de Agua Potable y Saneamiento aprobada por Asamblea Nacional." Government press release. May 19. Managua.

Redford, K. H. 1991. "The Ecologically Noble Savage." *Cultural Survival Quarterly* 15(1): 46–48.

Reding, A. 1991. "The Evolution of Governmental Institutions." *Revolution and Counterrevolution in Nicaragua*, ed. T. W. Walker, 15–47. Boulder, Colo.: Westview Press.

Ribot, J. C. 1999. "Decentralisation, Participation and Accountability in Sahelian Forestry: Legal Instruments of Political-Administrative Control." *Africa: Journal of the International African Institute* 69(1): 23–65.

Ribot, J. C. 2011. "Choice, Recognition and Democracy Effects of Decentralisation." *Sweden: Swedish International Centre for Local Democracy (ICLD)*, Working Paper 5.

Ribot, J. C., and A. M. Larson, eds. 2005. *Democratic Decentralization through a Natural Resource Lens*. New York: Routledge.

Robinson, Peter. 1988. "Willingness to Pay for Rural Water: The Zimbabwe Case Study." Unpublished paper. Harare, Zimbabwe: Zimconsult.

Robles, Frances. 2018. "In Nicaragua, Ortega Was on the Ropes. Now, He Has Protesters on the Run." *New York Times*, December 24. https://www.nytimes.com/2018/12/24/world/americas/nicaragua-protests-daniel-ortega.html?smprod=nytcore-ipad& smid=nytcore-ipad-share.

Robson, J. P., and G. Lichtenstein. 2013. "Current Trends in Latin American Commons Research." *Journal of Latin American Geography* 12(1): 5–31.

Rocha, J. L. 2007. "From Citizen-as-Ward to Citizen-as-Client with No Solutions in Sight." *Revista Envío*, July.

Rodríguez, F. J., J. A. Martínez, N. S. Silwany, O. A. Incer, S. Zeledón, and J. M. González. 2008. "Informe de Consulta y Dictamen: Ley Especial de Comités de Agua Potable y Saneamiento." Nicaraguan National Assembly. https://onlinelibrary .wiley.com/doi/abs/10.1111/j.1470-9856.2012.00700.

Romano, S. T. 2012. "From Protest to Proposal: The Contentious Politics of the Nicaraguan Anti–Water Privatization Social Movement." *Bulletin of Latin American Research* 31(4): 499–514.

Roth, D., R. Boelens, and M. Zwarteveen. 2005. *Liquid Relations: Contested Water Rights and Legal Complexity*. New Brunswick, N.J.: Rutgers University Press.

Roth, D., R. Boelens, and M. Zwarteveen. 2015. "Property, Legal Pluralism, and Water Rights: The Critical Analysis of Water Governance and the Politics of Recognizing 'Local' Rights." *Journal of Legal Pluralism and Unofficial Law* 47(3): 456–75.

RRAS-CA. 1998. *Agua y saneamiento rural en Nicaragua*. Managua: Red Regional de Agua y Saneamiento para Centroamérica.

Ruchwarger, G. 1987. *People in Power: Forging a Grassroots Democracy in Nicaragua*. South Hadley, Mass.: Bergin and Garvey Publishers.

Ruiz, D. 2009. "What's Going On in the Municipalities? And What's with the CPCs?" *Revista Envío* (339) (October). http://www.envio.org.ni/articulo/4077.

Seemann, M. 2016. *Water Security, Justice, and the Politics of Water Rights in Peru and Bolivia*. London: Palgrave Macmillan.

Semple, K. 2018. "Nicaragua Roiled by Protests over Social Security Benefits." *New York Times*, April 20. https://www.nytimes.com/2018/04/20/world/americas/nicaragua -protests-ortega.html?ref=nyt-es&mcid=nyt-es&subid=article.

Serra, L. 1982. "The Sandinista Mass Organizations." In *Nicaragua in Revolution*, ed. T. W. Walker, 95–114. New York: Praeger.

Serra, L. 1991. "Grass-Roots Organizations." In *Revolution and Counterrevolution in Nicaragua*, ed. T. W. Walker, 49–75. Boulder, Colo.: Westview Press.

Shiva, V. 2002. *Water Wars: Privatization, Pollution and Profit*. Cambridge: Pluto Press.

Schouten, T., and P. Moriarty. 2003. *Community Water, Community Management: From System to Service in Rural Areas*. London: ITGD Publishing.

Smith, C. 1996. *Resisting Reagan: The U.S. Central America Peace Movement*. Chicago: University of Chicago Press.

Solaún, M. 2005. *United States Intervention and Regime Change in Nicaragua*. Lincoln: University of Nebraska Press.

Stuart, R. A. 2009. *Consejos del poder ciudadano y gestión pública en Nicaragua*. Centro de Estudios y Análisis Político. Managua: EDISA.

Tendler, J., K. Healy, C. M. O'Laughlin, and Inter-American Foundation. 1983. *What to Think about Cooperatives: A Guide from Bolivia*. Arlington, Va.: Inter-American Foundation.

Tijerino, F. K. 2008. *Historia de Nicaragua*. Managua: Instituto de Historia de Nicaragua y Centroamérica y la Universidad Centroamericana.

Vanden, H. E., and G. Prevost. 1993. *Democracy and Socialism in Sandinista Nicaragua*. Boulder, Colo.: Lynne Rienner Publishers.

Van Koppen, B., M. Giordano, and J. Butterworth, eds. 2007. *Community-Based Water Law and Water Resource Management Reform in Developing Countries*. Boston: CAB International.

Walker, T. W. 1991. "The Armed Forces." In *Revolution and Counterrevolution in Nicaragua*, ed. T. W. Walker, 77–100. Boulder, Colo.: Westview Press.

Trask, R. R. 1993. "Revolution and Counterrevolution in Nicaragua." *History: Reviews of New Books* 21(2): 73.

Woolcock, M. 2001. "The Place of Social Capital in Understanding Social and Economic Outcomes." *Canadian Journal of Policy Research* 2(1): 11–17.

Woolcock, M., and D. Narayan. 2000. "Social Capital: Implications for Development Theory, Research, and Policy." *World Bank Research Observer* 15(2): 225–49.

World Bank. 1993. "The Demand for Water in Rural Areas: Determinants and Policy Implications." *World Bank Research Observer* 8(1.1): 47–70.

World Bank. 2018. "Rural Population (% of total population): Nicaragua." https://data .worldbank.org/indicator/SP.RUR.TOTL.ZS?name_desc=false.

World Health Organization and United Nations Children's Fund. 2017. "Progress on Drinking Water, Sanitation, and Hygiene." https://washdata.org/.

Index

About the Author

Sarah T. Romano is an assistant professor of political science and global studies at Lesley University. She is the recipient of several awards, including two Fulbright Scholars Awards.